THE COMPLETE CLASH

THE COMPLETE CLASH

Keith Topping

REYNOLDS & HEARN LTD
LONDON

For
Andy Cowper
and
Deb Williams

PHOTOGRAPHY CREDITS
BACK COVER – Nils Jorgensen (© Rex Features)
FRONT COVER – © Sipa Press/Rex Features

PICTURE SECTION
Page 1 – Michael Putland (© Retna)
Page 2 – © London Features International
Page 3 – top, Paul Cox (both © London Features International)
Page 4 – top, Fraser Gray (© Rex Features)
       bottom, © London Features International
Page 5 – top, David Fisher (© London Features International)
       bottom, © Yael/Retna
Page 8 – Ant Davie (© www.strummersite.com)

First published in 2003 by
Reynolds & Hearn Ltd
61a Priory Road
Kew Gardens
Richmond
Surrey TW9 3DH

© Keith Topping 2003
Reprinted with corrections 2004

A CIP catalogue record for this book is available from the British Library.

ISBN 1 903111 70 6

Designed by Peri Godbold.

Printed and bound in Great Britain by Biddles Ltd, Guildford, Surrey.

ACKNOWLEDGMENTS

Marcus Gray's *Return of the Last Gang in Town* enjoys a pre-eminent position in the literature about The Clash as the (only) standard biography of the band. Any author writing on The Clash inevitably owes an immense debt to Marcus Gray's ground-breaking research and scholarship.

The author wishes to express his gratitude to Marcus Hearn and Richard Reynolds for allowing him the unexpected opportunity to wobble on drunkenly about The Clash for 224 pages.

I'd also like to thank the following friends and colleagues for their encouragement and contributions to *The Complete Clash*: Ian Abrahams, Trev Atkinson, Chris Baty, Suzanne Breadon, Bethany Burgot, Suze Campagna, Neil Connor, Chris Cornwell, Martin Day, Diana Dougherty, Clay Eichelberger, Felicity Gauvain, Tony and Jane Kenealy, Kevin Keynes, Stephe Lindas, Kelly Lovell, John May, Leslie McGachan, John Peel, Alasdair Patrick, Steve Purcell, Mike Sargant, Phil Spanton, Andrew C Taylor, Lily Topping and Geoff Wessel.

Thanks to the many readers of the *Mojo* message board – http://www.mojo4 music.com/ – who enthusiastically shared their memories of seeing The Clash live with me. Several readers on the If Music Could Talk message board – http://boards.gcuber.com/board/ – also helped enormously. blackmarketclash.com website includes an exhaustive live resource on the band and is highly recommended to all Clash fans. www.geocities.com/j-blokhed/index.html includes details on many Clashbootlegs to have appeared over the years.

Special thanks to Ant Davie of www.strummersite.com, the official website of Joe Strummer and The Mescaleros, for additional picture research.

Thanks, also, to Spug, Swedge and Dekka, from Slime, plus Tommy Wonga, Matty, Korka, Willa, Ritchie Renkenstenk and Big Tye. Wherever the hell you all are these days.

CONTENTS

NOW, GET THIS!

FROM THE WESTWAY TO THE WORLD

'Putting The Beatles back together won't save rock 'n' roll.
Four kids playing to their contemporaries in a dirty
cellar might.'
Mick Farren — *NME* 1976

'All we want to achieve is an atmosphere where things can
happen. To keep the spirit of the free world (alive). We want
to keep out that safe, soapy slush that comes out of the
radio. All we've got is a few guitars, amps and drums.
That's our weaponry.'
Joe Strummer — *Time Out* 1978

Dates and places are vitally important in rock 'n' roll. It was 17 November 1978 at, of all places, Middlesbrough Town Hall. Myself and a crew of fellow teenage hooligans had caught the train down from Newcastle on the off-chance of getting tickets that somebody's cousin was supposed to have access to. We'd seen The Jam a couple of weeks previously and they had been special. Now, we hoped to catch a glimpse of their only rivals as The Best Band in the World. Cutting a long story short, we made it. As The Clash hit the stage playing 'Safe European Home', the guy immediately in front of me leapt up and threw back his arms in celebration. An elbow caught me square in the hooter. I spent the next hour on my knees, clutching my face in agony. I lost about a pint of blood and ended the night on the last train home to Tyneside with a red T-shirt that had once been white. That's my memories of seeing The Clash as a 15-year-old. Evidence from a low-quality tape of the show, found years later in Camden Market, suggests that it was magnificent – a passionate, furious performance from a band at the peak of their collective power.

But then, according to numerous accounts from all over the world, that was The Clash every night, of every tour. The Clash, as Lester Bangs once memorably wrote, were 'the only band that mattered.'

It was 23 December 2002. A phone call from my mate Abie brought the sad news. 'Have you heard?' he asked. 'Joe Strummer died yesterday.' The news produced a strange feeling in me. Not overwhelming grief as if someone close to me had suddenly been taken – rightly, those emotions belonged to Joe's family and friends. I never met the man; it would have been ludicrous (not to mention a little selfish) to experience direct loss. But I certainly did feel as if a, perhaps distant, friend had gone. A man who had, after all, been a presence in my life for a quarter of a century. That someone with as much life in him as Joe Strummer should have suffered an old man's death from a heart attack at the age of 50 seemed utterly wrong. 'That heart of his always worked too hard,' noted Pete Townshend.

Journalist Tony Parsons once referred to Strummer as 'the savage warmth at the heart of New Wave.' An interview with Gavin Martin, for *Uncut* in 1999, provides crucial insight into Strummer's complex character. He was, by all accounts, an immensely likeable person. A man of passion, sanguine humour, honour and no little courage. Joe seemed to be a genuinely decent geezer with his heart in the right place, especially when it came to his fans, for whom he always appeared to find time and energy even after the most gruelling of gigs. Martin describes a scene backstage at a festival in Finland: 'When it's time to find transport back to the hotel, Strummer escorts [a group of fans] past the doubtful-looking security guy. Fist thumping his chest he hollers, "I am the King of *Provinnsirock*... and these are my friends. Let them through."'

As literally thousands of fans over the years will testify, this was not some one-off performance for a journalist – it happened night after night. 'Joe wanted to know about the towns he was visiting. What it was like to grow up in Sheffield or Newcastle,' remembered The Clash's road manager Johnny Green in his affectionate memoir, *A Riot Of Our Own*. 'Fans would ask where we were playing tomorrow, and Joe kept a notebook of their names, telling doormen to put them on the guest list. Being accessible was all part of the punk movement, or at least The Clash's version of it.'

Just as touching is Martin's description of Strummer's meeting with Control, a Finnish Clash tribute band with whom he was happy to share a pint. This subsequently turned into *several* pints, all of which Joe bought, when he discovered that they had once played a gig to an audience of three. Strummer was genuinely moved. 'Those guys have been standing up for punk rock through some lean times. Imagine playing to three people? To me, that's what rock 'n' roll is all about.'

'A proud punk rebel with a big soft heart, Strummer was also a loving son and an attentive father,' wrote Martin, online, upon hearing of his old friend's death. 'As a musician, and as a human being, it was his ability to express his deepest feelings – anger or grief, sadness or fear – that made him special.' Joe Strummer's death brought a plethora of such tributes, many from other old friends like Allan Jones and Charles Shaar Murray, but it was the letters pages of the music magazines in the early months of 2003 that really expressed the sorrow felt by many at his parting. Joe Strummer was one of us, and now he was gone.

However, it has to be said, here and now, that *The Complete Clash* is not some revisionist attempt to paint The Clash as nothing more than Strummer's backing band. Philip Norman's *Shout* attempted the same underhand trick with John Lennon and The Beatles and brought a predictably pithy response from George Harrison. 'How many Beatles does it take to change a lightbulb?' Harrison memorably asked. 'Four. John, Paul, George and Ringo. Sorry, but that's the way it is.' Though they made one great LP before he joined, and played a lot of fine gigs after he left, for most fans of The Clash, the only years that matter are those between April 1977 and May 1982,[1] when the band contained Topper Headon along with Joe Strummer, Mick Jones and Paul Simonon.

'The rules of rock 'n' roll say you're only ever as good as your drummer,' Strummer noted in Don Letts' 1999 documentary *Westway to the World*. 'If we hadn't found Topper, I don't think we'd have got anywhere.' Mick Jones agreed, telling Chris Salewicz in 1985, 'I was just one component of what made up The Clash. It was never about just one person, or one attitude: You could see it on stage, the way we complemented each other.' Ultimately, to Strummer, The Clash were a perfect unit: 'It was like a chemical reaction between those four people,' he said. 'It was limping to its death from the minute that Topper was sacked.' When asked, by Charles Shaar Murray in 1999, what one decision that he had made in his life he would like to change, Strummer, poignantly, asked if he could have two. These would be, he continued, '*not* sacking Topper Headon and *not* sacking Mick Jones.'[2] Ten years

1. The 1980s, an up-its-own-arse decade of extreme proportions in most areas of life, but particularly music, badly needed one radical and dissenting voice. The Clash should have been that voice, but for their disintegration in 1983. It was thus left to a few outsiders, shouting from the wilderness – The Smiths, most obviously – to provide an antidote to American big-hair bands, passionless divas, pretentious videos and soulless synthesised pop.

2. 'Getting rid of Mick must have been an ego decision,' Strummer told *Wired* in 1988. For their part, both Jones and Headon used *Westway to the World* to acknowledge their own regrets at the circumstances that led to each leaving The Clash. Headon was especially frank, noting: 'If I'd kept my act together, I could see the band possibly still being together today ... I'd like to apologise to them for letting the side down.' He added, however, that being the sort of person he is, if he had the last 25 years to live over again, 'I'd probably do the same things.

previously, Strummer told MTV that during the first tour after Headon left, he began to realise that 'it was never gonna *burn* again... We tried to fix a clock that wasn't broken.' One of the most powerful and lasting images of *Westway to the World* remains a clearly emotional Strummer advising young bands that, if they find a formula that works, to do everything they can not to mess with it.[3]

Mick Jones was the one member of The Clash to taste any lasting musical success outside the band – with Big Audio Dynamite and its associated side-projects. A more complex and enigmatic, less heart-on-the-sleeve character than Strummer, Jones nonetheless shared much of his songwriting partner's vision of The Clash as more than just another group. 'We're regular blokes,' he told Lester Bangs in 1977, but you always sensed that Jones knew their destiny was to be greater than that. 'The dinosaur bands left you as they found you,' he said on the BBC's 1996 series *Dancing in the Streets*. 'You were the same after you'd heard them. The only difference was they were richer.'

Making sure that those who heard The Clash were never the same person after being witness to the wrath of their bombast was clearly as much of an obsession with Jones as it was with Strummer. Despite an unwarranted perception over the years that Jones was the narcissistic weak link in The Clash's proletarian façade, he frequently proved that he had solid and idealistic principles, too. 'The people involved in The Clash are my family,' he told Tony Parsons, who subsequently remembered that Jones had once almost quit The Clash in a petty argument with manager Bernard Rhodes, because their minder, Roadent, didn't have any socks.

Evolving out of Jones' schoolboy glam band, The Delinquents, The Clash's genesis also included The London SS, a band whose legendary status far outstripped any actual achievements (they never played a single gig, for instance).[4] Basically a loose unit of musicians around Jones, future-Generation X guitarist Tony James and Keith Levene, The London SS spent much of 1975 and early 1976 jamming; firstly in a squat in Davis Road, Shepherd's Bush and, after the acquisition of their manager, Bernard Rhodes, in a converted railway warehouse in Camden that became known as Rehearsal

3. 'We all wanted to do the documentary, but we couldn't do it in the same room. It's still too heavy,' Strummer told Caroline Sullivan in 1999. 'We haven't all been together since Topper left. It was touching, that bit where [Headon] apologised for getting addicted to hard drugs and screwing up the group. He'd never apologised before.' It would be 2001 – when The Clash were presented with Ivor Novello Awards for Lifetime Achievement – that Strummer, Jones, Simonon and Headon were together again in public.

4. 'One of the names that we had before The Clash was The Weak Heartdrops from a Big Youth song,' Jones told MTV in 1991. 'Another was The Psychotic Negatives, but neither of those worked.'

Rehearsals. At one time or another Jones' friend Chrissie Hynde (former *NME* journalist and future Pretender) and Rat Scabies and Brian James (who went on to form The Damned) were all involved along with future members of The Boys and Chelsea, and many other, less famous, characters.

The most important addition during this period was the arrival, in late 1975, of Paul Simonon, who had turned up one day with a friend, Roland, The London SS's drummer for that particular week. Jones thought that Simonon looked great and asked if he was a singer. After an audition, in which Simonon had a go at The Standalls' 'Barracuda' and Jonathan Richman's 'Roadrunner', it was decided that, no, Paul wasn't a singer. But he had a fantastically irreverent 'couldn't-give-a-shit' attitude, so Jones took it upon himself to teach his new recruit the bass.[5] 'Part of the punk thing was it didn't matter if you couldn't play,' Jones remembered in 1989.

The Clash became, as Chris Nelson wrote, 'razor-edged poets of a lost generation, those too young for the musical magic of the 60s and now facing a Britain wracked with racial violence, high unemployment and political turmoil.' They had the look, they had the ideas, they had the pugnacious attitude to get their message across. And, soon, they had the platform from which to deliver their manifesto, even if the message sometimes got buried in the cacophony that they created. 'The words are really great,' Strummer told Tony Parsons in 1977. 'But you can't hear them. Don't you think that's ironic?' In this regard, perhaps, The Clash's real achievement was that they took theoretical McLuhanism to its logical extreme. [5] However, the irony didn't end there. 'Unlike other punk bands, The Clash never trafficked in nihilism, never jabbed a safety pin through their ears, either literally or metaphorically,' wrote Michael Goldberg in 1982. 'The Clash always had more in common, politically and idealistically, with folk singers like Country Joe McDonald and Bob Dylan, than with the other angry young men of punk.'

A band of many contradictions then. 'They were political agitators who loved posing,' wrote *Uncut*. 'Pacifists who constantly confronted violence in music and in person, punk rebels haunted by the dilemma of "turning rebellion into money."' They were also, as *Mojo* noted, the first British group to cut a rap record and the first white faces to be painted on the wall of Lee Perry's Black Ark studio in Jamaica. Astounding achievements for a perceived gang of lowlife street-scum from North London. 'There was magic between Joe and Mick, a Lennon-McCartney thing,' their one-time manager Peter Jenner remembered in 1999. 'They complemented each other, the toughness

5. The philosophy of Canadian media-guru Marshall McLuhan (1911-80), author of *The Medium is the Message*, which states that the way people communicate with each other is more important than what they actually communicate.

of Joe and the musicality of Mick.'[6] In the same article, The Clash's photographer, and friend, Pennie Smith noted that there are two types of groups, romanticists and classicists. 'The Clash were romanticists. That whole mythology they built around them. Everything was chaotic, nothing was planned. That's what made them great.'

The influences that glued The Clash together were truly diverse and, possibly, this helps to explain the extraordinary cross-genre pollination that their music subsequently accessed. 'The Clash took the urban-scarred landscape of The Velvet Underground, added Stooges' nihilism [and] crossed it with the apocalyptic poli-tricks of the Rastafarian wing of reggae, which preached divine salvation and retribution cooked to a trance-induced beat,' wrote Lenny Kaye in 1991. Strummer's love of 1960s R&B, mod and beat music – The Beatles, The Stones, The Who, The Kinks, The Animals, The Yardbirds, etc – was something that he shared with Jones. But Strummer's time working the labyrinthine London pub-rock circuit with The 101ers had given him an appreciative, if somewhat eclectic, knowledge of, and fascination with, rock history. He may have worn a *Chuck Berry is Dead* shirt and sung of there being 'No Elvis, Beatles or The Rolling Stones' in 1977, but Strummer never lost his love of rhythm and blues, and rockabilly, much to The Clash's ultimate benefit.

Mick Jones' first musical influences were drawn from those same 6os bands, especially The Kinks, and subsequently from guitar heroes like Cream's Eric Clapton and Jimi Hendrix. In the early 1970s, Jones discovered the more peripheral, politically tinged histrionics of The MC5, the trash-rock of The New York Dolls and The Stooges and, in England, the good-time 'lads-together' boogie of Mott The Hoople and The Faces. Another significant influence was Mick Ronson's guitar work on the 1970-74 output of David Bowie. 'We all immersed ourselves in different parts of what's now known as popular culture,' noted Jones in *Westway to the World*. It was Jones' grasp of musical substance that provided the cohesion that held The Clash together. And it was Jones' talent and drive that turned a fairly orthodox band into something much greater.

'I didn't want the role of being John Entwistle or Bill Wyman, stuck in the background,' Paul Simonon told *Bassist* magazine in 1999. 'If that was what I'd been offered with The Clash I would've turned it down.' Simonon came from a different direction altogether to Strummer and Jones. A lugubrious

---

6. 'I would sit all weekend in the kitchen with a typewriter,' Strummer told MTV in 1991. 'All day and all night. The phone was hidden in a drawer. I'd emerge with one piece of paper and felt this thing was magical. I gave it to Jonesy and two or three days later it would sing. The words were no longer a strange poem, they had a tune.'

ex-skinhead, with mainly black friends, his music was always reggae, the sound of the urban ghettos of Jamaica and Brixton. Paul would subsequently get his enthused bandmates listening not just to Bob Marley, but also to more obscure reggae figures like Big Youth, Prince Far-I, Tapper Zukie and Toots and The Maytals. Once that connection had been made, the punk/rasta interface that The Clash worked so successfully would inspire entire careers from bands as diverse as The Police, The Ruts, Madness, The Specials and Culture Club. 'A lot of white people say reggae is boring, the bass is always the same,' Simonon told Eddie Izzard in 2003 on the Discovery Channel documentary *Mongrel Nation*. 'But when you're in a club you understand why the bass is that way. It's your footsteps.' Having been bold enough to cover Lee Perry and Junior Murvin's 'Police & Thieves' on their debut LP, The Clash couldn't have received a greater compliment than to be name-checked, along with The Damned and The Jam, in Bob Marley's Perry-produced 'Punky Reggae Party' late in 1977.

By contrast, Topper Headon's background was in soul and funk bands, and his true love was jazz. When he joined The Clash, the mix of radically polarised styles was complete. 'What other band has so successfully absorbed the music of so many cultures, digested it, and emerged with a startling, evocative language of their own?' asked *Creem*'s Susan Whitall in 1980. Musically, The Clash began to openly rebel against the straitjacket of punk's accepted format – speedy, three-chord chants – shortly after releasing their debut LP. This was, mostly, at Jones' instigation, but their new musical freedom was enabled, wholly, by Headon's versatility.

In short, The Clash, like every great band that's ever made records, took lots of little bits of all their favourite groups and artists and glued them together to produce something that was genuinely unique. 'Don't be afraid of the word 'paradox',' Strummer told *NME* in 1982. 'We're not just another wank rock group like Boston or Aerosmith,' he announced to *Rolling Stone* three years before, when asked about the band's concessions towards populism. 'We've got loads of contradictions for you. We're trying to be the greatest group in the world. At the same time, we're trying to be radical – we never want to be respectable. Maybe the two can't coexist. But we'll try.'

It was March 2003, and The Clash were inducted into the Rock & Roll Hall of Fame. 'We're all very proud,' Jones told *Rolling Stone* at the ceremony, which he attended with Simonon, original drummer Terry Chimes and Strummer's widow, Lucinda. 'But it's just not nice to be at something like this without Joe.'[7] U2's The Edge and Audioslave's Tom Morello presented their

---

7. Chimes used the occasion to make a very gracious speech acknowledging the absent Topper Headon as 'a genius'.

own thoughts on the band. 'I was used to buying heavy-metal T-shirts that had pictures of wizards and dragons,' noted Morello. 'The Clash shirt had just a few words over the heart. THE FUTURE IS UNWRITTEN. When I saw them play, I knew exactly what that meant.' Jones noted that he had attended the ceremony 'in honour of Joe's memory,' telling Mark Binelli that he had been particularly impressed by a tribute to Strummer at the 2003 Grammy Awards in February, a performance of 'London Calling' by Elvis Costello, Bruce Springsteen, Dave Grohl and Steve Van Zandt. 'I saw Tony Bennett clapping at the end,' he noted. 'That was nice. Joe may have chuckled!'

'If we make it then those kids know that they have a chance too,' Strummer told Mick Farren in 1981. This author hopes that Strummer would have continued to smile, benevolently, on this project and on others that he and his band inspired. And towards those fans who still keep the flame burning for a band who touched so many lives so deeply.

Keith Topping
His Gaff
Merrie Albion
August 2003

THE LEGEND OF THE LEGEND OF THE CLASH

T he story of The Clash is, literally, the stuff of legend. Of course, as with much rock 'n' roll mythology, much of that legend was completely self-perpetuated. But that's a revisionist view and it's also, frankly, boring. So let's stick with the legend for the moment.

It starts like this: There's a go-nowhere garage-band, led by a glam-rock obsessed guitar-hero of some talent. One day he and his trainee bassist are standing in the queue at Lisson Grove Labour Exchange[8] and they have brass neck to ask an experienced pub-rock singer to join their fledgling outfit. They would later even write some lyrics about the incident, relocating the meeting to the Portobello Road Market (presumably because this was considered more scenic than a dole office).[9] The rocker, in turn, is already becoming dissatisfied with his current band, who have just been supported by The Sex Pistols at the Nashville Rooms. He *knows* that a musical and cultural revolution is on the immediate horizon and he's actively looking for a vehicle with which to become a part of this. The garage-band's offer has come at just the right time. So he joins up, knocks a couple of years off his age, cuts his hair and helps to turn a bunch of the guitarist's bitter songs concerning ex-girlfriends into terrifying rants about urban alienation, tower blocks and other stuff like that. When Giovanni Dadomo writes that 'They're the first band who'll frighten The Sex Pistols shitless' in *Sounds* a couple of months later, the legend is more or less complete before the garage-band have even recorded a note and when they've only played one proper gig.

It's a fabulous tale and, as with a lot of the stories surrounding The Clash, it's about 80 per cent accurate.[10] But the jigsaw of truths, half-truths and

---

8. Misunderstanding the admiring looks that he was getting from Jones, Simonon and Viv Albertine, Strummer believed he was about to be attacked by these ruffians who were after his unemployment benefit. 'I was expecting them to tangle with me out in the street,' he remembered in *Westway to the World*. 'Paul looked a bit tasty, so I thought I'd smack Mick first and leg it.' Legend has it that, when the trio finally introduced themselves, Jones told Strummer, 'We like *you*, but your group's rubbish!' Some sources also place Glen Matlock at this meeting.

9. See 'All the Young Punks (New Boots and Contracts)'.

10. Jones and Simonon had already seen The 101ers – certainly when The Pistols supported (cont. overleaf)

outright lies that form the full story of how The Clash came to be features another vitally important figure. Because this improbable outfit was, at least in part, the conception of a Svengali-like manager who was looking to rival the impact of his colleague Malcolm McLaren's band. Mick Jones, Paul Simonon and Joe Strummer were three men with radically different backgrounds, yet one thing bound them together – and it was something that Bernard Rhodes spent a lot of time *not* publicising. It's a deep irony, but The Clash – that most English of bands – didn't, initially, contain a true Englishman among them.

Joe Strummer was born John Mellor in Ankara, Turkey, in 1952, the son of a middle-ranking civil servant. He spent most of his formative years at the City of London Freeman's School and most of his twenties adroitly laying a trail of false clues to avoid people knowing the full story of his background.[11] And with good reason: Strummer's middle-class roots inevitably made him a target for regular claims of hypocrisy, something he fought tooth and nail to reject. When asked by Annette Weatherman what poverty meant to him in 1977, he replied 'Fifty four pence, cos that's what I've got in my pocket right now.'

Despite a relatively comfortable middle-class upbringing, Strummer's childhood had been one of perceived rejection. His older brother took his own life when Strummer was in his teens, amplifying those feelings of abandonment that he had first felt at boarding school. It was through pop music that Strummer found his escape from the shallow mundanities of life. After a period playing in an R&B band called The Vultures in Newport, by 1974 Strummer had settled into London's Maida Vale squatting community which, as Pat Gilbert noted in 1999, was a 'world of bad plumbing, drug-busts and violent evictions.'

Three years younger than Strummer, Mick Jones' parents were a Welsh taxi-driver and a second generation Russian Jewish refugee. They divorced when he was eight and, from then on, Jones was raised by his grandmother. Paul Simonon's father was a Belgian immigrant. A talented painter, like his dad, Simonon, who was also born in 1955, also saw his parents divorce at an early age and he spent some time living in Italy as a teenager.

10. (cont.) them at the Nashville and also, according to Simonon in 1991, at The Red Cow pub. The actual approach to Strummer to join The Clash, however, was made by Rhodes and Keith Levene after a 101ers gig at the Golden Lion, on Fulham Broadway, on 30 May 1976. The benefits of the deal from The Clash's point of view were obvious, not only in the acquisition of a charismatic frontman. Additionally, Strummer brought with him The 101ers'

11. Over the years Strummer often alluded to the repressive atmosphere and harsh regime of his school life. 'My reports got worse and worse until I became the king of the long-term prisoners,' he told *Uncut* in 1999. 'Eight years in the joint, right? We were beaten like sheep. I've been beaten with wooden coat hangers, hockey sticks, leather slippers. Everything you could beat a person with. And I still came out shouting "Bollocks"!'

An enigmatic figure, Bernard Rhodes was, according to the man himself, brought to England from Russia in the 1950s by his mother, who worked as a seamstress in Soho. 'I was on the streets when I was 12,' he told *Mojo* in 1999. He also claimed to have known Mick Jagger at the London School of Economics and to have introduced Guy Stevens to the pop world during the mid-60s when Rhodes was active in London's emergent mod scene. Malcolm McLaren's T-shirt printer, Rhodes considered that McLaren was a good marketing man but that 'he stole all my ideas.'

In 1976, Rhodes was looking for his own band to visualise these ideas. Like McLaren, he was fascinated by the anarchist art-movement The Situationalists. [12] According to Tony James, Rhodes insisted that his bands read about existentialism, modern art and Dadaism. 'He'd say "You guys are wasting my time! Have you read any Sartre?"' James told *Mojo*. 'It taught us something important: you have to have a bigger idea. That was Bernie's lesson.'

It was Rhodes, too, who insisted that Strummer and Jones write songs about relevant social issues and the everyday lives of their audience instead of more traditional rock 'n' roll subjects. Urged on by Rhodes, Strummer in particular became one of punk's loudest voices and, as Gavin Martin noted, 'its most outspoken idealist, famously making grand, rash promises that often ended in pratfalls.' But, if Pat Gilbert's 1999 *Mojo* article is any indication, although given subsequent credit by the band for much of their success, Rhodes remains somewhat bitter about his dealings with The Clash. 'Their talent was to represent the kids. But they didn't,' he stated. 'I didn't realise Joe was such a coward [and] Mick was such an egomaniac. Paul was this pussy-whipped guy and the other one I couldn't stand because he was a provincial tosser.' [13] 'Sometimes I feel that I've only been a pawn in a game between Mick and Bernie,' Strummer told *Record Mirror*'s Jim Reid in 1986. 'If you wanna look at The Clash story, the Titans in the struggle have been Mick and Bernie.'

12. A politically and socially radical subdivision of the Surrealist movement, whose members included André Bertrand, Asgar Jorn and the Spur Group, the Situationalist International (1957-72) dealt in conceptual art. This was designed to, as Ian MacDonald described it, 'break the hypnosis of the mass-media 'spectacle' which it saw as a capitalist conspiracy to lull the workers into apathy.' Situationalist slogans appeared on the walls of Paris during the May 1968 uprising and, via McLaren and Rhodes' interest, Situationalism was a key part of the punk era's artwork and advertising. At the other extreme, the movement helped to spawn the Angry Brigade, a clandestine anarcho-syndicalist terrorist cell whose activities included a bombing campaign against capitalist targets like the fashion store Biba, Government ministers and high-ranking policemen.

13. It should be remembered that despite his somewhat rapacious reputation, Rhodes, in addition to The Clash, was also an important figure in the development of two of Britain's most popular bands of the early 1980s, The Specials and Dexy's Midnight Runners.

Rhodes 'imagined The Clash', as Joe Strummer put it in an MTV documentary. Yet what is often played down is the disproportionate control that the manager had over the band in those early days. Johnny Thunders, who accompanied The Clash on the Anarchy tour and saw this relationship at first hand, wrote 'London Boys', a song which spelled out The Clash's alleged dependence on their manager: 'You need an escort to take a piss/He holds your hand and he shakes your dick.' Rhodes' manipulation of The Clash didn't mean, however, that the band were mere puppets. The fact that The Clash were in a position to rebel and sack Rhodes in late 1978 (albeit to return to him three years later) clearly illustrates this. If there were going to be legends created around The Clash then, from a very early stage, the band themselves seemed more than capable of following a classic piece of punk dogma. Lesson 1: Do it yourself. Lesson 2: Do it *properly*.[14]

Strummer, Jones and Simonon had all attended art school – that was something they *could* talk about. These institutions had been a fertile breeding ground for the 1960s beat group scene – John Lennon, Keith Richards, Pete Townshend, Eric Burdon and Ray Davies had all emerged from art school.[15] As Ian MacDonald notes in his critically acclaimed book on The Beatles and 60s culture, *Revolution in the Head*, 'The key to the English art school experience is that it was founded on talent rather than official qualifications. In such an environment, one might interact with a wide spectrum of people, regardless of class or education.'

From day one, then, there was an element of traditional rock 'n' roll values within The Clash's sense of what they were doing, and why they were doing it. 'If The Clash [were, initially, cast as] a cadre of urban guerrillas raging against Britain's social malaise, they later developed their iconography into that of a more internationally alert agitprop army,' wrote Graham Fuller in 1987. 'They always worked hard at enabling their audiences to identify with them,' wherever that audience may, themselves, have been from. In this

14. The legend of The Clash extends far beyond the band themselves to touch the lives of many members of their inner circle. And not just other musicians (Jones' friendships with Chrissie Hynde, Tony James and Glen Matlock, and Strummer and Simonon's with Sid Vicious notwithstanding). People like their road crew (Johnny Green, Barry Glare, Robin Crocker and Roadent), PR man Kosmo Vinyl, their film-making pal Don Letts, clothes designer Alex Michon, photographer Pennie Smith and the various journalists whom they befriended and toured with (Caroline Coon, Tony Parsons, Lester Bangs) are all a vital part of The Clash's story, as this book will detail.

15. 'The last resort of malingerers, bluffers and people who don't wanna work,' noted Strummer in 1999 concerning art school. Jones, for his part, bemoaned the fact that he didn't meet any other musicians through it and that he attended after the first term simply to get the grant which he used to buy better guitars. However, it was through his friendship with fellow art student Viv Albertine that Jones first met Keith Levene.

regard, The Clash were the originators of an ethic that would later become associated with one of their would-be successors as 'The People's Band', The Stone Roses: 'It's not where you're from, it's where you're at.'

Another, often overlooked, context to the band's myth-building was the era in which they were bored. 'In 1974, it seemed like life was in black and white,' noted Strummer poetically in *Westway to the World*. He was mainly talking about the decrepit state of Britain's housing at this time, a situation that gave rise to widespread squatting, particularly in London, and out of which the punk movement sprang. But he could, just as easily, have been referring to the vast musical wilderness of the period, or to a social study of the early 1970s political wasteland: 'The three-day week, the blackouts, the Grunwick strike and pickets ... Pretty socio-politically active times,' Strummer told *Uncut* in 2002. 'When you see a film like *Rude Boy*, the beginning of that, it looks like it's a hundred years ago.'

The 1960s were long gone, and with them much of the radical agenda of those times had cracked and dissipated in a maelstrom of fractured sub-movements, confused manifestos and, not unconnected with all this, a surfeit of promiscuity and mind-bending drugs. The previous decade had seen British society breaking out of a straitjacket which had restrained it since Victorian times. Though it would be wrong to over-exaggerate the changes in everyday life (the fashionable clothes worn on Carnaby Street and the goings-on at the Ad Lib club had little to do with the lives of an average working-class family living on a council estate on an weekly wage of £25), it *was* a time of new ideas. The era saw a proliferation of foreign restaurants opening around the country (particularly Chinese, Indian and Italian), a new hedonism in the popular cultures of music, television, film, literature and the theatre, all aided by a relaxation in Britain's draconian obscenity laws and an increase in participation in sporting activity which saw the building of many new leisure centres.

All these changes happened during a decade of relative affluence and the first stirrings of social mobility. The development of comprehensive education had meant that for the first time young working-class men and women were leaving school and, instead of going into traditional blue-collar occupations, were finding employment in the better-paid white-collar sector. This was all the upside of what the 1960s had achieved. But, with the dawn of the 1970s, the negative aspects of this embryonic new society structure, still trying to define itself, were becoming apparent. The 'white-hot technology' of Harold Wilson's government hadn't produced the expected second industrial revolution. Instead, Britain's industrial base was winding down, with many traditional industries failing to adapt to a changing world. The poor, in Britain, were still poor and worked hard for little reward whether they worked in a nationalised industry or in the bowels of the capitalist system. 'Meet the new boss, same as the old boss,' according to one of the prophets of the new age, Pete Townshend.

There were people with agendas in all walks of life, and many of these were either confused or downright sinister. The Angry Brigade had tried to bomb their way to an anarchist utopia. It didn't happen.[16] Feminism, the one great popular social movement of the 1960s that had actually achieved a modicum of social change, still managed to bring out all the worst instincts on both sides of the gender lines. When Stokely Carmichael (1941-98), the Black Panthers' president, visited the UK in 1969, he was asked by a feminist journalist what place he saw for women in his vision of a harmonious, multiracial society. 'On your back, baby,' was his somewhat glib reply. The radical left were so torn by in-fighting and bland rhetoric that they couldn't organise themselves to fight the real enemy. So hopelessly concerned with right-on ideology were many of these groups that the *Monty Python's Life of Brian* parody of them ('Splitters!') is, actually, too truthful to be funny.[17]

The world was changing, and no one was immune from this process. On 17 October 1973, in response to the escalating Yom Kippur war, OPEC, the Arab oil-producing countries, summarily cut production and quadrupled the world price of oil. This, effectively, ended the relative affluence on which, as Ian MacDonald wrote, 'the preceding ten years of happy-go-lucky excess in the West had chiefly depended.' A less sentimental suggestion for 'the day that the 60s (conceptually) ended' than some symbolic musical event like The Rolling Stones' disastrous free concert at Altamont, the break-up of The Beatles or the death of Jimi Hendrix perhaps, but probably a more realistic one.[18] The resulting financial crisis in Europe sent inflation spiralling and led

16. The Trotskyist *Red Mole* newspaper's calls for solidarity with their comrades who had been accused in the Angry Brigade trials mostly fell on deaf ears. 'It is no use the organised left criticising the politics of the Angry Brigade, unless we also recognise why a lot of potentially good comrades reject the various Leninist organisations, and resort to bomb-throwing,' they wrote in 1972.

17. In its obituary for Strummer, the *Times* noted, perceptively, that 'in many ways, Strummer's songs were responding to the same events and sense of political drift that led to Margaret Thatcher's radical Conservatism.'

18. As a bizarre coincidence, on the same day – 17 October 1973 – England's football team drew 1-1 with Poland in a World Cup qualifier. This failure to reach the final stages of a tournament that England had won eight years previously may seem insignificant to some. But, just as that famous 'some people are on the pitch...' victory over West Germany in 1966 seemed to encapsulate the spirit of an entire era – when England (and, specifically, London) was, literally, on top of the world – so the gloom that settled over the country during the winter of 1973-4, with its three-day weeks, power cuts and general austerity, was inextricably tied to the failing fortunes of Sir Alf Ramsey's ageing side.

to all sorts of ramifications in unexpected places. It was the moment when the swinging 60s turned, almost overnight, into the sober and soon-to-be-unemployed 70s.

In such circumstances, many people tend to put their faith in anyone who offers easy solutions to society's problems. 'Vote for me, and I'll set you free,' as The Temptations had noted in 'Ball of Confusion' at the dawn of the decade. History, specifically the spectre of fascism in Germany, reminds us of this time after time. It should, therefore, be of little surprise that in this confused political climate, the right-wing repatriationist party, The National Front, enjoyed a spectacular rise in popularity in Britain. Formed in 1966 through a fusion of various existing far-right groups, in May 1977 the party polled over 100,000 votes in London's local council elections. A series of National Front marches in the late 1970s, often through multiracial areas of London like Lewisham, Southall and Lambeth, produced numerous angry confrontations with leftist groups like The Anti-Nazi League and the SWP. For the first time since the 1930s, Britain had political riots taking place on its streets.

'In Great Britain there is too little discussion of racial matters,' wrote American sociologist Thomas Cottle in 1978. 'To listen to some people is to believe there are no racial problems in the United Kingdom.' One of the great ironies, and a very revealing one, about British society during the 1970s was that, while the subject of class was now being openly spoken about (when it was, in reality, no longer the supreme overriding factor of social inequality), the ingrained reticence that once enveloped discussions of class had switched to the topic of race.

Those Britons of West Indian and Asian ancestry clearly, and rightly, felt that racist attitudes in white society had, by the late 1970s, spread far beyond the small minority who advocated violent confrontation with immigrant communities. Much of the National Front's support came from decaying urban areas where there were large immigrant populations, suggesting that tolerance was in short supply. In 1976, Mark Bonham-Carter, Chairman of the Community Relations Commission, warned that Britain's black population, 40 per cent of whom had been born in Britain, would not settle for second-class citizenship 'in exchange for higher living standards and the prospect of some employment. They are British, and they take the phrase 'equality of opportunity' for what it means.'

The Clash's integration of black culture into their music was, perhaps, inevitable. As their friend Don Letts noted in 2003, reggae was the only like-minded anti-establishment music around in 1976 for punks to listen to. When The Roxy opened, with Letts as its DJ, with the exception of one or two singles [19] there were, simply, no punk records that could be played. This led to reggae becoming the scene's music of choice. 'I've seen social development in this country, not through government or schools, but through music,' Letts told *Mongrel Nation*, noting that when he took Simonon, Strummer or John Lydon to reggae parties in the 1970s, they would often be the only white faces in the room. 'Now, you go to something similar and it's half white guys.' It was with this background that the initial punk movement formed its egalitarian anti-racist ideals, the punks being sussed enough to realise that white working-class youths like themselves were just as alienated, because of the class system, as the children of Caribbean immigrants. 'They were all standing together in the same dole queue,' added Letts, perceptively.

Strummer later considered that he had been 'fucked up the arse by the capitalist system', yet, as Marcus Gray notes, the main effect this had on Strummer was to turn him, not into a raging White Panther on the fringes of the revolutionary left, but, instead, into a nihilist who mistrusted *all* forms of the Establishment. 'We always go on the defensive when confronted with political stuff,' Strummer told *NME*'s Jack Basher in 1978. 'We see it as a trap, a hole to get shut up in.' When interviewed by Barry Miles in the same year, Strummer was very clear about what he was *against*. 'Fascists, [particularly the] racialist patriotism type of fanaticism. We're against ignorance.' Conversely, he was less direct about what he was actually in favour of. 'I'm *about* The Clash,' he noted, simply.

Jones was equally wary of being typecast as a member of a purely political band, telling *Melody Maker*'s Chris Brazier that, while he had leanings to the left of the political spectrum, his concerns were not only political. In 1981 he told *NME*'s Paul Rambali that 'I've still got a belief in the power of reason.' Simonon, too, had always professed himself to be more interested in personal politics than anything more compartmentalised.[20] 'We wanna be the apathy party of Great Britain,' Strummer told the influential punk fanzine *Sniffin' Glue* in 1976, and he was probably only half-joking. When interviewer Steve Walsh asked if The Clash were anarchists, as The Sex Pistols were claiming to be, Strummer caustically replied, 'I don't believe in all that anarchy bollocks.'

Punk, as Strummer subsequently noted, had a monochrome, myopic world-view. 'The day I joined The Clash was Year Zero,' he said in 1999. 'We were almost Stalinist in the way that you had to shed all your friends.' The past was dead. Only the future mattered – even if that was 'No Future', as The Pistols had declared. This was reflected in punk's choice of clothes – a

19. The Sex Pistols' 'Anarchy in the UK' and The Damned's 'New Rose' were both released in late 1976.
20. In 1980 Simonon told *Rolling Stone*'s James Henke 'When somebody says "You can't do that!" we think you should stand up and ask why, not go "Well, all right."'

rejection of the ubiquitous flares that mark out the mid-70s as the era that taste forgot. It gave rise to one of the band's most quoted pieces of propaganda, from that same *Sniffin' Glue* interview: *Like trousers, like brain*. 'The new look,' Strummer said, later, 'was Mod. Fast. Trim. Going places.'

During their first meeting with Caroline Coon, a journalist who would help their career immeasurably, Strummer and Jones verbally abused the founder of Release as a reactionary representative of everything that they were trying to destroy. 'They said, "You old hippy, [your] movement failed",' Coon remembered in 1999. 'They were anti-drugs, anti-denim, anti-*Top of the Pops*; there was this wonderful dialogue as two generations clashed.' This dismissive attitude towards those whom they regarded as Establishment stooges knew few boundaries. 'They'd even laugh at Maurice Oberstein [the head of CBS who had signed them],' *Rude Boy* co-director Jack Hazan told Pat Gilbert. 'He loved them, but they treated him appallingly. They thought they were rock 'n' roll commandos, but sometimes I think they couldn't differentiate between who was good and who was bad.'

Yet this single-minded determination to do things on their own terms (or, at a pinch, on Rhodes') led, almost from day one, to The Clash being open to accusations of hypocrisy. The day they signed to CBS, 25 January 1977, was, according to *Sniffin' Glue*'s editor Mark Perry, 'the day that punk died.' Charges of 'sell-out' were never far from The Clash's door, often over the most trivial of matters – taste in clothes, changes in musical direction, etc. The kind of stuff that bands are normally applauded for being open to. Partly, this reaction was The Clash's own fault: if you constantly bang on about how in-touch you are with 'The Kids' because you're living in the gutter with them, and then you sign with a record label for an advance of one hundred grand, it's, naturally, going to be taken the wrong way by some of your audience. Often, though, banal accusations of selling out say far more about those making such claims than they do about The Clash themselves. While Perry's motives were, no doubt, sincere, it was noticeable that in the fanzine's next issue his co-editor, Danny Baker, mounted a spirited defence of The Clash's wish to reach more ears than they could by blasting out incendiary sets at The Roxy. 'Punk was about change,' Simonon told *Rolling Stone* in 1980. 'Rule number one was: there are no rules.'

In 1981, Strummer told Vic Garbarini that it was the fans who had killed punk rock. 'They wanted it to stay the same, and that ended our interest in it. Now they've got what they deserved: a lot of rubbish, basically.' [21] As early as June 1977, Jones had conceded to *Search and Destroy* fanzine that, while The

---

21. Those people – both journalists and fans – who bemoan The Clash's move away from two-chord thrashes and lyrics about council estates to something more subtle will, presumably, be delighted to know that copies of the compilation LP *The Oi Story* can be obtained for as little as 50p at your local junk shop.

Clash wanted to listen to their fans, 'lately they've started to say, "Why aren't you doing this now?", "Why have you copped out?" We call them 'Social Conscience Botherers'.' For Strummer, this was clearly a vexed problem. 'Can we do the thing all the time?' he asked Wolfgang Büld rhetorically in 1980. 'No. That way, you're dead.' The problem was exacerbated for The Clash as their fame increased and they reached out to new converts further and further from home. 'Every time we come to a town, they say "We've been waiting five years for you,"' Strummer told Roz Reines in Australia in 1982. 'The message of punk was Do It Yourself. Somehow it's been distorted. Now you get carbon copies of skinheads and punks in far-flung corners of the globe. They're not dealing with their own town, they're wishing they could be somewhere else.'

This emergent theme, of The Clash turning out to have feet of clay in the eyes of some of their fans because they wished to expand their musical landscape, is the mirror image of a more spiteful trend. That is, The Clash turning out to have feet of clay in the eyes of some music journalists because they dared to have ambitions to play bigger venues than The 100 Club and sell more than a fistful of records. Over the years several writers who were caught up in the excitement and rush of the early punk movement in London have cast a jaundiced eye over what became of the utopian musical future that they imagined in 1976. As early as May 1977, *NME*'s Neil Spenser was the first to do so and many others followed. Even when the band themselves tried to introduce a little reality into the myth, they were often doomed to failure. 'I kept trying to stress that we're not in there with John Reed and *Ten Days That Shook the World*,' Strummer told Richard Cromelin in 1988. 'We'd be in the alley with Charlie Parker shooting up junk ... I felt worried that people thought we were Che Guevara.'

In *England's Dreaming*, Jon Savage suggests that The Clash, post-1978, simply became a 'very good rock band', but that before this they were actually something more. Savage notes that it's hard when you define a period so accurately. 'The Clash seem locked in time,' he had written in November 1978, reviewing *Give 'Em Enough Rope*. 'They have an audience which is loyal to the point of fanaticism: they often seem to relate to each other on the basis of mutual reinforcement. Trapped in this circle, The Clash's solution is rock 'n' roll. From being radicals, they become conservatives.' There is a hollowness to some of these charges, however. Criticising The Clash for no longer being bored with the USA, but rather becoming keen to incorporate a wider musical heritage, a few pages later Savage lambasts The Jam for being, in his words, 'Little Englanders'. [22] You can't have it both ways, surely?

---

22. Frankly any writer who describes Paul Weller continuing to 'blight' the British music scene deserves, in this author's opinion, to have their views taken with a pinch of salt, no matter how good they are. And Savage, let's be fair, is good!

Marcus Gray's 1995 Clash biography, *Last Gang In Town,* spends much time and effort debunking many of the myths that Rhodes and The Clash carefully-created for themselves. He does it well and the book is not, contrary to some contemporary reviews, a negative, salacious exercise in hero-desecration à la Albert Goldman's books on Elvis and Lennon. It's excellently researched and well written, just as *England's Dreaming, The Boy Looked at Johnny* and *Psychotic Reactions* all are. What it *is,* however – and this is something that it shares, especially, with Savage's book – is fundamentally flawed by the belief that almost anybody who enjoys The Clash's music is actually *bothered* about whether they were true to the ideals that they professed to have. So they told a few pork pies about their background? Big deal. 'All this blathering about authenticity is just *a bunch of crap* [my italics],' noted Lester Bangs in 1977. Who are we mere mortals to argue?

Were The Clash a bunch of hypocrites? Possibly they were. Mick Jones *did* live on the 18th floor of a tower block overlooking The Westway with his grandmother, Stella. So what if, before that, they had a much nicer house somewhere else? It doesn't make 'Deny' or 'Complete Control' or any of the dozens of songs that Jones wrote in 111 Wilmcote House any the less extraordinary. Kosmo Vinyl's infamous comment, that The Westway was to The Clash what Trenchtown was to The Wailers, a spiritual place, may be an example of crass hyperbole, but there's undeniably an element of truth in the assertion. Does it matter that Joe Strummer had a, rather unhealthy, interest in terrorist chic circa 1978? The Rolling Stones flirted with exactly the same dangerous cocktail a decade earlier, and got away with it. The Manic Street Preachers would do so all over again 20 years hence. *Plus ça change, plus ça la même chose.* The Clash allowed one of their songs to be used in a commercial to sell jeans and, as a consequence, made a bit of money from it. It must be said that, on a list of people who have sold their soul to The Man, that still leaves them pretty low down the pecking order. In a business of charlatans, rogues and manipulators, The Clash were as close to the real deal as it was possible to be. 'If you don't like The Clash, you don't like rock 'n' roll,' wrote *Sounds* in 1977. 'It's as simple as that.'[23]

When an American journalist in the late 1990s noted that 'if you catch them on a really good night, U2 sound like what they are, a fair-to-middling Clash tribute band,' it may have been damning U2 with faint praise. But there's no doubt that Bono and the boys successfully followed, almost to the letter, The

---

23. The Clash, inevitably, got so sick of questions concerning whether they had sold out that by 1981 they weren't even bothering to answer them seriously. In what circumstances does a group sell out, Jones was asked by one earnest journalist in New York in 1981. 'When there are no further tickets available,' Jones replied straight-faced. 'That, by definition, constitutes a sell-out.'

Clash's chosen identity as 'The People's Band' and their subsequent assimilation of assorted disparate influences into their music to gain a truly global audience. 'The modern definition of 'made it' is filling 100,000-seat stadiums,' Strummer told Bill Flanagan in 1988. 'U2 do it five times a week ... I'd say we sold a *speck* overall of what U2 sell now. [But] *we* made it in another way. We made it in the culture.' That goes for other would-be Clashes too – bands who throw all the right poses and give good interview, but who need to develop the music to go with the aesthetics. 'Oasis are really great, but I don't know if they've got the same amount of depth we had,' Jones told *Guitar World* in 1995. 'I came into the punk scene because punk stayed with you. A lot of the other music of the time left you as it found you.'

The Clash certainly had articulate principles and in many cases they carried these through as far as was practical (and sometimes way beyond, to the exasperation of a succession of managers). Nine times out of ten, their attitude to their fans was above and beyond the call of duty – at many gigs, famously throwing open the back door to those without tickets. They released first a double LP and then a triple at the cost of normal albums, and they always kept the ticket prices to their concerts as low as possible, despite usually featuring a minimum of two support bands, thus often losing money even on sell-out tours.

The Clash's idealism was real, but they probably realised early on that they were part of an industry that kills rhetoric just as easily as it fuels excessive ego. There may have been a lot of leftist ideology in their lyrics, but it was obvious to anyone with half a brain that The Clash, themselves, were not doctrinaire Marxists. 'Toeing any [party] line is a dodgy situation. I'm not into policy or I'd have joined the Communist Party years ago,' Strummer told *Musician*. 'I've done my time selling the *Morning Star* at pit-heads in Wales.' By the time that Jones wrote 'Complete Control' in June 1977, The Clash pretty much knew what the game was about. And they were prepared to play that game, even sometimes by other people's rules, because it enabled them to reach out to new converts. That was their priority. The music always came first.

The Clash quickly ceased to be the danger to society that they had been perceived to be in 1977. By late the following year, tabloids such as the *Sun* and the *Daily Mirror* were running complimentary articles on them – the former calling Simonon 'the James Dean of punk', the latter describing Strummer as 'a Cockney Bogart'. The comparison to stars of Hollywood's golden age probably wasn't a conscious comment on The Clash's hope to fit into a mythological hybrid American landscape, but it is interesting in view of the route that the band were to take. Virtually alone among the punk elite, The Clash took enthusiastically to America. There they found, as *Uncut* noted, a spiritual home in a land of misfits, outlaws and frontiersmen. 'We were revolutionaries on behalf of punk rock,' Strummer would tell Charles Shaar Murray two decades after their US debut. 'There was no MTV, no radio – it was hard to break in America. We did it [by] playing every shithole between Kitchener, Ontario and the Everglades.'

King Crimson's Robert Fripp made an interesting point when he was interviewed, along with Strummer, by Vic Garbarini in 1981. British musicians, by and large, are more politically aware because British society's class system is so rigid and ingrained that one almost feels obliged to comment on it, and to define one's position within it. America, by contrast, is a commercial culture and a great deal of social mobility results. In other words, Britain has a completely class-conscious system in which everyone but *nouveau riche* vulgarians knows their place. In December 1976, the novelist Lynne Reid Banks, in a letter to the *Observer*, summed up a widely held opinion: 'Class is so deeply embedded in our national subconscious it is poisoning every aspect of our lives. Not just industrial relations and politics, but our choice of districts to live in, jobs, schools, friends – even which bar to drink in. It's a kind of civil war we are perpetually fighting, wearing out our energies and emotions, wasting our time and money.' For the working classes, escaping this pigeonholing is only an option for those who have – as James Bolam's character, Terry Collier, memorably noted in the 1976 film of *The Likely Lads* – 'cracked it through football or rock 'n' roll.'

In America, by contrast, the only culture that really matters is money culture. 'In the United States, The Clash have no clear political connections or milieu to help them maintain definition in the face of success,' wrote Tom Smucker in 1980. This was something that many British critics seemed (and, in some cases, still seem, even two decades later) to have a major problem with. There was something about the way The Clash openly drew on American culture to get a foothold on the other side of the Atlantic that seemed designed to bring out the racist Little Englander in the UK music media. It's as though some writers regard The Clash as being their own personal property because they saw them once down The Roxy, and they are really miffed that anyone else, especially anyone else *American*, can find anything in the band to admire. [24]

Frequent suggestions that The Clash should stick to British subjects in their lyrics was 'evidence of a blinkered and parochial view', noted Marcus

---

24. There's always been an element of sniggering amusement at American foibles by even the best of British music writers. See, for instance, Ian MacDonald's rather haughty dismissal of American humour in *Revolution in the Head* ('audiences are clearly cued, in inferior TV sitcoms, by a ponderous archness guaranteed to set English teeth on edge').

Gray. He did add, perceptively, that this had possibly been inspired by The Clash's own pro-British, anti-American rhetoric on 'I'm So Bored With The USA'. Nevertheless, 'to see where you've come from, you have to go someplace else,' Jones told New Zealand journalist Duncan Campbell in 1982. 'Otherwise you don't understand that the world doesn't finish at the end of your street.'

Critically, for The Clash, America was a different world: The Clash's repertoire, wrote Greil Marcus in 1979, consisted of 'harrowed rhythms and coarse vocals' which propelled 'a foray of songs aimed at the bleak political realities and social ennui of English life, making social realism – and unbridled disgust – key elements in the punk aesthetic.' Even many of the old guard of US rock journalists took enthusiastically to The Clash, *Rolling Stone* veteran and Who biographer Dave Marsh describing them as the first great new rock band to have emerged since the 1960s. The Clash must have found it hard to believe their luck. At the very moment when, in the UK, Nick Kent was describing what he considered to be a spurious attempt by The Clash to self-aggrandise their own myth, and Jon Savage was preparing notes for a subsequent career of writing retrospectives on how good the band used to be, Strummer was telling *Rolling Stone* that 'England's become too claustrophobic for us. Everything we do is scrutinised.'

American audiences (and critics), by contrast, seemed hungry for the cathartic urban anarchy which they identified with punk and, from 1980 onwards, America was where The Clash's head, if not always their heart, usually lay. When one considers the nonsense they were having to put up with back home – Ian Penman's notorious 1981 comment in *NME*, 'What do they see when they look in the mirror? Third world guerrillas with quiffs?' for example – who could blame them? 'If we were just going to be another Stones or another Who,' Strummer told a Detroit newspaper in 1979, 'it would be a bore. That's why we're going to turn left where we should've turned right.'

A problem for most music writers, and I include myself in this, is avoiding the risk of hyperbole in what we write about. It's an easy trap to fall into. Such is the power, passion and emotion that truly great music provokes, after a while it's possible to start making sweeping, grandiose statements that simply don't hold up in the cold light of day. That often happened to The Clash throughout their career and beyond, and there is a strong feeling that a portion of the backlash they felt from the English music press during the early 1980s was, in part, due to embarrassment from the journalists themselves at having got so carried away in the first place.

The Clash were a great band, don't just take my word for it, their influence and the affection with which they are held speaks for itself. But, because of that, it's easy to believe that their importance lay beyond their music. Very few bands ever changed the world to any significant degree. And those that did – The Beatles and The Rolling Stones are the obvious examples – usually did so in a social and cultural context rather than, specifically, through their music. 'There's so much corruption: councils, government, industry, everywhere,' Strummer told Barry Miles in 1978. 'It's got to be flushed out. Just because it's been going on for a long time doesn't mean that it shouldn't be stopped.' The fact that, in 2003, the situation is just the same, if not worse, clearly demonstrates that music changes very little in the great scheme of things.

When it is suggested that a band has changed the world, what such comments realistically mean is that, for the two minutes and 58 seconds that a song is played, the listener's world was altered. That, mentally, they were taken to a different place, whether that was through the imagery the lyrics or music inspired, or through more down-to-earth associations from memories of, for example, when the song was first heard. That's certainly true of The Clash. For a certain age group, particularly in England, many of these songs are the soundtrack of our youth, floating out from transistor radios and cheap record players, accompanied by memories of the first experiences of drink, sex and life. Those of us from the council estates for whom something like 'Stay Free' – along with, for example, The Jam's 'Saturday's Kids' and The Undertones' 'Teenage Kicks' – chronicled, with almost obsessive detail, our teenage lives. What we did, where we went, how we felt. What The Clash, and their music, changed was not the world, but rather, some people within it.

Of course, every now and then a particular song does change the world, however peripherally. It doesn't happen very often, but it must have caused Strummer a moment's introspection when one of his contemporaries, Jerry Dammers, wrote just such a song, 'Nelson Mandela'.

In the end, maybe, a bit of the cynical post-punk-idealism world even got to Joe Strummer. But only a little bit. In 1986 he admitted that he was disappointed not to have been invited to play on the Red Wedge package that Dammers and Paul Weller had put together to encourage young voters to become politically active. Yet he had enough common sense to note that 'After eight fucking years of Thatcher, surely that's all you need to tell you to vote Labour? If you don't, a few decent rock 'n' roll shows ain't gonna change your mind.'

Strummer's passion, integrity and dignity remained till the end, and was abundantly evident at one of his last live appearances a month before he died.[25]

---

25. 'The spirit of rock 'n' roll helped to stop the Vietnam War,' Strummer told the *Times* in one of his last interviews. 'Perhaps it's crazy for me still to feel like that. But I can't help it. Someone's got to keep the faith.'

It was a benefit concert for striking firemen[26] and Mick Jones joined him on stage, for the first time in 20 years, to play 'Bankrobber', 'White Riot' and 'London's Burning'.

Those qualities remain, too, with Jones, Paul Simonon and Topper Headon. They're all older and, perhaps, wiser. Three middle-aged men who were once – along with a fourth, now sadly deceased, man – members of one of the greatest rock 'n' roll bands of all time. That fact needs no embellishment.

26. Fire-fighters' union leader Andy Gilchrist later said that he had first become politicised after seeing The Clash at the Rock Against Racism carnival in April 1978.

THE SONGS FROM A TO Z

ALL THE YOUNG PUNKS (NEW BOOTS AND CONTRACTS)
[Strummer/Jones]
LP: *Give 'Em Enough Rope*

With its title drawn from a combination of David Bowie's 'All the Young Dudes' (the song which gave Jones' beloved Mott The Hoople their first hit) and Ian Dury and The Blockheads' 1977 LP *New Boots and Panties*, 'All the Young Punks' saw The Clash's self-mythology machine hit maximum overdrive. Further lessons in rock 'n' roll history occur via Jones' Eric Clapton-style guitar solo (played on his 'heart attack machine' Les Paul) while, musically, the song sounds not unlike an out-take from *The Who Sell Out*. The lyrics, when they aren't telling the erroneous, if admittedly poetic, story of The Clash's origins, are a cunning mixture of the *this is what the biz is all about*-shenanigans of **Complete Control** and the *can't work/won't work* defiance of **Career Opportunities** and **Janie Jones**. Most memorably, however, 'All the Young Punks' describes the Bernard Rhodes/CBS contract as resembling something dreamed up by the Mafia. Everyone may, indeed, want to bum a ride on 'the rock 'n' rollercoaster', as the song suggests, but there is always a price to be paid for such fantasies. To The Clash's horror, that price in their case seemed to involve working until they dropped.

Recorded at Basing Street, the *Rude Boy* movie features Strummer performing an impassioned vocal-take to a pre-recorded backing. 'All the Young Punks' briefly featured in The Clash's live set, introduced at the beginning of the On Parole tour in June 1978. A few shows later it was dropped.

AMMUNITION
[Strummer]

Sometimes referred to as **Live Ammunition**, this song about the international arms trade was an important part of the post-Mick Jones line-up's live set during 1984. Strummer would often preface performances of the song by speaking of his growing concern at the decade's mainstream political shift to the right (with specific reference to Margaret Thatcher and Ronald Reagan) and encourage young people to use their votes wisely. Introduced at Santa Monica in January 1984, rumours circulate that a studio version of 'Ammunition' was recorded during the *Cut the Crap* sessions, but the song remains unreleased. With its anti-warmongering theme and rousing 'Thank you, chief' chorus, 'Ammunition' went down well with The Clash's concert audiences and, if it *was* recorded, its absence from *Cut the Crap* is mysterious.

ARE YOU READY FOR WAR?
See **Are You Red.. Y**.

ARE YOU RED.. Y
[Strummer/Rhodes]
LP: *Cut the Crap*

Initially performed as **Are You Ready For War?** on the 1984 tour, like **Ammunition**, the song first appeared live at Santa Monica on 27 January and remained in The Clash's live set for most of that year. A highly simplistic examination of escalating world conflict, the song refers to Ronald Reagan's Strategic Defense Initiative ('Star Wars') programme – an update of the 'satellites that burn' theme of **Charlie Don't Surf**. Strummer's lyrics are, frankly, dreadful – full of inelegant rhymes ('sentimental', 'regimental' and 'continental', for instance), vernacular clichés (the Kremlin and vodka) and crass metaphors. Worse still, 'Are You Red.. Y's music is about as far removed from what one would expect from The Clash as it's possible to be. Peppered, richly, with of-the-era sequenced keyboards and percussion in the place of actual human beings, 'Are You Red.. Y' displays all the worst excesses of a dreadful musical era. In this world, style is dead, flair is dead, *enigma* is dead, all buried in unmarked graves and replaced with somebody playing space invaders. Even the guitar sounds suspiciously 'manufactured'. Live, the song was tackled slightly slower and with a much more human-sounding arrangement.

ARMAGIDEON TIME
[Willie Williams/Jackie Mittoo]
B-SIDE: 12/79

A reggae hit for Jamaican singer Willie Williams in 1978, 'Armagideon Time's quasi-biblical lyrics were right up The Clash's collective street. The song was refined during the Clash Take The Fifth tour, first being played in September

1979 at the *Tribal Stomp Festival* in Monterey: 'A soundcheck job, that turned into an encore job, that turned into a studio job,' as Johnny Green noted. Definitive proof that the band's commitment to mixing punk with contemporary reggae didn't end with **Police & Thieves** and **Pressure Drop**, recording of 'Armagiddeon Time' took place at Wessex Studios on 5 November 1979 during the mixing sessions for *London Calling*. The song featured Mickey Gallagher[27] on keyboards and tubular bells played by Headon.

'I [had] this theory that all great singles should be two minutes and 58 seconds long,' remembered Clash aide Kosmo Vinyl, who was in the control room. Strummer liked that idea and told Kosmo to stop the group when they reached the time limit. At exactly 2:58, Vinyl hit the studio intercom and said 'Time's up, let's have you out of there.' The song almost ground to a halt, only Simonon's bass continuing. 'Okay, okay,' shouted Strummer angrily, off-mike, 'don't push us when we're *HOT!*' The annoying interruption over, the song continued for another exhilarating minute, ending as one of The Clash's most majestic studio performances. 'I thought, I'm dead, I've ruined a perfect take,' Vinyl wrote in the *Clash On Broadway* booklet. 'But nobody said a thing about my voice being all over it.'

Released as the B-Side of the **London Calling** single, 'Armagideon Time' remained a live favourite for much of the rest of The Clash's career. The song would often be performed with the stage in near darkness, Johnny Green holding up a lone torch to illuminate Strummer's face.

A searing version, recorded on 27 December 1979 at the Hammersmith Odeon, subsequently appeared on the TV film and LP of the event (*Concerts for the People of Kampuchea* – Atlantic K 60153, March 1981). A five-minute version recorded on 18 February 1980 at the Lewisham Odeon graces *From Here to Eternity*. Featuring Mikey Dread's additional toasting, this shows how the song was regularly performed throughout the 16 Tons tour. In 1982, when The Clash toured the US with The Beat, Ranking Roger (with whom Jones would subsequently work in BAD) provided the toasting accompaniment. The song was also, occasionally, performed live in a brutal medley with **The Magnificent Seven**. 'Armagideon Time' was subsequently used in the Strummer-compiled score for the John Cusack movie *Grosse Pointe Blank*.

---

27. Gallagher began his career in the South Shields group The Chosen Few (along with future Lindisfarne songwriter Alan Hull) before a brief spell, in 1965, as Alan Price's replacement in The Animals. Gallagher later played with Skip Bifferty, Frampton's Camel, Bell & Arc and Loving Awareness before joining Ian Dury and The Blockheads in 1977. Kosmo Vinyl recommended Gallagher to The Clash.

ATOM TAN
[The Clash]
LP: *Combat Rock*

One of the *Combat Rock* songs never to be performed live, 'Atom Tan' was a slow soul groove, with a dragging beat, angular guitar phrases and call-and-response vocals.

Recorded at Electric Lady in November 1981, the lyrics are a complex series of riddles and conundrums that appear on the surface to concern the pressures and paranoia of modern life. On closer inspection, however, there's a much darker and more enigmatic undertone, with suggestions of suicide and sexual violence ('chained by love'). Then again, the song's description of someone suffering a heart attack live on television which 'looked like Hollywood' is yet another brick in the wall of *Combat Rock*'s de rigueur media obsessions (see **Red Angel Dragnet** et al). Subsequent allusions to The Lone Ranger and Batman merely reinforce this point.

BABY, PLEASE DON'T GO
[Big Joe Williams]

This R&B classic is best known via the 1965 version by Van Morrison's Them. The Clash jammed the song during the soundcheck for the 21 September 1979 New York Palladium show.

BANKROBBER
[Strummer/Jones]
B-SIDE: [Netherlands] 6/80. **SINGLE:** [UK] 8/80

'Bankrobber' was another link in the chain of Clash lyrics that urged listeners to stop working in dead-end jobs and to experience life to the fullest (see **Career Opportunities**, **Janie Jones**, **Clash City Rockers**, **All the Young Punks**, **Clampdown**). Described in *Last Gang In Town* as 'an outrageous slice of Staggerlee-goes-to-Hollywood myth-making' (see **Wrong 'Em Boyo**), 'Bankrobber' was introduced to The Clash's live set during the Christmas 1979 gigs at Acklam Hall and the Hammersmith Odeon. Strummer's opening verse is the only real competitor to **Four Horsemen** as the funniest thing he ever wrote, with its noble allusions to Robin Hood, stealing from the rich to give to the poor, shattered by the hilarious final line.

The rest of the song, which references John Updike's 1960 novel *Rabbit Run* and Butch Cassidy and the Sundance Kid's Hole In The Wall hideout in the Wyoming Big Horn mountains, maintains this sly, tongue-in-cheek, laddish attitude. But it does so while sticking two metaphorical fingers up at the concept of 'a lifetime serving one machine' and not forgetting to grovel to The Man afterwards. The song is largely carried by Simonon's pitching and yawing bassline, and various production tricks, although Jones' contribution, an understated bottleneck guitar riff, is worthy of considerable attention.

The recording of 'Bankrobber', on 1 and 2 February 1980 at Pluto Studio in Manchester, was the first occasion that The Clash worked with Mikey Dread.[28] 'Mikey got a great vibe going in the studio,' noted Mickey Gallagher. 'He made rhythms by shaking a matchbox, or using a squeaky toy. He would make the hi-hat sound he wanted with his mouth.' Dread, who also played tambourine on the record, persuaded The Clash to slow down the song into more of a reggae groove. 'Bankrobber' was intended to be the first offering in 'the singles campaign that never was'. 'We decided to record a single a month. As one dropped out of the charts, we would release another one,' remembered Kosmo Vinyl. 'We delivered it to CBS but they wouldn't release it. They said it sounded like all of David Bowie's records played backwards at once. Eventually they put it out, but only after we had sneaked it out as a B-Side in Holland and it was going to chart on import sales alone.'

The single was finally released in the UK on 8 August 1980 and became The Clash's second successive single to narrowly miss the top 10 (making number 12). 'The moaning hook line and some cleverly introduced buzzing noises make this a likeable addition to an honourable catalogue,' wrote David Hepworth in *Smash Hits*. 'They sound more human all the time.' In *Sounds*, by contrast, Strummer's assertion that his daddy was a bankrobber was somewhat ridiculed by the reviewer: 'Actually, John Mellor's daddy was a Second Secretary of Information at the Foreign Office. One of *my* mate's daddys *was* a bankrobber. He ended up in little pieces after a gangland feud.'

A video was shot by Don Letts, which mixed images of The Clash recording the song in Pluto, playing it on stage (at the Lewisham Odeon on 18 February) and two masked robbers (Johnny Green and Barry Glare) holding up a bank on Lewisham High Street. Tragically, *Top of the Pops* weren't interested in

---

28. Michael Campbell began his career as a DJ on JBC in Jamaica, where his late-night radio show, *Dread at the Controls*, proved to be both popular and controversial. After recording material with Lee Perry in 1978, Dread started his own label and his debut LP, named after his radio show, was a big hit with the UK reggae community. By early 1980 he had worked with Sugar Minott, Ed Fitzroy and Earl 16.

showing it. Thus, in one of the great slapstick comedy moments of UK television history, resident dance troupe Legs and Co.[29], dressed in stripy spandex and gangster hats, threw money in the air and wiggled their bottoms in time to the music on the 18 August 1980 episode.

'Bankrobber' became a huge live favourite of The Clash's later years. A furiously uptempo rockabilly cover version was performed by The Pistoleers in 2003 and the song has also been covered by Audioweb and The Soul Merchants.

THE BEAUTIFUL PEOPLE ARE UGLY
[The Clash]

Recorded at Electric Lady in late 1981 during the sessions for what would become *Combat Rock*. This slight number, which seemed to have been inspired by elements of calypso and funk, was ultimately excluded from the finished LP and remains unreleased.

BE-BOP-A-LULA
[Vincent/Davis]

An echo-drenched 1956 standard by Gene Vincent and The Blue Caps, 'Be-Bop-a-Lula' has been covered by just about every self-respecting rocker since. Strummer played the song with The 101ers and, inspired by The Clash's first lengthy tour of the US in late 1979, he and Joe Ely led the band through encore versions of the song during the Hollywood and San Francisco shows. It was also performed by The Clash on their 1985 Busking tour.

BILLY
[Bob Dylan]

Recorded, with Guy Stevens, during the early *London Calling* sessions. The song, from Dylan's 1973 soundtrack *Pat Garrett & Billy The Kid*, would have probably been Strummer's choice, having previously played it with The 101ers.

BLITZKRIEG BOP
[The Ramones]

The huge influence of The Ramones debut LP on The Clash, particularly Strummer and Simonon, has been well documented. By way of acknowledgment, during 1978 The Clash often performed the New York group's best known song as part of a live medley with **Police & Thieves**.[30]

BLONDE ROCK 'N' ROLL
[The Clash]

A Jones song from the 1980 New York *Sandinista!* sessions. Sung by its composer in a duet with his girlfriend, Ellen Foley, 'Blonde Rock 'n' Roll' was cursed by slight lyrics and an uncertain medium-paced rhythm. It remains unreleased.

BRAND NEW CADILLAC
[Vince Taylor]
LP: *London Calling*

'Vince Taylor was the beginning of British rock 'n' roll,' Joe Strummer told *Mojo* in 2000. 'Before him there was nothing. He was a miracle.' Born Brian Holden in London in 1939, his parents emigrated to the US when Brian was seven. They ended up in California, where his sister married animation legend Joseph Barbera. Obsessed with rock 'n' roll and Elvis Presley, Brian began a singing career. A trip back to London in 1958 brought him a name-change, a backing band (The Play-Boys) and a residency at the Two i's coffee bar in Soho. Taylor's second single for Parlophone, 'Pledging My Love', contained on the B-Side his own composition, 'Brand New Cadillac', an instant classic thanks to Taylor' histrionic vocals and guitarist Tony Sheridan's tense riff. Although it was never a hit in England, the song, and others like it, made Taylor a rock 'n' roll superstar in France during the early 1960s. Sadly, by 1962, Taylor had begun to spiral into mental illness, on one occasion infamously going on-stage in a white shroud and announcing that he was Jesus Christ. His story inspired David Bowie, who met Taylor in the mid-60s and had a long conversation with him about aliens, to create the character of Ziggy Stardust.

'I met [Taylor] in The Pig's Foot restaurant in the early 80s,' remembered Strummer. 'He talked to me for over five hours about how the Duke and Duchess of Windsor were planning to kill him with poisoned chocolate cake.' Taylor's final years were spent as a virtual recluse in Switzerland, where he died in 1991. Strummer would, subsequently, play a character based on Taylor in the 1997 movie *Docteur Chance*.

30. The medley debuted at Aylesbury during the On Parole tour, in June 1978.

Surprisingly, perhaps, it wasn't Strummer who brought 'Brand New Cadillac' to the attention of The Clash. Rather, it was Simonon who, in early 1979, was investigating the early rock 'n' roll music that Strummer had enthusiastically introduced him to. (Simonon discovered the song on a reissue single released by Chiswick in 1976.) 'Brand New Cadillac' was a 'look at my car' song in the tradition of Eddie Cochran's 'Something Else', but with a novel twist – it's the singer's *girl* who has the car and, with it, she's heading out of his life. Strummer had a field day, throwing around the positively filthy lyrics – certainly by 1959 standards – with abandon. He even forgets to be angry with his baby's new possession at one point, asking *'Jesus Christ! Where'd ya get that Cadillac?'*

The Clash worked up a furious version during the Pimlico rehearsals and the song was the first thing to be recorded – in just one take – with a hugely impressed Guy Stevens at Wessex. It subsequently entered the band's live repertoire at the Rainbow in July 1979, although the song was only performed on a couple of occasions during the Clash Take The Fifth tour. From 1980, however, it became in indispensable part of the band's set. Strummer remained obsessed with 'Brand New Cadillac' and continued to play it live with his 90s band, The Mescaleros.

BROADWAY
[The Clash]
LP: *Sandinista!*

The closest The Clash ever got to jazz (more New Orleans than modern or trad, admittedly), 'Broadway' is a mellow, beautiful product of the all-encompassing New York atmosphere of the *Sandinista!* sessions. 'We stayed at the Iroquois Hotel,' wrote Barry Glare in the *Clash On Broadway* booklet. 'Outside was a heating vent. There was always this one particular bloke, standing or sleeping on it. I remember one night we came back from the studio about four in the morning and Joe was looking at this guy quite intently. I always thought 'Broadway' was about him.'

In 'Broadway', Strummer meets an old tramp who 'testifies' with his life story. The clever wordplay and social observation that follows is some of the most perceptive that Strummer, a gifted human observer at the best of times, ever wrote. The burned-out-boxer metaphor of the song's second verse suggests either an attempt to match the imagery of Paul Simon's 'The Boxer' or perhaps that Strummer had seen an early cut of his friend Martin Scorsese's *Raging Bull*, filmed in New York the previous year. (During the band's residency in the city in 1981, Strummer twice dedicated 'Broadway' to heavyweight boxer Leon Spinks who, two years earlier, had been stripped of his titles after a drug scandal.) The song includes many poetic images of New York city life; the misty rain-covered streets, the bright lights, the bars, the cars and the girls. One almost feels, given the circumstances, that 'Broadway' should be sung (as Scorsese's film was shot) in monochrome.

'Broadway' is also, interestingly, an almost-archetypal example of an English *avarice* song, yet it's tinged with the disillusionment and regret of the narrator having seen beyond the façade of materialism and discovering that there is nothing there. 'Did you put your money in?' asks Strummer pointedly, the implication being that if you don't, you don't get to play.

Introduced to The Clash's set during the New York shows in June 1981, the song's dramatic structure was used to devastating effect as the opening number during the Paris residency and the UK tour later that year. The song made an occasional live appearance thereafter and was revived for the Brixton Miners' Benefit gigs in December 1984 and the Clash's 1985 dates.

THE CALL UP
[The Clash]
SINGLE: 11/80. **LP:** *Sandinista!*

Featuring The Voidoids' Ivan Julian on guitar, 'The Call Up' opens and closes with a US marines' marching chant. 'The registration for the draft in America affected a lot of our fans,' noted Jones in 1991. 'I remember going to a demonstration on the Upper West Side.' The song's fiercely anti-war sentiments echo John Lennon's similarly themed 'I Don't Want To Be A Soldier'. Lyrically slight, and featuring somewhat obvious anti-establishment rhetoric ('who gives you work, and why should you do it?' is yet another link in the extended **Career Opportunities** chain of the rejection of dead-end employment), 'The Call Up', nevertheless, includes touching observations. Love, it concludes, is more important than fighting for a cause ('there is a rose that I want to live for'). 'The Call Up' made its live debut in Berlin in May 1981 and featured during the subsequent New York residency. Thereafter, the song made only occasional concert appearances until it became a fixture again during the Combat Rock tour.

Don Letts' video for the single, shot in black and white, featured Simonon dressed as a cowboy, Headon as a World War II pilot and Jones... well, it's difficult to tell exactly *what* Mick is supposed to be – his costume includes a Mounties hat and a leopardskin wrap. This was filmed at the warehouse of singer Chris Farlowe, an enthusiastic collector of military paraphernalia.

CAPITAL AIR
[The Clash/Ginsberg]

See GHETTO DEFENDANT.

CAPITAL RADIO ONE
[Strummer/Jones]
SINGLE: NME CL-1 4/77.

Strummer recognised the importance of radio – especially the BBC's World Service[31] – from an early age, and the power of the medium became a subject he addressed in a number of songs.

Recorded, along with **Listen**, at CBS on Sunday 3 April 1977 – specifically to be used on a give-away single in association with *NME* – the recording was Terry Chimes' final studio performance with The Clash. 'Capital Radio' immediately secured a place in the band's live set on the White Riot tour, and it remained there for most of the rest of the band's career.

The song's simple format allowed for much experimentation and 'Capital Radio', along with **Police & Thieves**, became the main concert vehicles for Strummer's love of adding stream-of-consciousness raps and throwing in references to other songs.[32] The version recorded at the Lewisham Odeon in February 1980, and featured on *From Here to Eternity*, is a spectacular case in point. In it, Strummer acts out ringing up his local station and asking to hear 'The Woolly Bully' by Sam The Sham & The Pharaohs ('not Sham 69!'). Unfortunately, The Man, he say 'no'. Covered by The Hyperjax, the lyrical influence of 'Capital Radio' on Elvis Costello's similarly themed 'Radio Radio' seems certain. The song's climactic chant would also inspire Stiff Little Fingers' 'Can't Say Crap on the Radio'.

---

31. The BBC's motto is 'And Nation Shall Speak Peace Unto Nation.'

32. At the Lyceum, in December 1978, Strummer dedicated a fierce performance of 'Capital Radio' to a litany of radio DJs, suggesting, in an extended coda, that they all had the power of life and death over their audiences. Other notable performances include one from London in July 1979 in which Strummer alluded to Johnny Cash's 'I Walk the Line' and Shirley Ellis' 'The Clapping Song'.
At another gig, at Atlanta in October 1979, the song included references to numerous soft-rock acts currently cluttering up US radio, much to Strummer's apparent disgust, as well as a quotation from Muddy Waters' 'The Mannish Boy.'

CAPITAL RADIO TWO
[Strummer/Jones]
EP: *The Cost of Living*

By early 1979, copies of the original *NME* 'Capital Radio' EP were selling for ludicrous amounts of money. As the song was such a live favourite, The Clash decided to record another version for inclusion on *The Cost of Living* EP. Recorded at Wessex in January, 'Capital Radio Two' was a rearrangement much in the style of The Clash's on-stage performances of the song, as opposed to the short sharp shock of the original. For example, the remake begins with a delicate, decorative snatch of acoustic guitar, an idea which grew out of an arpeggioed introduction that Jones occasionally experimented with during live performances of 'Capital Radio' on the Sort It Out tour.

Thereafter, the recording includes a cod-funk/disco coda, which suggests that Jones had been listening closely to Bernard Edwards and Nile Rodgers' contemporary productions for Chic. During this sequence, Strummer alludes to both of Olivia Newton John and John Travolta's massive 1978 hits from *Grease*, 'You're The One That I Want' and 'Summer Nights', and to The Sweet's 'Blockbuster'. All this comes after Joe has told Jonesy that he's realised the band will never get on the radio playing all this punk nonsense ('I've been studying the charts, using my mind and my imagination').

CAR JAMMING
[The Clash]
LP: *Combat Rock*

First recorded – along with **This Is Radio Clash** and **Sean Flynn** – at Marcus Music in April 1981, and completed in New York in December 'Car Jamming' included references to such diverse subjects as Agent Orange[33] and Lauren Bacall. The song features Jones' girlfriend Ellen Foley on backing vocals.

'Car Jamming' entered The Clash's live set at the beginning of the Down The Casbah Club tour in May 1982 and was a regularly feature during the rest of the year.

33. A highly poisonous herbicide used as a defoliant in Vietnam and, subsequently, the subject of REM's 'Orange Crush'.33. A highly poisonous herbicide used as a defoliant in Vietnam and, subsequently, the subject of REM's 'Orange Crush'.

THE CARD CHEAT
[Strummer/Jones]
LP: *London Calling*

The zenith of *London Calling*'s 'outsider' theme, 'The Card Cheat' takes the outlaw figure central to much rock mythology directly from some Last Chance saloon in a Johnny Cash murder ballad. It then sticks him in the midst of Ingmar Bergman's *The Seventh Seal* for one final game of chance with fate. In this context the placement of 'The Card Cheat' on *London Calling*, just three songs after the ostensibly similar **Wrong 'Em Boyo**, is a masterstroke. The central character of 'The Card Cheat' seems to be an older and more cynical version of the characters in songs like **Jimmy Jazz** and **Rudie Can't Fail**, reaching the end of his long and winding road with bitter regret at his underachieving life.

Originally called 'King of Hell', the song's imagery of death and renewal (as in the coming dawn) is among the most imaginative and striking that Strummer ever conceived. Indeed, there is really nothing else like this anywhere in The Clash's canon. The final graphic twist comes in the fourth verse when, having failed to keep himself from 'the darkest door', the gambler reluctantly joins the ranks of the many men from history's pages, from the Hundred Year War to the Crimea, who have 'stood with no fear/In the service of the King.' The obvious implication is that, like us all, the gambler flees from death, desperate for time to run more slowly. That he ultimately fails, as every man must, is just another part of the gamble. This is further emphasised by the subsequent repeat of the first verse, a return to solitude and futility, with not a hint of redemption in sight.

Strummer noted in at least one contemporary interview that he had recently been reading the pessimistic prose of poet Sylvia Plath (1932-63). In the years following her suicide, Plath had become a feminist heroine and martyr. In reality, she was simply a victim of the recurrent psychodrama of her tragically wounded personality. Her final series of poems, written in the months before her death – including 'Lady Lazarus', 'Ariel', 'Edge' and 'Daddy' – define a militantly nihilistic metaphysic, from which death provided the only dignified escape. To the subsequent inspiration of at least two generations of moody teenagers.

If the tortured melodrama of Strummer's words don't impress (and they should), then Jones' haunting arrangement pushes Strummer's lyric to an altogether more complex level. Recorded late in the *London Calling* sessions (by which time it was Jones, along with Bill Price, who were, de facto, producing the record), the idea was to create a Phil Spector-style Wall of

Sound. By double-tracking every instrument, Jones achieved this with considerable clout. ('That's the secret,' he noted in 1991. 'Two of everything.') To this end, Headon's drum patterns were based on one of Spector's most imitated productions, The Ronettes' 'Be My Baby'. A clever countermelody fanfare was provided by The Irish Horns, to underscore the lyric's military connotations. Impossible to reproduce live with the epic grandeur of the recorded version, 'The Card Cheat' remains one of the best Clash songs never to be played on stage by the band.

CAREER OPPORTUNITIES
[Strummer/Jones]
LP: *The Clash, Sandinista!*

'Who'd have thought five years previously when we'd written it in Camden Town that we'd play 'Career Opportunities' at Shea Stadium?' Strummer asked in 1999. 'These are the things that make the world interesting.' As with the band's name, the title for 'Career Opportunities' came from Simonon looking for inspiration in headlines in the *Evening Standard*. Jones stated that the song, a marginally mutated 12-bar blues, was 'written in half an hour in Rehearsals,' though a section of lyrics concerning pensions was dropped after Simonon refused to sing them. Strummer commented that he wrote the bulk of the lyrics while Jones and Simonon went to Kentucky Fried Chicken for potato croquettes.

Many commentators completely misread 'Career Opportunities' as a song about unemployment. It isn't. Like **Janie Jones**, the song actually concerns someone stuck in a job that they don't want. The lyrics had been partly inspired by Jones' experiences a few years previously when he had a temporary job as a Clerical Assistant in a DHSS benefit office in Praed Street, Paddington. At the time the IRA were beginning to use incendiary parcel devices as their latest terror weapon. Government offices were on a state of high alert for potential letter bombs and Jones, as the most junior (and, he alleged, most subversive-looking) employee, was given the job of opening the post. 'Most of the letters the Social Security get are from people saying their neighbours don't need the money,' Jones told Tony Parsons in 1977. 'The whole thing works on spite.' The song also included an allusion to Hughie Green's ghastly TV talent show *Opportunity Knocks*.

The bile that 'Career Opportunities' displays towards dead-end jobs ('Do you wanna make tea at the BBC?') intrigued Caroline Coon, who suggested to Jones in November 1976 that someone had to do the dirty jobs. 'Why?' asked Jones, observing that technology had advanced to the point where a few people with machines could handle a factory's output. 'There's a social stigma attached to being unemployed. Like 'Social Security Scroungers' every day in the *Sun* ... Go up North and the kids are ashamed that they can't get a job.'

'Career Opportunities' was first recorded at the Polydor demo sessions with Guy Stevens. This version subsequently appeared on *Clash On Broadway*. 'Everyone was disappointed with the demos,' noted Roadent. 'We felt [they were] too bland, too straight.' Introduced to The Clash's live set at Birmingham in October 1976, 'Career Opportunities' was still being played on the Busking tour almost nine years later. Along the way it would, as Strummer noted, be performed in huge US stadiums, a far cry from the London squat in which it was written. On 13 October 1982, The Clash played the song at Shea Stadium and the result – including a topical reference to that year's Falklands War – can be heard on *From Here to Eternity* (and seen on *The Essential Clash* DVD).

What has often been described as a karaoke version of 'Career Opportunities', a piano-led romp featuring Mickey Gallagher's sons, Luke and Ben, singing suitably amended lyrics referring to 'my school's rules', was recorded in 1980 at Wessex. Probably intended as nothing more than a band in-joke, it was included on *Sandinista!* The usual critical line is to dismiss this performance as a sacrilegious desecration of an important piece of social observation. Actually, it's quite *funny* in an ironic, postmodernist sort of way. Whether that was the intention or not remains unclear, The Clash being by no means immune to gross miscalculations of taste. 'Career Opportunities' has been covered by Stigmata, on the *City Rockers* tribute LP, and by The Farrell Brothers on the *This Is Rockabilly Clash* compilation.

CHARLIE DON'T SURF
[The Clash]
LP: *Sandinista!*

In February 1980, Strummer told *Sounds*' Robbi Millar that he had become obsessed with Francis Ford Coppola's *Apocalypse Now*. 'It doesn't leave you,' he noted. 'It's like a dream.' [34] Taking its title from a line of dialogue spoken in the film by Robert Duvall's surf-obsessed US cavalry officer Colonel Kilgore, 'Charlie Don't Surf', unlike the wholly pacifist **The Call Up**, is a song which actually *celebrates* war. At least, wars of liberation. Sung, by Jones, in the

34. Coppola's controversial epic is loosely based on Joseph Conrad's *Heart of Darkness*. Special forces assassin Captain Willard (Martin Sheen) is sent up the Nang River to 'terminate with extreme prejudice' maverick (and insane) US Colonel Kurtz (Marlon Brando). A visual tour de force, the film becomes a mesmerising odyssey of often surreal encounters as Willard discovers the true madness of war.

character of a Vietcong soldier who has been indoctrinated to 'keep the strangers out', the song takes a dispassionate view of America's cultural and military imperialism in South East Asia (and elsewhere – Africa, Jones notes, is choking on Coca-Cola). America, the song concludes, wishes to impose its own religion and belief systems on others. By extreme force, if necessary ('Charlie's gonna be a napalm star'[35]). The Clash, however, realise that the face of war is changing, with global superpowers and satellites that can 'make space burn'. First played live at Gothenburg in May 1980, 'Charlie Don't Surf' was a key part of The Clash's 1981 set, featuring during the residencies in New York, Paris and London.

Footnote: In 1988 Strummer told *Musician* that one night he was in a restaurant when he saw Roland Orzabal of Tears for Fears. 'You owe me a fiver,' Strummer told the startled Orzabal. 'He asked why. I said, "'Everybody Wants To Rule The World' – 'Charlie Don't Surf' – middle eight, first line." He reached into his pocket, got out five and gave it to me.'

CHEAPSKATES
[Strummer/Jones]
LP: *Give 'Em Enough Rope*

The most sloppily recorded song on *Give 'Em Enough Rope*, 'Cheapskates' features a stuttering, uncertain bassline and heavy use of feedback to mask the lack of a contrasting rhythm guitar part. In this regard, at least sonically, it actually sounds not unlike Sandy Pearlman's best known recording, Blue Öyster Cult's '(Don't Fear) The Reaper'.

Lyrically, 'Cheapskates' begins with a vicious put-down of Bernard Rhodes as a tight-fisted manipulator, picking up dog-ends in the rain, and someone who has 'never read a book'. (At the Lyceum in December 1978, Strummer introduced 'Cheapskates' with a vicious swipe at Rhodes: 'This song was written by a used car salesman who lives up the Camden Road. Well, he gave us the *idea* for it.') Soon, however, the lyrics become more opaque and veiled as Strummer attacks someone who is supposed to be a star, 'not a cheapskate bleeding queer.' This mysterious outsider also, according to the lyrics, attacks The Clash to save their own sense of cool. There have been suggestions that these lines referred, pointedly, to Jones, but Strummer always denied that, claiming the song was addressed to members of the music press concerning their overt criticism of The Clash in early 1978.

35. Probably inspired by another of Kilgore's most quoted lines: 'I love the smell of napalm in the morning.'

47

The band, Strummer went on to claim in 'Cheapskates', don't date models or indulge in cocaine. The latter point, in Jones' case at least, was simply not true – indeed, by the middle of the following year Strummer would tell the press that all the band 'had their moments' with cocaine. 'That song was written during a period of heavy drug-taking,' Jones told Garry Bushell on *Give 'Em Enough Rope*'s release. 'The lyrics are meant to be a satire on that.'

Introduced into the live set in June 1978, 'Cheapskates' was performed regularly during the rest of the year, but was dropped prior to the band's first trip to America.

CHEAT
[Strummer/Jones]
LP: *The Clash* [UK only]

Often said to be the only song on *The Clash* never played live. Actually, that's a fallacy – the song was regularly performed on the White Riot tour, and occasionally on the Get Out of Control tour. 'Cheat' was written, according to Simonon, just before The Clash went into CBS to record their debut LP in March 1977. A variant, both lyrically and musically, of **Hate & War** (which predates 'Cheat' by three months), 'Cheat' also draws inspiration from a phrase found in a much-reproduced flyer for King Mob, a Situationist splinter group which Strummer would have been aware of through Rhodes. The opening line – 'I get violent when I'm fucked-up' – and the following allusions to the surly silence that speed often produces, suggest an epic in the making. Sadly, 'Cheat' soon, lyrically, falls into a cycle of banal clichés and bathetic repetition (note, the particularly uninspired fourth verse with its limp insult 'you stupid fool').

Regarded by Strummer as 'a filler', the recording of 'Cheat' was, nonetheless, The Clash's first experiment in sonic distortion. The solo, one of Jones' most frugal, is a distant cousin of Mick Ronson's on Bowie's 'Suffragette City' and the guitars were heavily treated with phasing effects.[36] 'Simon [Humphrey, The Clash's recording engineer] came up with that,' Terry Chimes remembered in 2002. 'Someone said something about phasing and he said "Let's put some on and see what it sounds like."' 'Cheat' was covered in the late 90s by Clash devotees Rancid.

---

36. Phasing is a form of audio-manipulation in which a signal is processed via two conveyance routes, producing a 'shadow' signal slightly out of synch to produce a swirling, otherworldly sound. Pioneered by maverick producer Joe Meek on such groundbreaking singles as The Tornados' 'Telstar' (1962), it became a much-used effect during subsequent years: See The Small Faces' 'Itchycoo Park', The Who's 'I Can See For Miles' and The Beatles' 1966 output in general.

CITY OF THE DEAD
[Strummer/Jones]
B-SIDE: 9/77

The Clash songs written during the summer of 1977, and released over the next year as singles and B-Sides to bridge the gap between *The Clash* and *Give 'Em Enough Rope*, were largely the work of Mick Jones.

Strummer subsequently admitted that he was suffering from clinical depression during this period, and was very disillusioned about the future of the punk scene. (See, for instance, his extraordinarily negative interview with Caroline Coon in *Melody Maker* in March 1977.) The movement had burst out of the London clubs and gone national but, as a result, nobody seemed sure what to do with it. Many members of The Clash's provincial audience were behaving at gigs exactly in the way that the tabloid press had told them they ought to: spitting and being mindlessly aggressive. During this period, Strummer had taken to reworking the lyrics of **What's My Name** to ask his audience 'What the hell is wrong with you?/You're doing what you're supposed to do.'

With this background, 'City of the Dead's nihilistic imagery of loveless relationships, alcoholism, dread-filled streets, paralysed courage and a wind of ugly tension, makes absolute sense. During the Get Out of Control tour, Jones would occasionally introduce 'City of the Dead' as concerning 'being dead from the neck up.' With its title drawn from an obscure 1960 British horror movie, one of the song's verses concerned 1977's popular craze of 'punk-bashing'. Egged on by various scum tabloid journalists, for a few weeks during that summer anyone wearing anything even resembling punk clothing was a prime target for a severe and public kicking, usually by Teddy Boys. [37] Jones himself suffered one such attack, as he confirmed in *Westway to the World*. It was a bad time to be different, as 'City of the Dead' notes ('What we wear is dangerous gear/It'll get you picked on anywhere').

The verse concerning New York Johnny and his wish to 'cop' (ie, to score some junk) had its genesis in a couple of highly unsavoury backstage incidents on the Anarchy tour. Nick Kent remembered in *The Face*, in 1986,

37. On 6 June 1977, the *Sunday Mirror* ran a piece entitled 'PUNISH THE PUNKS' which, basically, encouraged the newspaper's readers to make their disgust at the phenomenon known to any punks they should come across. Within a week, somewhat predictably, several violent incidents had taken place, including attacks on high-profile figures in the punk movement like Jamie Reid and, on 13 June, Johnny Rotten. To the ultimate shame of Crown Prosecution Service, no *Mirror* journalist was ever charged with incitement to cause violence. Nor, for that matter, was Labour MP Marcus Lipton, who was quoted in the *Daily Mirror* as saying that 'if pop music is going to be used to destroy our established institutions, it ought to be destroyed first.'

that Johnny Thunders was in the habit of waving a syringe 'in the face of some uninitiated, impressionable shrill' and asking 'Are you a boy, or are you a man?' Other parts of 'City of the Dead' were possibly inspired by Jones' fractious relationship with his then-girlfriend, Viv Albertine. This was a period of real unhappiness for Jones. 'Mick used to cry and cry about Viv,' Johnny Green remembered. The cynicism of 'City of the Dead's opening lines certainly sound like a man suffering from a bleeding wound. Jones would subsequently seek solace in a series of short-term relationships and the hedonistic joys of booze and cocaine while living with Tony James in a flat off the Portobello Road.

The first Clash song to feature additional instrumentation – saxophone and piano[38] – 'City of the Dead' was recorded at CBS in August 1977, along with **Complete Control** and an initial version of **Pressure Drop**. A fabulously full production, certainly one of the best things that The Clash had recorded to that point, 'City of the Dead' throws in everything but the kitchen sink, production-wise, to create a big sound. The most obvious influence, musically, is Bruce Springsteen, not a name normally bandied around by punk rockers in 1977, but Jones was certainly a fan.

The song made its live debut on the European dates in September and featured, off-and-on, in The Clash's live set for the next year (it was particularly popular in the US, where many fans told Jones and Strummer that they associated the song with their own home town). The band themselves were less keen on performing it and weren't pleased when Barry Glare and Johnny Green inserted 'City of the Dead' as the opening number on the set-list for a show at Boston in September 1979. The song made a brief reappearance in The Clash's set during 1980. A great version, probably recorded at the Lyceum on 3 January 1979 – though the CD suggests 28 December 1978 – appears on *From Here to Eternity*. This clearly demonstrates the power of the song in a live context.

CLAMPDOWN
[Strummer/Jones]
LP: *London Calling*

A boisterous Jones tune that had been knocking around for some weeks during the Vanilla rehearsals, the instrumental was initially called 'Working

---

38. The piano on 'City of the Dead' was played by Elvis Costello and The Attractions' Steve Nieve, whom Jones knew from his guest slot on The Attractions' 'Big Tears'. The *NME* reported a rumour that Attractions producer Nick Lowe may also have contributed to 'City of the Dead' but this remains unconfirmed. When introducing the song at Middlesbrough on the Sort It Out tour, Strummer told the audience 'You're the saxophones!'

and Awaiting' and then, equally briefly, 'For Fuck's Sake' before Strummer added words.

'The nuclear meltdown at Three Mile Island got me started,' noted Strummer in 1991. On 28 March 1979, at the Three Mile Island nuclear power plant near Harrisburg, Pennsylvania, a series of mechanical, electrical and human failures led to what was subsequently described as the worst atomic accident in history. Watching news reports from Harrisburg, it seemed to Strummer that the world was, indeed, 'waiting to be melted down.' But that was merely the first stage of a whistle-stop tour of human insanity.

Opening with Spike Millgan's catchphrase from his influential TV comedy show Q5 ('What are we gonna do now?'), 'Clampdown' voiced a complex series of snapshots of a world teetering on the brink of disaster. This included Strummer's most misunderstood lyric ('Taking off his turban/They said is this man a Jew?'), an observation, with epiphanic clarity, about national stereotyping and illogical suspicion that incurred unjust accusations of anti-Semitism. According to Johnny Green, Strummer had assured him that 'Clampdown' was really a song about wheel-clamps, which were just beginning to appear on London's streets during the late 1970s, and about those who wielded them. As a metaphor for mean-spirited authority, literally ball-and-chaining people's freedom, there are few better examples, anywhere.

In fact, Strummer's targets in 'Clampdown' were numerous and wide-reaching, taking in the horrors of religious indoctrination, the sinister shadow of fascism, the judiciary, corrupt politicians and those 30-something bullies who can't believe their luck when they find themselves in a position of power over somebody weaker than themselves. The latter may have been suggested by Simonon, who told *Melody Maker* in 1988 about a job that he had briefly held after leaving school in the John Lewis warehouse. 'There was a lot of shop-floor fascism. I got the shit end of the stick.'

Strummer used another verse to loudly celebrate his confidence that some of those happy to work for the clampdown would, ultimately, get what's due to them. Indeed, the song may begin with a resigned fatalism which suggests that the machinery of the state produces an automated conveyor belt of repressed robots, too scared to voice discontent. Yet, in positively stressing that 'anger can be power', Strummer's belief that resistance is not only possible, but an obligation, is little short of life-affirming. A holistic protest song with a message of hope through civil disobedience. Bob Dylan would have been well-proud.

One of The Clash's most powerful flat-out rockers, 'Clampdown' entered the band's set at Minneapolis in September 1979. 'Seeing as we're a so-called political band, this is a so-called political number,' Strummer told the audience at Atlanta two weeks later. Thereafter, 'Clampdown' remained an integral part of The Clash's repertoire until 1985. A live version, filmed at the Lewisham Odeon on 18 February 1980 by Don Letts, appears on *The Essential Clash* and *Westway to the World*. At Auckland, in February 1982, Strummer sang his mumbled introduction a capella, an intriguing experiment that was subsequently abandoned.

'Clampdown' was subsequently covered, imaginatively, by The Indigo Girls, and by Hot Water Music and Sinisters.

CLASH CITY ROCKERS
[Strummer/Jones]
SINGLE: 2/78 LP: *The Clash* [US only]

'Rockers is a reggae rhythm,' noted Strummer. 'It doesn't make sense if you think [the song] is about people in leather jackets.' The most positive set of lyrics from a period of generally morose and disillusioned songs (see **City of the Dead**), 'Clash City Rockers' was The Clash's first deliberate attempt at self-mythology *in song*. (**Garageland** and **Complete Control** have some prior claims but, while both are sung in the first person, neither contains as overt a self-homage as 'Clash City Rockers'.) As such, the song followed in the grand traditions of 'Bo Diddley', 'The Monkees Theme' and 'Bob Dylan's 115th Dream'. The lyrics aren't Strummer's best, but they do continue several of the themes that he had explored in *The Clash* – notably a rejection of dead-end employment and informing the listener that they have a purpose in life. Despite the wish to 'burn down the suburbs with a half-closed eye', 'Clash City Rockers' is about moving forward and accentuating the positive in life rather than the empty, negative, *destroy* rhetoric of many of The Sex Pistols' lyrics. The middle section, based on the nursery rhyme 'Oranges and Lemons', includes references to David Bowie, Gary Glitter and Jamaican toaster Prince Far-I, whose *Under Heavy Manners* had been a big influence on the band visually and lyrically during the previous year. The song's closing riff is a dead-ringer for Status Quo's 'Caroline'.

Introduced to the live set at Mont de Marsen in August 1977, 'Clash City Rockers' was recorded during sessions in October and November at CBS. Following an on-the-road bust-up at the end of the Get Out of Control tour, Jones and Simonon weren't on speaking terms and during at least one of these sessions Strummer had to spend much of his time shuttling backwards and forwards across the studio relaying instructions (and insults). The recording features some piano vamping to bolster the main riff, probably played by Jones.

The single was scheduled for release in February. However, while Jones and Strummer were in Jamaica in December, Bernard Rhodes decided that the recording was 'too flat.' 'We varispeeded the master about one-and-a-half per cent,' Micky Foote remembered. However, when Jones heard the result, he was incandescent with rage. 'He went absolutely mental,' Johnny Green noted. Having, very publicly, faced-off with their record company over artistic freedom, The Clash now considered that they were being subverted from within. Although it was too late to halt the release of the single, the original mix of 'Clash City Rockers' would be used on all subsequent releases. And, although Foote continued to work for Rhodes, it was the end of his career as The Clash's producer.

Always popular live, 'Clash City Rockers', became The Clash's opening song at the Christmas 1979 gigs, and on most of the 16 Tons tour, and it remained in The Clash's set pretty much all the way to 1985. A version recorded at The Orpheum Theater in Boston on 7 September 1982 features on *From Here to Eternity*. Nevertheless, the song did have its critics. 'It's no good speaking up for the common man if the common man isn't putting his hands into his pocket,' wrote *NME*'s Bob Edmands in reviewing the single. He added sarcastically, 'Watch for this act on *Top of the Pops*. They're gonna be bigger than Darts.' Saves The Day's rather approximate cover appears on the 1999 tribute LP *City Rockers*, while another cover, by Jakkpot, can be heard on the tribute compilation, *Backlash*.

COMPLETE CONTROL
[Strummer/Jones]
SINGLE: 9/77 **LP:** *The Clash* [US only]

The debacle over CBS's release of the **Remote Control** single in May, without bothering to ask The Clash, fuelled the fires of the band's most incendiary piece of *realpolitik*. In three minutes and 13 seconds, Mick Jones' warning to every band about to sign to a record label about the waiting dangers is loud and clear. The song's ultimate message is distilled into one of The Clash's most quoted couplets: 'They said, we'd be artistically free/But it's just a bit of paper.'

In 'Complete Control', The Clash wearily survey a desolate landscape of crushed punk idealism, acting as caustic, cynical observers to the compromised world that they are themselves now a part of. A possible inspiration for this can be found in some of John Lennon's pre-and-post Beatles song-as-diary creations ('The Ballad of John and Yoko', 'God', 'New York City'). Yet there's a deeper story in this state-of-the-union address to all the young punks: 'Bernie and Malcolm [McLaren] got together and decided to try and control their groups,' noted Strummer in 1991. 'Bernie [had] a meeting in The Ship in Soho, after The Anarchy tour. He [said] he wanted complete control ... I came out of the pub with Paul collapsing on the pavement in hysterics at those words.' The seed was sown for a revolution from within.

The song was written in Jones' bedroom at Wilmcote House after The White Riot tour in June. 'Complete Control' also included allusions to the band's numerous run-ins with the law (like the Newcastle Holiday Inn malarkey) and their seemingly official policy of opening the back door at gigs on the White Riot tour to fans without tickets. Told by Rhodes to 'write what affects you,' Jones complied. 'All this stuff *was* affecting us.' There was also an inevitable, and surprisingly mature, comment on media perceptions of punk and of the band themselves, peppered by some of Strummer's most funny ad-libs ('You're my guitar hero!' and, memorably, 'This is Joe Public speaking').

Recording took place at Sarm East Studios in Whitechapel in August. It was Headon's first with The Clash, and he puts in a powerhouse performance, driving the song forward, particularly immediately after the pseudo-dub middle-section as the band comes crashing back to full speed. Although Micky Foote engineered the session, the production was, officially at least, in the hands of Lee 'Scratch' Perry, the eccentric Jamaican dubmaster who had co-written **Police & Thieves** and who was currently producing Bob Marley and The Wailers in London.

How much Perry actually contributed to 'Complete Control' has been the source of much subsequent debate, although all involved seem to have got on well with him. 'Lee was shit hot,' Foote noted. 'He took this equaliser and twiddled the bass dial around. The whole studio was shaking! He nearly blew the control room up.' Foote added that Perry was 'well into it, dancing and kung-fu kicking.' Strummer, however, later joked that Perry was in and out of the studio in about 15 minutes. Subsequently, according to Jones, 'we went back and fiddled about with it. It was good what Lee did, but his echo sounded underwater slightly on us. We brought out the guitars and made it sound a bit tougher.' Jones' own interest in getting different sounds from his guitar came to the fore, particularly in the arpeggios used in the countermelody ('I don't trust you...').

The Clash's first Top 30 hit (number 28), 'Complete Control' became one of their most popular live anthems, first introduced to the set in August 1977 at Mont de Marsen. A piece of violent polemic about what a big bad world four young guys had found themselves a (perhaps willing) part of, it was the band's opening number for most of 1978 and a regular encore thereafter. A splendidly spunky live version, with a dramatic tension-building guitar introduction, recorded in June 1981 in New York, opens *From Here to Eternity*. (This version was used as the soundtrack to a composite video of various Clash clips assembled by Don Letts for *The Essential Clash* DVD.) The song was briefly dropped from The Clash's set in late 1982, but it returned after Jones' departure and was still being played live in 1985.

'A definition of how much fury and determination are worth, and of how good they can feel,' wrote Greil Marcus in 1978. 'This is rock to rank with 'Hound Dog' and 'Gimme Shelter'. Music that, for the few minutes it lasts, seems to trivialise both.' 'Complete Control' has been criticised, subsequently, for its naïveté regarding the corporate music industry. (John Peel, for instance, suggests that The Clash *must* have known that CBS were not a foundation for the arts but had signed them to make as much money as possible.) Yet even if the song's anger is *faux naïf*, it still packs a considerable punch. Indeed, as Jon Savage wrote, 'Instead of a piece of cynicism, 'Complete Control' becomes a hymn to Punk autonomy at its moment of eclipse.'

A 1998 cover by Kowalskis has to be heard to be believed.

COOL CONFUSION
[The Clash]
B-SIDE: 6/82 [US only]

Unreleased in the UK until it appeared on *Super Black Market Clash*, 'Cool Confusion' was recorded during the *Combat Rock* sessions at Electric Lady in November and December 1981. The lyrics were partly inspired by a visit to New York's Studio 54 disco. 'I started to notice that stars with big egos would always swan into places, make an appearance, and swan out again,' remembered Strummer. 'Whenever we went out, we'd always be in a place for the duration.' The lyrics are quite interesting, with references to Kung Fu in the car park, Cinderella's shoe and sniffing glue in a bag. Certainly, 'Lend me your star for a turn/As heroes fix their hair,' is worthy of a much better song. The song seems to be an attempt at a Lee Perry-style 70s dub with lots of production tricks hiding the fact that there isn't much of a tune underneath.

THE COOL OUT
[The Clash]
B-SIDE: 3/81 [US only]

Another track unreleased in the UK until its inclusion on *Super Black Market Clash*. This Wessex instrumental remix of **The Call Up**, from February 1981, features the production credit of 'Pepe Unidos', an alias for Simonon, Strummer and Bernard Rhodes. The chief point of interest is the opportunity for closer inspection of Jones' impressively choppy *Shaft*-style guitars.

COOL UNDER HEAT
[Strummer/Rhodes]
LP: *Cut the Crap*

With its swaggering opening line ('Rebels on the corner, rebels to the core'), 'Cool Under Heat' ludicrously presents its orator as a *Wild Ones*-style 'what've yer got' Dionysian warrior. A rebel without a cause or a care. Or, seemingly, too many brain cells. The song's theme stresses how completely together it is for the angry young punk rebel in *Cut the Crap*'s cretinous imaginary world, to be, you know, cool. The song suggests that when the angry young punk rebel and his (presumably angry young punk) girl have a fight, it's a good idea to cool off afterwards in the rain. It also contrasts various ways to scratch a living in 'a fat man's city'. Musically directionless, histrionic and turgid, occasional lines dripping with poetic majesty ('pitiless eyes of the cityless souls') crop up just to remind the listener that, yes, this *is* a Joe Strummer song.

Amid such banal sentiments as 'soon the present will be the past', it's difficult to believe that this is the man who wrote the blindingly ironic lyrics of **The Magnificent Seven** and **Death Or Glory**. 'Where's his knack for a pungently well-turned phrase?' asked a disappointed Mat Snow in his *NME* review of *Cut the Crap*. 'Cool Under Heat' also includes a pointless allusion to Carl Perkins' 'Blue Suede Shoes', painfully obvious fist-in-the-face guitar riffs and, in its bloated, grandiloquent chorus, layers of dirge-like chants. Like many of the songs on the disastrous *Cut the Crap*, 'Cool Under Heat' is a blot on an otherwise impressive CV. The song was played live by The Clash during the Busking tour in a stripped-down acoustic arrangement that, while it doesn't wholly rescue what remains a thoroughly bad song, is at least a shade easier on the ear.

CORNER SOUL
[The Clash]
LP: *Sandinista!*

'Corner Soul's brooding militant Rastafarian groove takes a leaf from **War in a Babylon** and the collected works of British roots-reggae bands like Third World, Steel Pulse and Misty. A series of provocative soundbites ('total war must burn on the Grove'), 'Corner Soul' anticipated by more than a year the riots that would leave Britain's inner cities burning during the summer of 1981. [39] Considering what would happen in Brixton, Toxteth, St Paul's and elsewhere, 'Corner Soul' captures perfectly the pent-up fury on the streets. But amid all this, Strummer – always a romantic dreamer at heart – wonders if he will have to take his machete to chop his way through the path of life.

The question 'Is the music calling for a river of blood?' is a direct reference to an infamous speech made by Tory politician Enoch Powell in Birmingham on 20 April 1968. Powell's despicably racist assertion that immigration would inevitably lead to a race war in Britain coincided with the emergence of the neo-fascist National Front and outbreaks of 'Paki-bashing' in towns like Luton, Leicester and Bradford. [40] No proper understanding of the political climate in which The Clash wrote their songs is complete without taking Powell and his alarming, yet widely held, views into account. [41]

With Headon's military-style drumming and Jones' echo-drenched production, 'Corner Soul' was a popular addition to The Clash's live set on the Radio Clash tour in April 1981. It also featured during the New York residency in June but was dropped thereafter.

THE CROOKED BEAT
[The Clash]
LP: *Sandinista!*

Often described as Simonon's sequel to **The Guns of Brixton**, yet, apart from the two songs sharing a South London location and the singer's monotone

39. The starting point for this summer of discontent occurred in July 1981, when a concert by skinhead band The 4-Skins, at the Hamborough Tavern in Southall, turned into a riot in which the venue was burned to the ground. In the run-up to the concert, several racist attacks had been carried out, stoking local tension. The fact that the police allowed the concert to go ahead in such a climate led the *Guardian* to comment the following day: 'At the very least this is incompetence on a pretty grand scale.'

40. This outrageous term first entered popular consciousness in 1970 with reference to a series of attacks in Bethnal Green. The *Observer*, unsympathetically, wrote that 'any Asian careless enough to be walking the street alone at night is a fool.'

41. Sacked from the Shadow Cabinet for his repatriationist statements, Powell (1912-98) became a pariah on the fringes of British politics for several years. However, for a certain proportion of the population Powell was (and remains) the best Prime Minister Britain never had (a Gallup poll published shortly after his sacking alleged that 75 per cent of Britons were broadly sympathetic to the sentiments he expressed and, following his sacking, there were many working-class demonstrations in solidarity). A Greek scholar and a distinguished army officer, Powell was a brilliant orator and a potent symbol for the emerging radical right. In the third volume of his political diaries (*Against the Tide: 1973-76*), Anthony Wedgwood-Benn notes that Powell was a champion of 'right-wing working-class people', adding '[they] listen to him, fascinated by his intellect and clarity. He mesmerises Labour MPs like rabbits caught in a headlamp.' Powell re-emerged as a member of the Ulster Unionist party in 1974.

voice, there's very little to link them. Taking its lyrical inspiration from the nursery rhyme 'There Was A Crooked Man', the song includes examples of witty wordplay that are almost worthy of Strummer, along with several less inspired lines ('badges flash and sirens wail/They'll be taking one and all to jail'). At least the references to 'the towers blocks of my home town' can claim to maintain some astute links to The Clash's Westway roots – see also **Up In Heaven (Not Only Here)**. Never played live, 'The Crooked Beat' was one of the last songs recorded for *Sandinista!* at Wessex (September 1980) and shows signs of having been written hastily, firstly to give Simonon some royalties and, secondly, to fill space. At five minutes and 29 seconds, the song is actually two separate pieces: the song itself and an echo-saturated dub version, produced by Mikey Dread. Dread himself provides the authentic Trenchtown patois (*'rub-a-dub... bang-biddling-biddling. MURDA!'*) that ends the song.

DANCING SHOES
[Bob Marley]

A Wailers single first released in 1966. 'We decided to try to rock it up, to Ramones-it if you like,' Strummer remembered in 1978. 'We used to play it a fair bit, but only to ourselves at Rehearsals, it was an attempt to fuse a style out of something, but we realised it was getting nowhere so we dropped it.'

DEADLY SERIOUS
[Jones]

A short, furiously fast song about music's importance which features Pete Townshend's ubiquitous 'I Can't Explain' riff at its core. (See also the contemporary **I Know What To Think Of You**.) A rejection of the empty hedonism inherent in much rock 'n' roll, 'Deadly Serious' has a feel of the righteous zealotry of the recently converted. In this case, an author who had just seen the light of The Sex Pistols. Regularly played live in 1976, the song would later mutate into **Capital Radio**.

DEATH IS A STAR
[The Clash]
LP: *Combat Rock*

'It's about the way we all queue up at the cinema to see someone get killed,' Strummer told Roz Reines in 1982. 'These days, the public execution is the celluloid execution. I was examining why I want to go and see these movies.' A half-spoken, mainly acoustic dirge, with the sound of crickets chirping in the distance, 'Death is a Star' was a damn strange way to end *Combat Rock*'s tour of The Clash's vision of the American Gothic experience. Yet, conceptually, it's a cornerstone of the LP. All *Combat Rock*'s recurring themes are present and correct; references to Americana (the 'one-stop-only motel'), the movies ('stalked through the back lots'), drug culture and war – particularly in the jungles of Vietnam. Yet in the midst of Strummer's whimsical delivery of the song comes one of his most poetic lines: 'Make a grown man cry like a girl/To see the guns dying at sunset'.

Jones' 1920s-style jazzy piano and plaintive Spanish guitar and Headon's use of snare brushes manage to carry the song through, despite the stop-start format, towards a vaguely structured conclusion. 'Death is a Star' is a striking, if rather solemn and downbeat, end to the often bombastic and radio-friendly world of *Combat Rock* and it was never performed live.

DEATH OR GLORY
[Strummer/Jones]
LP: *London Calling*

Humour was *always* an underrated part of The Clash's story. Beneath their urban guerrilla poses and pop star army fatigues, they could be a right bunch of sarky buggers. This was particularly true of Strummer, whose wry wit is often there bubbling away under the surface of many of the band's finest lyrics (see **Safe European Home**, **The Magnificent Seven**, **Rock the Casbah**, etc). This was never better illustrated than in the two lines that ensure 'Death Or Glory' will *never* be played on a radio near you: 'I believe in this, and it's been tested by research/That he who fucks nuns will later join the church.'

'Death Or Glory' begins with Strummer reflecting on how time changes everything and that nothing escapes this process. The teenage hood who makes his bargain with the world is ultimately assimilated into the unwanted adult reality of marriage and buying sofas. Like Alex, the anti-hero of Anthony Burgess' *A Clockwork Orange*, the only way to escape the follies of youth is, seemingly, to grow up. Yet the song also incorporates images of painful domestic violence which, Strummer suggests, results from the frustrations of being told to settle down too quickly. Lester Bangs believed, with no supporting evidence, that the lyrics concerning a gimmick-hungry yob were directed at Sham 69's Jimmy Pursey.

The song also takes a caustic look at the difficulties of not selling out, something much on the band's mind at the time. Often seen as a key piece of 'The Clash As Self-Mythologisers' argument, 'Death Or Glory' is, in fact, a song about purpose and perseverance. One of Strummer's most heartfelt and emotional pieces, 'Death Or Glory' also benefits immeasurably from a terrific band performance – as on much of *London Calling*, Simonon's bass is outstanding. Legends abound, too, over the recording of the song, with an excited Guy Stevens throwing chairs around in the studio to create an ambience of tension.

Strummer was obviously fond of the song and told *Eccentric Sleeve Notes* fanzine in July 1982 that The Clash had always wanted to play 'Death Or Glory' live but hadn't had time to rehearse it properly. Perhaps because of the song's complexity, it was seldom a feature of the band's set. First unveiled at The Rainbow in July 1979, its only appearances thereafter were a few performances on the 16 Tons tour in 1980 and during the pre-US festival dates in 1983. A 1999 cover version by Dave Smalley features on the Clash tribute LP *City Rockers*.

DENY
[Strummer/Jones]
LP: *The Clash* [UK only]

Written by Jones in the period just prior to Strummer joining The Clash, 'Deny' was, initially, a song about denial in all its forms. It appears to have been aimed at Jones' then-girlfriend, possibly the same mysterious girl who inspired **I'm So Bored With You**. The song's muse is clearly a drug addict, something that Jones seems to have a hard time dealing with. It's probable that an additional influence on both the structure and the lyrics of 'Deny' was The Sex Pistols' 'Liar', which Jones would have heard via its author, his friend Glen Matlock. Jones has also stated that Chrissie Hynde 'probably helped with the end bit.' Certainly 'Deny' places the object of its scorn and concern squarely in the midst of punk London, with a direct reference to the 100 Club. Strummer's arrival meant adapting the song to something more in keeping with Rhodes' insistence that The Clash sing about reality, yet it maintained the disgust and betrayal of the original lyrics.

'From his grandmother's flat on the Warwick and Brindley Estate, Mick Jones had an eagle's-eye view of Harrow Road, North Kensington and

Paddington, dominated by the elevated Westway,' wrote Jon Savage. 'The Clash's urban hyperrealism was quickly overlaid by a more conventional sense of social relevance.' Certainly with songs like 'Deny', The Clash were singing about relevant issues far removed from the subsequent cartoon rhetoric of many second generation punk bands who seemed to believe that only songs about tower blocks, being bored and waiting at the DHSS had any currency with their audience. 'Deny's *just say no* message may seem hypocritical in light of Jones' subsequent flirtation with cocaine and Headon's helpless heroin addiction in the 1980s, but its patent horror at the needle, and the damage done, shouldn't be underestimated.

Recorded in the quasi-live environment of *The Clash* sessions at Whitfield, the fade-out included Strummer ad-libbing references to 'a 12p comic', that being the price of a Marvel or a DC in 1977. The song also made interesting use of fade-in, a studio trick first used by The Beatles on 'Eight Days A Week'. There are also Who references – on an LP full of them – the rhythm guitar riff being a distant cousin to 'The Kids Are Alright'. A fixture in the band's set from their first gigs in 1976, when it was often used as their opening number, 'Deny' remained in the set during the White Riot tour but was then replaced by the newer material written in the summer of 1977.

DICTATOR
[Strummer/Rhodes]
LP: *Cut the Crap*

Once again, as with songs like **Cool Under Heat** and **Are You Red.. Y**, this song contains crassly inelegant sledgehammer lyrics ('the more guns I got the better', 'from my armour-plated Cadillac') where once Strummer would have chiselled out something witty and dangerous. An allusion to Sergio Leone's *For a Few Dollars More* suggests that Strummer was attempting something cinematic along the lines of *Combat Rock*'s Vietnam trilogy, but here it just doesn't work on any level.

Musically at least, 'Dictator', with its radio samples and stabs of brass, has some merit to it, although the less said about the tuneless cacophony of the first 20 seconds the better. A vague Latin tinge points the listener in the direction of the geographical region the song is commenting on, though the horribly synthetic drum-sound negates much of the intended swing.

'Dictator' was performed by The Clash, in a much harsher and more heavy metal arrangement, during the Out of Control tour and at the late 1984 European gigs. Live, the song was more frantic, and perhaps more spirited, than the subsequent studio recording.

DIRTY PUNK
[Strummer/Rhodes]
LP: *Cut the Crap*

The fact that the dirty punk about whom Strummer sings in this, one of the marginally better *Cut the Crap* songs, intends to 'rock your neighbourhood' and to get himself a big car with which to drive 'up your boulevard' suggests that he comes from the American suburbs. This is confirmed, subsequently, when the song comments upon the stereotypical American neurosis of dysfunctional families – momma screaming while daddy smashes the TV screen and hunky clean-cut brother gets drunk. These clichés are no more or less lumpish and unrefined as those in other songs on the LP, but at least in the context of 'Dirty Punk's subject matter, they make a vague kind of sense.

'Dirty Punk' is a brash, over-the-top example of the thrashy end of 1980s US hair-metal. It's also a verse too long, and Nick Sheppard's guitar solo is a one-dimensional throwaway that would have had Mick Jones turning in his grave if he'd been dead. Nevertheless, there is some spirit in 'Dirty Punk', particularly the feedback-drenched coda, that's wholly missing from many of the *Cut the Crap* recordings. The only live performances of 'Dirty Punk' came at The Clash's two Brixton Miners' Benefit gigs in December 1984.

DO IT NOW
[Strummer/Rhodes]
B-SIDE: 10/85

A vaguely ska-inspired melody, recorded in Munich during the *Cut the Crap* sessions in January 1985. 'Do It Now' was subsequently left off the LP and appeared as the B-Side of the **This Is England** single. Although by no means a classic, it's an adequate enough little song about logical positivism with a plea to 'turn the music up'. It's certainly preferable to some of the more silly political rants that make up *Cut the Crap*, although the song is cursed with the same musical deficiencies (an over-reliance on nail-through-the-ear bellowed vocals to get the point across). Interestingly, the 2000 CD reissue of *Cut the Crap* includes 'Do It Now' as the final track. The song was never played live.

DRUG-STABBING TIME
[Strummer/Jones]
LP: *Give 'Em Enough Rope*

First demoed at Rehearsal Rehearsals in January 1978, with Gary Barnacle on saxophone, unlikely as it may seem 'Drug-Stabbing Time' bears more than a passing resemblance to Hawkwind's 1973 single 'Urban Guerrilla'. In part a piece of cinéma verité set to music, the song describes a police drug-bust (it's possible that Strummer had seen some of the early footage shot by Mingay and Hazan for *Rude Boy* which included just such a scene, or he may have been writing from some personal experience). 'Drug-Stabbing Time' makes clear The Clash's healthy disdain for hard drugs ('Nobody wants a user/Nobody needs a loser') and the paranoia that they induce. All of which was fine and laudable, but the common knowledge of Jones' predilection for Charlie at the time that the song was recorded serves, as Marcus Gray notes, 'to rob [it] of much comedy value.'

First played live during the On Parole tour, unlike several of the *Give 'Em Enough Rope* songs, 'Drug-Stabbing Time' survived in The Clash's act into 1979, being played on the Pearl Harbour tour. Dropped thereafter, it was revived for a one-off performance at Monterey in September 1979.

ENGLISH CIVIL WAR
[trad. arr. Strummer/Jones]
SINGLE: 2/79 **LP:** *Give 'Em Enough Rope*

The American Civil War (1861-65) produced many things; death on a large scale and a theoretical end to slavery being two of the more notable ones. Although the Yankees won, the South had all the best songs – 'The Battle Hymn of the Republic' and 'When Johnny Comes Marching Home', to name but two. [42] Elvis Presley adapted the former as part of his 'American Trilogy'. The latter was a song that Strummer had learned at school. 'It was such a good tune,' he later noted. 'I suggested we update it, to see what it sounded like.' Strummer's ambitions, however, were marbled by another history lesson. In the 1650s, for the only time in its history, Britain was a Republic. Attempts by King Charles I to dissolve Parliament in 1642 had led to a lengthy civil war in which the Parliamentarians' military wing was the New Model Army, commanded by Oliver Cromwell. They eventually defeated the Royalists and, after much debate, Charles was executed. It all came to a

---

42. Ironically, 'When Johnny Comes Marching Home' was actually written by a Massachusetts Unionist, Irish-born Patrick Sarsfield Gilmore (1829-92). However, it was popular with both sides during the conflict and, subsequently, became associated with the Confederates.

pretty crappy end, unfortunately, and within 12 years, the monarchy had been reinstated. But this was a clear historical precedent for People Power.

The rise of the far right in Britain in the mid-1970s was truly alarming to those on the left of the political spectrum, like The Clash. 'War is just around the corner,' Strummer told Terry Lott of *Record Mirror* in 1978 after 'English Civil War's first live performance at the Rock Against Racism show in April. 'Johnny hasn't got far to march. That's why he's coming by bus or underground.' In the same interview, Strummer also referred to a recent race riot in Tower Hamlets and to Britain's top tennis player Buster Mottram, who had openly supported the British National Party. 'It's a folk song, that's all,' Strummer concluded. When asked what The Clash thought about suggestions that the power of the National Front had been exaggerated, Jones replied, 'In 1928, Adolf Hitler got 2.8 per cent of the votes. By 1939, there was no one voting for anyone else.'

Sadly, within two weeks of 'English Civil War's public debut, one of the most highly publicised racial murders in British history took place. Altab Ali, a young Bengali, was stabbed to death in London, heralding a series of anti-racist demonstrations. After press coverage of claims by the British National Party that the GLC was planning to house Bengalis in what were described as ghettos, some 150 Asian youths rampaged through the Brick Lane area in June, smashing windows and damaging shops and cars. The National Front welcomed the idea of keeping Bengalis separate from whites, as, seemingly, did the *Daily Telegraph*, which argued that a 'harmonious, multiracial utopia cannot exist outside the minds of those who are striving to bring it about.'

As with most of the recordings on *Give 'Em Enough Rope*, 'English Civil War' features a jigsaw puzzle of interlocking guitar parts with Jones' solo veering perilously close to the heavy metal idiom The Clash had so strenuously avoided thus far. The song was considered to be 'a wise enough, if a miscued and rock 'n' rolly, warning of all things uniformed and sinister,' by *NME*'s Danny Baker on its release as a single in January 1979. The picture sleeve featured a still from John Halas' classic 1955 animated adaptation of Orwell's *Animal Farm*.

A fixture in the band's live set between 1978 and 1980, and played occasionally thereafter, The Clash tried an interesting experiment for the Take the Fifth tour of the US, returning 'English Civil War' to its roots by playing it in slow, acoustic folk style. This was to the bemusement of some fans, particularly those in Detroit who, according to Strummer, 'booed us for not sounding like Ted Nugent.' At Dallas in October 1979, Strummer introduced the song as 'Dining At The Atomic Holocaust'. An exciting, fast-paced version was recorded live at the Lyceum on 3 January 1979 for possible inclusion in *Rude Boy*. Although not used on that occasion, it *was* included on the *Clash On Broadway* CD. The 2001 Salvation DVD release of *Rude Boy* included footage from this performance as a bonus. The song also featured prominently in the 1979 segment of the classic 1996 BBC drama *Our Friends in the North*.

ESCAPADES OF FUTURA 2000
[The Clash/Futura 2000]

The Clash first met groundbreaking New York street-artist Futura 2000 during the *Sandinista!* sessions and commissioned him to design a backdrop for them during their residency in the city the following year. Subsequently, at the Paris and London Lyceum shows in late 1981, The Clash would perform in front of a canvas backdrop. During their sets – and in an example of performance pop-art either a decade behind the times or two decades in front of them – Futura worked (up a ladder) with his spray cans, providing a splash of garish Technicolor to proceedings. Once he had finished, Futura would occasionally join The Clash to perform the so-called **Graffiti Rap**, a make-it-up-as-we-go-along stab at rap improv.

Impressed with the spontaneity of the results, when The Clash were recording *Combat Rock* in January 1982, they invited Futura to the studios. Not only did he provide a powerful, authentic black voice to the closing rap in **Overpowered By Funk**, he was also given the opportunity to record a rewritten version of the stage collaboration, now under the title 'Escapades of Futura 2000'. The song was eventually released as a single in May 2003 (Celluloid CYZ 104).

THE EQUALISER
[The Clash]
LP: *Sandinista!*

'Marx was something of an old fart,' Strummer told Vic Garbarini in 1981 with specific reference to this song. 'He was an authoritarian and a centralist, and what he proposed was essentially the same as capitalism, except with a different set of people in charge. In any kind of realistic political change you have to start on the inside, by changing the central value system. Change has to be a personal choice.' A valid, and sensible, social policy from a man with his heart in the right place. Just what one would expect from Strummer, frankly. It's surprising, therefore, that 'The Equaliser' includes such an avalanche of naïve posturing in its lyrics.

The song, an echo-drenched, bass-heavy reggae tune, is a proposed call to arms to the oppressed workers of the world to throw off the chains of their gangbosses and go on strike. This 'us and them' situation has gone on too long, the song urges, so throw down your tools and get yourself a better life. Because, of course, *that's* never been tried before. The politics of 'The Equaliser' are for the Under Six age group, with simple moral certainties and totally unrealistic aims. That Strummer was a social idealist who, perhaps, had read one too many pamphlets and believed in the unattainable, is evidenced by his subsequent Rock Against the Rich tour in 1988. That concept was beset by ludicrous hypocritical values (who, exactly, constitute 'the rich' in the first place?) and by in-fighting with the very political groups which the tour was, in theory, supposed to be in sympathy with. Strummer emerged from the experience of having his concerts picketed by Class War and the Social Workers Party with his eyes much clearer than they had been previously. When asked by a Q reader in 1999 if his irony-meter had been on the blink during this period, Strummer recalled that the tour had largely been organised 'down the pub [after] a fifth pint of Guinness.'

'The Equaliser's simplistic evocation of the redistribution of wealth (seemingly so that Strummer could rhyme 'tools' with 'jewels') and its naïve assumption that a mass withdrawal of labour was achievable or realistic, are signs of bland sloganeering, something that Strummer had seldom indulged in previously (although it would subsequently be a hallmark of *Cut the Crap*). And certainly never without a dose of balancing wit. In this regard, he wasn't alone – soon afterwards Paul Weller would write the thematically similar, and equally blinkered, 'Trans Global Express', which also called upon 'the workers' to strike for their futures. The workers, inevitably, took absolutely no notice.

'The Equaliser' also, sadly, laid itself open to charges of anti-Semitism (see **Death Or Glory**) with the line 'See the world, it's not yours/Say the stealers of Zion'. Never played live by The Clash, 'The Equaliser' was a product of the political confusion of the era in which it was written, the early days of Thatcher's Britain. People don't write songs like this any more, perhaps because we've all realised that, while the sentiments may be laudable, pissing into the wind ultimately produces only wetness and a faint odour.

EVERY LITTLE BIT HURTS
[Ed Cobb]
LP: *Clash On Broadway*

When The Clash were staying at the Gramercy Park Hotel in New York while recording *Sandinista!*, Jones was visited by his friend Chrissie Hynde, who was in town with The Pretenders. This reminded Jones of 'Every Little Bit Hurts' a song that he and Hynde rehearsed four years previously at his grandmother's flat while both were in the fledgling London SS. A Motown single for Brenda Holloway in 1964, it's likely that Jones knew the song from The Spenser Davis Group's cover version of a year later. 'It was one of Jonesy's favourite songs,' remembered Norman Watt-Roy. 'We just did it, no run through, just one or two takes.'

FINGERNAILS
[Joe Ely]

The Clash first heard about Texas country singer Joe Ely's LP *Honky Tonk Masquerade* through their roadie Johnny Green, who was a fan of Ely's wry songs. Ely subsequently met The Clash when his band played London's The Venue in early 1979 and the two bands became friendly, socialising and attending each other's sessions. Ely supported The Clash on several occasions, such concerts often including him joining his friends on stage for performances of Ely's 1978 single 'Fingernails'. With its amusing lyrics about the difficulties of playing piano with long fingernails, the song was first played by The Clash and Ely at Monterey in September 1979. Subsequent performances occurred later on the same tour in Texas and Los Angeles, in 1980 in London and in 1982 in Dallas. Ely remained a close friend of the band, and Strummer in particular, contributing backing vocals to **Should I Stay Or Should I Go**.

FINGERPOPPIN'
[Strummer/Rhodes]
LP: *Cut the Crap*

Quite possibly the worst song ever written by anyone, 'Fingerpoppin'' is a trite, one-dimensional exposé of male and female coital rituals. 'Are they urban tribes of fighting troops?' asks Strummer. No, Joe, actually they're boys and girls doing what boys and girls have done for millennia. 'Fingerpoppin'' features an embarrassingly clumsy neo-funk backing track, in which the constituent components sound as though they're trying to escape into a different song. The Clash always sounded a bit ridiculous when they tried to play disco but, at least when Headon and Jones were in the band, they had the musical skill to just about pull it off.

With its imitation slap-bass the present song sounds uncannily like a Level 42 B-Side. Given the notoriously crap state of the UK charts in the 1984-5 period, this would probably have been a fair-sized hit had it been released as a single. The song's first and only live performance came at one of the Brixton NUM benefit shows in December 1984. The miners, subsequently, lost. 'nuff said.

FIRST NIGHT BACK IN LONDON
[The Clash]
B-SIDE: 4/82

Initial recordings for 'First Night Back In London' took place on the Rolling Stones Mobile at The Clash's rehearsal rooms at Ear Studios in September 1981. The song was completed at Electric Lady in December and mixed by Jones for possible inclusion on *Rat Patrol From Fort Bragg*. A recording of clashing styles – a lolloping reggae beat, synthetic disco drums – the song appears to be an autobiographical account of a taxi ride that turns into a drug bust. This suggests that Headon's contribution may have extended beyond musical suggestions. Having said that, The Clash's general disenchantment with England is clear in the lyrics ('as soon as I get home I call Heathrow/want a standby fare to Borneo'). A highlight of the recording is Jones' echo-saturated guitars, which are reminiscent of the sound that Andy Summers achieved on The Police's Clash-influenced 'Walking On The Moon' two years earlier.

54-46 THAT'S MY NUMBER
[Frederick Hibbert]

Inspired by Toots Hibbert's 1966-68 prison sentence for possession, this Toots and The Maytals' song was quoted from in the lyrics to **Jail Guitar Doors**. Often, when The Clash performed the latter live, Strummer would throw in additional lines from this song.

48 HOURS
[Strummer/Jones]
LP: *The Clash* [UK only]

"'48 Hours' only took about 24 minutes,' Jones said on *Westway to the World*, illustrating the speed at which he and Strummer would craft a song once a basic theme had been established. Written at Rehearsal Rehearsals, '48 Hours' was another meditation on the theme of dissatisfaction with conventional working lives, already articulated in **Janie Jones** and further elaborated in **Career Opportunities**. It describes the feeling of desperate obligation to cram as much fun as possible into Saturday and Sunday before the dreaded 'jail on wheels' of Monday comes around again. In that regard, the song is a minor variation on The Easybeats' 1966 classic 'Friday On My Mind', which was often performed by Strummer in The 101ers. '48 Hours' later gave its title to the influential punk fanzine *48 Thrills*. [43] It was also a likely inspiration for The Jam's 'Here Comes the Weekend' and Sham 69's 'Hurry Up Harry'.

First introduced into The Clash's set at the Screen On The Green in August 1976, '48 Hours' was a mainstay throughout the rest of 1976 and the White Riot tour. It was then dropped, but made a reappearance in The Clash's repertoire in Los Angeles in April 1980 and on the tour of Europe the following month.

FOUR HORSEMEN
[Strummer/Jones]
LP: *London Calling*

If *London Calling*'s apocalyptic edge (see **London Calling**, **Clampdown**, **Death Or Glory**) depresses the listener, then the present song restores the balance with hilarious self-mockery in the face of such potentially pretentious twaddle. The idea of The Clash as The Four Horsemen of the Apocalypse is ludicrous enough in itself, but the presentation here – of Four Horseman who are, like, having a really rotten day – is one of the funniest moments in rock 'n' roll. Those po-faced people who fail to spot the humour inherent in the output of bands like The Smiths and Happy Mondays, really ought to be tied to a chair, with 'Four Horsemen' on repeat, until they get the joke.

Strummer's lyrics take the biblical imagery of Revelation Chapter Six and give it a *Monty Python* twist, presenting The Clash as hard-drinking, hard-drugging, hard-loving prophets. ('One was over the edge, one was over the cliff/One was lickin' 'em dry with a bloody great spliff!') And they're coming to your town. Dismissed by sour and jaded music journos as self-aggrandising folly, 'Four Horsemen' is actually The Clash's finest stand-up comedy moment – a bit of Tommy Cooper for the punk generation. Cherish it.

43. Editor Adrian Thrills toured extensively with The Clash during 1977 (he even managed to sell Lester Bangs a copy of his fanzine for 20p). He then turned professional, writing his own weekly column, *Thrills*, in *NME*.

The sole live performance of 'Four Horsemen' occurred in the unlikely surroundings of a large field in Turku, Finland, at the Russrock Festival on 4 August 1979.

FUJIYAMA MAMA
[Burrows]

Wanda Jackson's 1957 novelty hit was performed on stage by The Clash at the Tokyo Sun Plaza dates in early 1982, backing Simonon's future wife Pearl Harbour, who had recorded a version of the song on her 1980 LP *Don't Follow Me I'm Lost Too*. It probably seemed like a good idea at the time.

GALLINI
[Strummer]

Rehearsed, although seemingly never performed live, during 1984 by the post-Jones Clash.

GARAGELAND
[Strummer/Jones]
LP: *The Clash*

The Clash's third gig, at the Screen On The Green in August 1976, was reviewed by Charles Shaar Murray for *NME*. One of Britain's finest rock journalists since his teens when he wrote for the underground magazine *Oz*, Murray was, nevertheless, unimpressed with The Clash. They were, he noted, 'the kind of garage band who should be speedily returned to the garage, preferably with the motor running.'

In interviews during the next few months Strummer appeared to take Murray's comments very personally and Murray was persona non grata around The Clash for some time afterwards. 'He was saying that our whole work of art was so piss-poor we should be executed immediately, which is pretty severe criticism, don't you think?' Strummer told Gavin Martin in 1999. 'At least it was clear-cut. There was no fucking around with poncy intellectual bollocks. He said what he meant. But so did we.' Perversely, two years later Murray would be describing The Clash as 'the greatest rock band in the world' in the same magazine. He subsequently became friendly with the group, and Strummer in particular. Fitting, therefore, that his sarcastic throwaway comments about wishing to see them dead should provide the inspiration for this glorious eulogy to the power and passion of music and celebration of being in a band.

But underneath the fists-in-the-air arrogance of its chorus, 'Garageland' is actually quite a painful and sad song. Beginning with one of Strummer's finest opening lines ('Back in the garage with my bullshit detector'), 'Garageland' is a, possibly unconscious, farewell to a scene that was expanding and, therefore, dying. The song's wailing harmonica suggests the cries of a funeral or a wake. In this context, Jones' Beatles-style harmonies, and the riff's debt to Mott The Hoople's 'All The Way From Memphis', suggest a stepping back into rock history from the badlands of punk's 'the past is dead' propaganda. The contracts had all arrived, the groups were contemplating wearing suits, the punks had all come out of the garage and gone into the studio, thereby castrating the DIY ethic of their origins. 'The truth is only known by guttersnipes' sang Strummer, defiantly. But, by the time the song was written in early 1977, he must have known that the truth was a more complex commodity than this suggested. In placing such a revisionist and radical departure as the closing song on *The Clash*, a definite statement was being made. The future, it suggests, lies this way. Jones told Kris Needs after the completion of the LP that 'Garageland' had to be the last song because it indicated 'where we're moving to next.'

The line concerning an old bag was, according to Simonon, inspired by an elderly woman who lived downstairs at the Davis Road squat and who constantly complained about the noise. Debuted live at the Harlesden Coliseum in March 1977, 'Garageland' was, thereafter, an almost permanent fixture in The Clash's set, normally used as an encore. An impressive, much slower version – emphasising the song's bluesy Mixoldydion roots – was performed in *Rude Boy*. 'Garageland' was subsequently covered by The Sick.

GATES OF THE WEST
[Strummer/Jones]
EP: *The Cost of Living*

Based, loosely, on Jones' pre-Clash song **Ooh, Baby, Ooh (It's Not Over)**, 'Gates of the West' is one of the more convoluted Clash recordings, and also one of their best. It was first attempted (under the title 'Rusted Chrome') at Basing Street in April or May 1978 during the *Give 'Em Enough Rope* sessions. Although Jones subsequently suggested that the song was 'our reaction to being in America', it was, in fact, mostly written before The Clash ever got to the States. Further work *was* done on the song by Jones and Strummer in September 1978 in New York. It was finally completed, and mixed by Bill Price, at Wessex in January 1979.

Although the opening bass riff is a clear lift from Booker T And The MG's **Time Is Tight**, the main influence on 'Gates of the West' is Bruce Springsteen, both lyrically and musically (see also **City of the Dead**). The song certainly wouldn't be out of place on one of The Boss's mid-70s LPs like *Born To Run* or *The Wild, The Innocent and the E-Street Shuffle*. 'I should be jumpin', shoutin', that I made it all this way/From Camden Town station to 44th and 8th,' sings a wide-eyed Jones, echoing Ian Hunter's similar line in 'All The Way From Memphis': 'From the Liverpool docks to the Hollywood Bowl'. 'Gates of the West', clearly, sees the challenge of giving Eastside Jimmy and Southside Sue the new sounds that they crave as a significant moment in The Clash's development. Jones' lyrical imagery is at its most poetic ('The city casts a shadow of the perfect crime'). With references to Little Richard, and the great musical heritage that The Clash felt had been devalued by a decade of stoned hippies and complacent corporate rock, standing at the gates of the west they envisage a return to the glory days when they themselves got a foothold in the land of the free. A prophecy of their own future, 'Gates of the West' is The Clash's first step on the road to the musical freedom of *London Calling*, and the internationalist concepts of *Sandinista!* and *Combat Rock*.

Released on *The Cost of Living* EP, 'Gates of the West' failed to find a place in The Clash's live set, despite its obvious popularity with fans – particularly in America. In September 1979, at the New York Palladium, a fan's request for the song caused Strummer to admit sadly that the band couldn't play 'Gates of the West' live because 'it's a bit complicated!'

GHETTO DEFENDANT
[The Clash/Allan Ginsberg]
LP: *Combat Rock*

Initially written and rehearsed during September 1981 at Ear Studios, 'Ghetto Defendant' was, at that stage, a mid-paced reggae tune, featuring Jones' plaintive harmonica, whose lyrics largely concerned New York's spiralling drug crisis. Strummer used the opportunity to blame the addicts' depression for the breakdown of community street spirit in a similar manner to pious sentiments voiced in **One More Time**. 'It's heroin pity not tear gas nor baton charge/That stops you taking the city,' notes Strummer, angrily.

The Clash had first met Allen Ginsberg in June 1981 when the legendary beat poet had joined them on stage during a show at Bond's to recite some poetry, over which the band played an impromptu musical backing (usually referred to as **Capital Air**). 'When we were recording *Combat Rock*, Ginsberg came to the studio with Pete Orlofsky,' remembered Kosmo Vinyl. 'He wanted The Clash to back him on a record, but he ended up on ours instead.' Strummer invited Ginsberg to be 'the voice of God' on the song. 'Ginsberg wrote his own bit to 'Ghetto Defendant' but he had to ask us what were the names of punk dances,' Strummer recalled in 1991. 'He just did it on the spot, it was *good*.' Ginsberg's words included a litany of international areas of confrontation in 1981 – Guatemala, Honduras, Poland, El Salvador, Afghanistan. '[Strummer] said "You're the greatest poet in America, what can *you* do with this,"' Ginsberg told *Rolling Stone*. Ginsberg took the opportunity to include a reference to his own favourite existential-symbolist poet, Arthur Rimbaud, 1854-91, author of *A Season In Hell*. According to Ginsberg's biographer Barry Miles, the poet actually attended several sessions and a number of collaborations were recorded but, apart from 'Ghetto Defendant', none has seen the light of day.

Introduced during the Paris residency in September 1981, 'Ghetto Defendant' was a vital part of The Clash's 1982 live repertoire.

GLUE ZOMBIE
[Strummer]

Played at several shows in 1984 (its debut was at Glasgow Barrowlands in February), this virulently passionate anti-drug song ('I lost my friends to the smell of gasoline') was one of the best numbers Strummer wrote after Jones left the band. Musically a distant cousin of Joe Jackson's 'It's Different For Girls', 'Glue Zombie's Beatlesque guitars and charming one-note bassline made for a simple yet effective song that, with a bit of work in the studio, could have developed into something really interesting. Sadly, for reasons unknown, the song was not recorded during the *Cut the Crap* sessions (or, if it was, the recording remains unreleased). From the evidence of a live recording from 1984, it could have considerably improved the LP.

GRAFFITI RAP
[The Clash/Futura 2000]
See THE ESCAPADES OF FUTURA 2000.

GROOVY TIMES
[Strummer/Jones]
EP: *The Cost of Living*

'What sparked the song was that they started to put fencing around English football grounds,' Strummer noted. 'It looked horrible, like cages, with the fans inside. It distressed me.' The Hillsborough disaster, which resulted in the deaths of 95 Liverpool fans a decade later, proved that his instincts were correct.

Dominated by Jones' acoustic guitars, 'Groovy Times' is one of The Clash's most clever and underrated pieces. The imagery contained is of urban decay, of miserable boarded-up high street shops, see-through police riot shields, frantic housewives wanting their daily bacon and broken glass on concrete pavements. In this regard, the song is yet another restating of the running Clash themes of alienation and monotony.

Yet 'Groovy Times' is a much subtler song than ostensibly similar material on *The Clash*. In many ways the song is a pointer forward to the gentler and more positive sound-world of *London Calling*, and to songs like **Clampdown** with their urge for popular revolt against conformity. 'Groovy Times' also includes an amusing allusion to Bill Grundy ('the King of early evening ITV') and his shattered career, post-'the filth and the fury', fronting Sunday evening religious programmes. One of Jones' most urbane melodies, with its angelic chorus and foot-tapping medium-paced beat, the song would have had hit single written all over it. If, that is, it had been recorded by anybody other than The Clash.

First recorded as little more than a demo (under the title 'Groovy Times Are Here Again') during the *Give 'Em Enough Rope* session at Utopia Studios in May 1978, the song was completed, with Bill Price, at Wessex in January 1979. 'Bill had worked with all the right people,' remembered Jones. 'He was really good, and an English gentleman, although we used to drive him to the edge.' The harmonica was credited to Bob Jones. 'That's me,' added Mick Jones. 'It's a Bob Dylan joke.' Like **Gates of the West**, 'Groovy Times' was never performed live by The Clash.

THE GUNS OF BRIXTON
[Simonon]
LP: *London Calling*

During rehearsals for *London Calling*, Simonon came up with an innovative reggae-style bass riff that the rest of the band developed into an instrumental.

A few days later, Simonon presented Strummer with a set of lyrics that he had written. 'They're fantastic,' Strummer noted, 'but they're yours. You sing them.' A confirmed non-singer, Simonon demurred at first but, after a few days of cajoling by the rest of the band, he plucked up the courage to try. 'I don't consider myself a singer,' he noted. 'The vocal mike was right up against the glass panel of the control room and sitting two feet behind the glass was some American CBS bloke. That's probably why the vocals came out the way they did.'

Simonon's first song relocated Ivan, the Jimmy Cliff character from the film *The Harder They Come*, to South London for a brush with the Met. It was do-or-die stuff ('when the law break in/how you gonna go?'), full of startlingly violent imagery (Black Marias, Death Row, crushing, bruising, Heaven and Hell). The bassline subsequently became famous more than a decade later, when Norman Cook (aka Fatboy Slim) sampled it for his Beats International hit 'Dub Be Good To Me'. 'I was surprised that it became a number one,' Simonon told *Bassist Magazine*. 'So, really, I *have* done *Top of the Pops*! I met up with Norman and we came to an arrangement which was much needed at the time. But I thought it was a really good idea and it was quite reassuring for that to happen to my first song.' In July 1990, Simonon commissioned DJ and former Haysi Fantayzee singer Jeremy Healy to remix 'The Guns of Brixton' and it was released as a single, entitled **Return to Brixton**, though it was only a minor UK hit.

The song became Simonon's major showcase live with The Clash after its introduction to the set in September 1979 at Chicago, and remained a firm favourite thereafter. Usually, Simonon and Strummer would swap instruments on stage, allowing the bassist to concentrate on bellowing the vocals with little subtlety but always with great enthusiasm. A splendidly representative version, recorded in June 1981 in New York, features on *From Here to Eternity*. The song has been covered by Dropkick Murphy, Rancho Deluxe, The Honeydippers and Davey Dreamnation (as 'Guns of Davey').

Footnote: According to the credits of the 1989 *London Calling* CD (Columbia 460114-2), 'The Guns of Brixton' was written, not by Paul Simonon, but rather by Paul Simon.

GUNS ON THE ROOF
[The Clash]
LP: *Give 'Em Enough Rope*

On 30 March 1978, two of Headon's friends from Dover, Steve and Pete Barnacle, were at Rehearsal Rehearsals with a high-powered air rifle that they intended to sell to Headon, who was fascinated with such weaponry. Together with Simonon and roadie Robin Crocker, they went up to the roof and began having a few practice shots at some passing pigeons. These, it subsequently transpired, were expensive racing pigeons owned by George Dole, a mechanic who worked in the neighbouring garage. Having been spotted by officers of the British Transport Police, the group's activities were reported to the CID. Believing that a bunch of anarchist guerrillas were taking pot-shots at trains on the mainline to Euston, the authorities sprang into action. What followed, wrote Johnny Green who witnessed the raid, was like 'a scene from *The Sweeney*.'

Headon, Simonon, Crocker and the Barnacle brothers were arrested, taken to Kentish Town station and charged with possessing an illegal weapon and attempted manslaughter. [44] Soon afterwards the band began jamming at Rehearsals on yet another variant of the 'I Can't Explain' riff previously used on both **Capital Radio One** and **Clash City Rockers**. As a joke, the song was given the title 'Guns on the Roof'. Actually, the lyrics that Strummer eventually came up with concerned more weighty themes: political torture, oppression, martyrdom, assassination, instant justice and corruption – a kaleidoscopic indictment of the global arms trade and of covert military actions. As *Last Gang In Town* noted, the song is Strummer's most sensation-alist and histrionic musing on the subject of terrorism, not that it is without some accurate observations. However, Strummer's simplistic belief that assassins are a by-product of corrupt societies, while having some merit, is not the whole answer (as **Tommy Gun**, written several months prior to 'Guns on the Roof', confirms). Sadly, the choice of title undermined the song's concerned message, with most reviewers assuming that it directly related to the pigeon-shooting incident instead of something more serious. Strummer's opening line, swearing by almighty God to tell the truth, as a defendant would in court, didn't help with this misconception.

A template for U2's entire career, 'Guns on the Roof' was introduced to The Clash's set on 30 April 1978 at the *Rock Against Racism* gig in Victoria Park. The song was occasionally played live during the remainder of 1978. Initial performances, like one at Birmingham in May, were still very much work-in-progress – the song lacking its subsequent middle section. It also lost much of the protracted drama of the studio version in the hurly-burly of a live event. 'Guns on the Roof' was regularly performed on the Pearl Harbour tour, but was dropped thereafter.

---

44. These charges were subsequently dropped after the police produced no evidence to support them. When the case came to court in June 1978, Headon, Simonon and Pete Barnacle, who had actually done the shooting, were fined £30 each and had to pay Mr Dole £700 compensation for the loss of his pigeons.

THE HARDER THEY COME
[Jimmy Cliff]

The theme song from the 1972 movie that, along with its attendant soundtrack, greatly helped to popularise reggae in Europe and America. The Clash regularly performed the song at soundchecks in 1979 and 1980. It remained a favourite with Strummer, who often included 'The Harder They Come' in the live sets of The Mescaleros. The film *The Harder They Come* is name-checked in **The Guns of Brixton**.

HATE & WAR
[Strummer/Jones]
LP: *The Clash*

'The only things we've got today.' Written in November 1976, 'Hate & War' turned the hippy mantra of 'love and peace' upside down to illustrate the contrast between the optimism of the late 1960s and the grim and sober reality of Britain just a few years later. 'It was a good punk rock blast to have a song called that,' Strummer told *Uncut* in 2002.

'I wrote the lyric in a disused ice cream factory that I'd broken into,' Strummer remembered in 1991. 'It was just behind the Harrow Road [Foscote Mews]. I wrote it in the dark by candlelight and the next day took it to Rehearsals and Mick put a tune to it.' In *Last Gang In Town*, Marcus Gray suggests that the song may have been written specifically to back up some of The Clash's recent media pronouncements on 'creative violence.' Gray also comments on the almost xenophobic use of terms like 'wops' and 'kebab Greeks', expressing surprise that The Clash were never challenged over such seemingly racist language (particularly in light of the misunderstanding, in the media and elsewhere, concerning **White Riot**). With its allusions to 'the hate of a nation' and city houses falling down, 'Hate & War' fitted in nicely alongside songs like **London's Burning** and **1977** as an evocation of The Clash's angry working-class voice. But it's not simply an exposé of social injustices; it's far more bitter. In 'Hate & War', The Clash are on the barricades and, if you're not with them, you're going to get your head kicked in.

Musically, 'Hate & War' displays *The Clash*'s most undisguised early example of the influence of reggae on Strummer and Jones' writing, both via the choppy rhythm guitars and in Strummer's quasi-dub *hate-hate-hate* backing vocals. Introduced into The Clash's set during the Anarchy tour, the song was a mainstay during 1977 but was dropped the following year, only to reappear in a radical rearrangement on the Pearl Harbour tour. (The band also performed 'Hate & War' on the *Alright Now* TV show during this period.) It was resurrected, on occasions, thereafter – for some of the 1980 European dates; at Newcastle in 1982; for the 1983 shows with Pete Howard and, with Strummer on lead vocals, the 1985 festival dates that would prove to be The Clash's live farewell. The song has been covered by Murphy's Law.

HATEFUL
[Strummer/Jones]
LP: *London Calling*

Written during the Pimlico rehearsals in April 1979, 'Hateful' is a dry variant on Lou Reed's 'I'm Waiting for the Man' and is The Clash's most pointedly anti-drugs song, with its portrayal of helpless heroin addiction and the limited life expectancy of those caught in its web. That the song obviously had personal meaning for its author, Strummer, can be seen in the line 'This year I lost some friends', a reference to the death of Sid Vicious in February. A jaunty tune, which belies the song's disturbing and cynical message of dependency, 'Hateful' was only performed live during the three July 1979 London shows at Notre Dame Hall and The Rainbow. No Doubt's 1999 cover version appears on *Burning London – The Clash Tribute*. Kid Dynamite also covered the song.

HEARTBREAK HOTEL
[Axton, Durden, Presley]

In late 1977 Strummer was asked to do some soundtrack work for a low-budget German arthouse movie, Diego Cotez's *Grutzi Elvis*. His contributions were two versions of Presley's 'Heartbreak Hotel', a song that had previously featured in The 101ers set. One had a Cajun-style backing of German session musicians. The other, described as 'a terrorist-style recording', is rumoured to be a Clash out-take from the sessions that produced **Clash City Rockers**.

HEART AND MIND

In November 1978, Jones mentioned to *Sounds*' Garry Bushell that The Clash had 15 unreleased songs at various stages of completion. 'Heart And Mind' was one of the titles mentioned. Whether the song was ever finished, or if it mutated into something else, will probably never be known.

HITSVILLE UK
[The Clash]
SINGLE: 1/81 **LP:** *Sandinista!*

Jones' laudable attempt at recreating a 60s soul-groove in the style of early Motown, the tune for 'Hitsville UK' is a distant cousin of Holland, Dozier and Holland's 'This Old Heart Of Mine (Is Weak For You)', a hit for The Isley Brothers in 1965.

The song begins with a stab of cod-gospel organ, after which Headon's inscrutable parody of an authentic period drum sound, Simonon's fluid bass and a glockenspiel (played by Jones) carry the tune. Sung as a duet by Jones and his then-girfriend Ellen Foley, Strummer's lyrics celebrate musical independence in all its forms and include yet another embittered attack on CBS (albeit somewhat more veiled than either **Complete Control** or **Death Or Glory**). 'Hitsville UK' namechecks several British independent record labels like Small Wonder, Factory and Rough Trade and rejoices in a group's ability to knock off a powerful piece of work in two minutes and 59 seconds without expense accounts, hype or 'slimy deals with smarmy eels'.

Recorded at Wessex in August 1980, 'Hitsville UK' was not an obvious choice for the second single from *Sandinista!* (it was probably chosen with America in mind). The band did little to publicise it and the song was never performed live by The Clash.

HIT THE ROAD JACK
[Ray Charles]

An R&B classic, 'Hit the Road Jack' was used by Strummer in a medley with **Police & Thieves** at several dates on the 16 Tons tour in 1980. The Clash also backed Pearl Harbour on a version during their Paris residency in September 1981.

HOUSE OF THE JU-JU QUEEN
[Strummer/Jones]

A song written specifically by Strummer for The Clash's former muse Janie Jones. Recorded at Wessex on 28 December 1982, along with a version of James Brown's **Sex Machine**, the single eventually came out during December 1983

(Big Beat NS91), credited to Janie Jones And The Lash. The back cover featured a charming photo of a leather-clad Janie spanking some nuns. Perhaps predictably, it died a death, minimising the chance of any further musical collaboration between the parties. The song itself is full of sniggery S&M innuendo, although Mick Jones' guitar solo is worthy of a much more interesting song. Featuring Mickey Gallagher and fellow Blockhead Charley Charles on drums, as well as Simonon, it's a Clash recording in everything but name. A home demo version of 'House of the Ju-Ju Queen', featuring Strummer on vocals, appeared on Ms Jones' compilation LP *I'm In Love With the World of Janie Jones*.

How Can I Understand the Flies?
[Strummer]

An integral part of The Clash's 1976 live set was this primal, Ramones-influenced wall-of-sound thrash. Introduced by Strummer at The Roundhouse in September as 'a summer song', it appears to concern the squalid living conditions in the Orsett Terrace squat that Strummer was sharing with Palmolive, Sid Vicious, Keith Levene and Simonon. 'How can I go to sleep/ With the flies buzzing around my head?' Strummer asked plaintively.

By the time the band got into the studio, songs like this had been supplanted by more politically pointed material.

I Don't Want Your Money
See I Never Did It

I Fought the Law
[Sonny Curtis]
Single: 7/79 [US only] **EP:** *The Cost of Living* **LP:** *The Clash* [US only]

While Strummer and Jones were in San Francisco in 1978, overdubbing *Give 'Em Enough Rope*, they discovered that The Automatt studio had a fabulous jukebox. One of the records they particularly enjoyed playing was The Bobby Fuller Four's 'I Fought the Law.' [45] 'It made a great impression on us,'

---

45. Texan Bobby Fuller (1942-66) died, in mysterious circumstances, just five months after 'I Fought the Law' was a hit, in July 1966. Friends suspected that he had been murdered, possibly at the hands of organised crime.

remembered Jones. Written by The Crickets' guitarist Sonny Curtis (allegedly in just half-an-hour), 'I Fought the Law (and the Law Won)', to give the song its full title, was a country-rock standard by the time The Clash got their hands on it and made it their own.

A venomous song when played live, Strummer would often change a key line to indicate that he had killed rather than lost his baby, an almost certain reference to his friend Sid Vicious' sorry end. 'I Fought the Law' went straight into The Clash's set when Strummer and Jones got back from the States for the Sort It Out tour, starting in October 1978. 'When Mick and Joe first played it on acoustic guitars, I said "I'm not doing that, it sounds terrible",' remembered Headon. 'Of course, as soon as we got drums on it, it sounded great.' Indeed it did, and Headon's contribution to the song is immense. The opening thunder of drums helps to destroy the accepted wisdom that punk rock killed the drum solo. [46] Additionally, the moment in the second chorus when Strummer sings of 'Robbin' people with a...' and, before he can add 'six gun', Headon interjects a rapid staccato of side-toms, is one of the most thrilling in The Clash's discography.

An incendiary version of 'I Fought the Law' recorded at The Lyceum on 3 January 1979 – one of the most exciting rock 'n' roll performances by anyone, anywhere, under *any* circumstances – graces *Rude Boy*, *Clash On Broadway* and *From Here to Eternity*. A studio version followed later the same month, the song becoming the lead item on *The Cost of Living* EP and the band's first single in the US. Confusingly, The Clash dropped the song during the Pearl Harbour tour, preferring to concentrate on highlighting older material. But it was back with a vengeance for the Notre Dame Hall gigs in June 1979 and, thereafter, remained in The Clash's set pretty much for the rest of their careers (often in a fine medley with **Koka Kola**).

I KNOW WHAT TO DO

See I KNOW WHAT TO THINK OF YOU

---

46. Headon's 'lead-drums', in the style of The Who's Keith Moon, are just one example of clever and intricate drumming far removed from the stereotypical 'biff-bang-crash' punk backbeat. While no punk drummer ever got anywhere near to the excesses of Ginger Baker or John Bonham, for example, John Maher's solo on Buzzcocks' 'Moving Away from the Pulsebeat', or, in live performance, Rick Buckler of The Jam's work on songs like "'A' Bomb In Wardour Street' and 'Little Boy Soldiers' reminds us that the drum-solo was still alive and kicking as late as 1979.

I KNOW WHAT TO THINK OF YOU
[Jones]

A rather moody and slow R&B song with a staccato riff obviously modelled on The Who's 'I Can't Explain' and a double-time middle section that owes much to Van Morrison's 'Gloria'. Predominantly a relationship song, the lyrics include the dramatic line 'standing in the hospital room, dead or alive,' which indicates that drugs may have been part of the equation too. Played at several 1976 shows, including The Screen on the Green. Speeded up, the song's chord sequence would subsequently become the basis for **Clash City Rockers**. Also known as **I Know What To Do** and **You Know What I Think About You**.

IF MUSIC COULD TALK
[The Clash/Mikey Dread]
LP: *Sandinista!*

The spontaneous excitement of the early *Sandinista!* sessions, and of New York generally, reached its zenith with this extraordinary talkin' blues broadside in the manner of Bob Dylan's 'Talkin' New York'. Taking the instrumental backing-track **Shepherds Delight**, recorded with Mikey Dread at Pluto two months earlier, Strummer added a stream-of-consciousness lyric about New York, full of startling images, dice-throwing metaphors and hard luck tales. (He even indulges in some lewd banter with a girl he meets in a bar, asking if she needs a country cowboy 'who's just thin and tight in those bus depot jeans?') Putting some of his double-tracked vocals in the left stereo channel and more in the right – à la The Velvet Underground's 'The Murder Mystery' – Strummer thus created one of the most interesting pieces of music on the LP.

Among a plethora of lyrical references are Bo Diddley, actor and hellraiser Errol Flynn (1909-59), Joe Ely 'and his Texan men', the sale of London Bridge to Lake Havasu City in Arizona, Sir Isaac Newton's discovery of gravity when an apple fell on his head, Buddy Holly And The Crickets, Elvis Presley's 'Are You Lonesome Tonight?', Jim Morrison (the man who said he was a voodoo shaman) and Samson (sans Delilah). But 'If Music Could Talk' is also directly about The Clash themselves. The song alludes to Electric Lady studio, Headon's growing heroin addiction ('my drummer friend comes shooting by'), namechecks lighting man Warren 'Stoner' Steadman and references Strummer's 'Spliffbunker', where the lyrics were most probably written. Gary Barnacle's jazzy saxophone, overdubbed at Wessex in August, flits in and out of a backing track dominated by Headon and Simonon. Needless to say, 'If Music Could Talk' was impossible to reproduce live.

I'M NOT DOWN
[Strummer/Jones]
LP: *London Calling*

Early 1979 was a depressing time for Mick Jones. Just before Christmas his Pembridge Villas flat had been burgled and many of his most cherished possessions had been lost. Soon afterwards his relationship with Viv Albertine, which had been off-and-on several times during 1977-78, finally ended. Just as Strummer had experienced a period of introspection and doubt at the end of 1977, so Jones was, temporarily, going through a fallow time. While he could be relied upon to provide the tunes that Strummer needed, for the moment his own lyrical well seemed to be dry. 'I'm Not Down' was perhaps an attempt to kick-start his enthusiasm for songwriting. In many ways, the song is an update of **Hate & War**, a defiant gesture in the face of mounting disappointment. With its reference to judgment day, there's a possibility that the placing of 'I'm Not Down' immediately after **Four Horsemen** on *London Calling* was a deliberate attempt to prolong the former song's dour wink at the audience. Yet 'I'm Not Down', while hardly a happy song, is nevertheless one in which Jones notes that, while he may have lived the kind of day 'when none of your sorrows will go away', life tends to balance out the positives and negatives.

The verse concerning the singer facing a jeering gang, refusing to run and being beaten, appears to be autobiographical and may refer to an incident that Jones mentions in *Westway to the World* in which he was whacked over the head with a blunt instrument by an enraged rocker. A pleasingly spiky performance on record, 'I'm Not Down' made its live debut at the London shows in July 1979. [47] The fact that, by the time of the US tour three months later, it had been dropped, possibly indicates that the song's author was on the road to recovery from his doldrums (however, see **Train In Vain**).

I'M SO BORED WITH THE USA
[Strummer/Jones]
LP: *The Clash*

Turning self-mythology into an art form was something The Clash did better than anyone else. There are few finer examples of this than 'I'm So Bored

---

47. Strummer seems to have been amused by the depressing lyrics of 'I'm Not Down'. Introducing the song before its public debut, he asked if anyone in the Notre Dame audience was contemplating suicide.

With The USA' A fine song with a terrific story behind it. During Strummer's first meeting with Jones and Simonon at the Davis Road squat (probably on 1 June 1976), Mick played Joe several of his compositions, including 'I'm So Bored With You'. This was a bitter, if slight, variant on Bob Dylan's 'Don't Think Twice, It's Alright' and concerned Jones' relationship with a nameless soon-to-be-former girlfriend, an ex-public schoolgirl (see **Deny**). Strummer, momentarily distracted as Jones played the song, misheard the title as 'I'm So Bored With The USA' 'That's great. What a fine thing to say,' Joe noted and, on the spot, added some verses to Mick's now-amended chorus. As late as 1999, in *Westway to the World*, both men were still sticking to, basically, the same story.

However, live Clash recordings from August and September 1976 catch the song still under the original title and still, ostensibly, about the end of a relationship. At the band's second 100 Club show on 20 September, the familiar 'USA' chorus had arrived and by October the song had metamorphosed, with references to Cambodia, the CIA, the Watergate conspiracy and the contemporary US cop shows *Starsky and Hutch* and *Kojak*. With the line 'I'll salute the new wave', The Clash also gave punk its alternate, and more socially acceptable, label. Ironically, the phrase makes more sense when seen in the context of an earlier lyrical draft in which the preceding verse had concerned the American West Coast surfing scene. 'Although we'd been brought up on American TV shows,' noted Jones in 1999, 'there was too much of an American influence [on Britain in the 70s]. There were too many McDonalds.'

In the context of 1976 punk rhetoric, an admiration for anything American was about as uncool as it was possible to get (cf The Sex Pistols' sneering dismissal of the CGBG punk scene and its 'hippy-drug-heroes', 'New York'). 'For a relatively young nation, the USA is remarkably slow when it comes to tapping talent – even though sucking the cents out of every available European culture is the national pastime,' wrote Parsons and Burchill in *The Boy Looked at Johnny*. It should also be noted that Subway Sect lyricist Vic Godard alleged in a 1977 interview with *ZigZag* that The Clash had 'nicked' his song 'USA'. The veracity of this claim has yet to be proven. On the other hand, the lifting of 'I'm So Bored With The USA''s stinging rhythm guitar riff from The Beatles' 'The Word' sees The Clash banged to rights.

'I'm So Bored' was first demoed, using marginally different lyrics, with Micky Foote on 8-track at Beaconsfield's National Film and Television Studios in January 1977. (Julien Temple's black-and-white footage of Strummer, Jones and Simonon overdubbing the vocals on this version appear in *Westway to the World*.) A permanent fixture in The Clash's live set from 1976 until 1978, thereafter the song would only occasionally be visited during shows in Britain. In America, however, it became the band's regular set opener on three successive tours. 'We started the show with 'I'm So Bored With The USA' because we wanted to find out if they had a sense of humour in America,' Strummer noted in 2001. Violent Society and XX Cortez both produced spirited cover versions in the late 90s.

I'M SO BORED WITH YOU

See I'M SO BORED WITH THE USA

I NEVER DID IT
[Jones]

Sometimes credited as **I Don't Want Your Money**, this was another staple of The Clash's early stage set that was jettisoned by the time they got into the recording studio. A fast, Ramones-style assault, the lyrics catalogue the protagonist's disillusionment with an old friend who had sold out for a superficial lifestyle. 'I could've been as rich as you,' yells Strummer. Complete with Mick Jones' Beatle-style vocal harmonies, the song normally ended with a Terry Chimes drum solo which segued into **How Can I Understand the Flies?**

IN THE POURING RAIN
[Strummer]

First played at the Glasgow gig in February 1984, 'In the Pouring Rain' also featured on the subsequent US tour. A mid-paced ballad with some mature meteorological metaphors in Strummer's lyrics and a fine Nick Sheppard guitar solo, this song, like **Ammunition** and **Glue Zombie**, may have vastly improved *Cut the Crap* had it been selected for recording and inclusion. Sadly, it was not.

INOCULATED CITY
[The Clash]
B-SIDE: 10/82 LP: *Combat Rock*

Similar in tone and spirit to **The Call Up**, Jones' 'Inoculated City' attempted to break the chains of command in the military by attacking that old Nazi-style standby 'I was just following orders'. A template for this may have been XTC's

1980 UK hit 'Generals and Majors'. Jones' anger at the futility of conflict ('No one knows what they're fighting for') and the crassness of politically motivated interference in such matters is evident,[48] although this seems to have temporarily robbed him of inspiration as the rest of the lyrics are rather flat and one-dimensional. The song's ornate foundation, jaunty chorus and chanted unison vocals (by Jones and Strummer) somewhat belie its earnest subject-matter. Rehearsed during the Ear Studio sessions, 'Inoculated City' was introduced live during the Paris residency in September 1981 and also featured on the subsequent UK tour.

Jones' growing interest in sampling saw the inclusion of the soundtrack from a TV toilet cleaner commercial for '2,000 Flushes' over the song's instrumental bridge. A clever piece of social comment on rampant commercialism (the scatological nature of the product probably helped), the sample led to legal problems with Flushco Inc. As *Last Gang In Town* notes, it forced the band into 'sneaking around the US like wanted men' to avoid being served with a writ. The sample is said to have been subsequently withdrawn from some US imprints of the LP until a settlement was eventually reached.

THE ISRAELITES
[Desmond Dekker/Leslie Kong]

One of the records on the jukebox at Rehearsal Rehearsals was this reggae standard by Desmond Dekker and the Aces. With its famously impenetrable lyrics (comedian Lenny Henry has noted that for years he, along with many other people, thought the chorus said 'Ooo, me ears are alight'), it was the UK's first reggae number one (in April 1969). John Lennon famously used the song's bassline in an effort to show the American musicians he was working with on *Sometime In New York City* how to play reggae. The Clash often thrashed out a spirited version in rehearsals and soundchecks. The band's only recorded performance of 'The Israelites' was on 4 March 1979 on the Tyne Tees Television show *Alright Now*. Pretty good it was too, with Strummer handling the lyrics confidently. Sadly, it featured right at the end of the show as the credits rolled. As a result, the performance only lasts for about a minute.

---

48. The Clash were fortunate in the timing of 'Inoculated City's release in May 1982, the contemporaneous Falklands War giving the song a relevance that it may not have otherwise had.

IVAN MEETS GI JOE
[The Clash]
LP: *Sandinista!*

Headon's first songwriter credit for The Clash (he wrote all the music) and also his first vocal contribution to the band's recorded output. A Clash disco record was probably the last thing their fans expected in 1980, but signs of a developing interest in funk and rap had been there for a while. 'People prefer to dance than to fight wars,' Jones had told *Rolling Stone*, and Strummer's droll lyrics use such notions to good effect.

Namechecks occur for New York's Studio 54 and The Clash's favourite Parisian discotheque haunt, Le Palace. Casting the world's two superpowers as contestants in a bizarre dance competition, the song's metaphorical parallel assessment of mutually assured destruction is in stark contrast to its punchy, infectious beat. References crop up to atomic and chemical warfare, Soviet dictator Joseph Stalin (1879-1953) and Marvin Gaye's 'Hitch Hike'. Steve Bell's hilarious cartoon that accompanied the song on the *Armagideon Times* lyric sheet makes the most of Strummer's glowing imagery.

Introduced to The Clash's set in April 1981, the song was a live fixture during the rest of that year and the Far East tour in 1982.

JAIL GUITAR DOORS
[Strummer/Jones]
B-SIDE: 2/78 **LP:** *The Clash* [US only]

'Jail Guitar Doors', was originally written by Strummer with the help of The 101ers when he was still in that band.[49] The Clash played it during their first rehearsals but, at the time, Strummer had decided that such songs were outdated and that he wanted a clean break from his past. In 1977 Jones, who admired the song greatly, rewrote the lyrics and sang the version recorded at CBS in September. 'We took pieces of 'Jail Guitar Doors' and rewrote a different verse,' Strummer told *Uncut* in 2002. An unholy alliance between The New York Dolls, Bowie's 'Rebel Rebel' and, in terms of subject matter,

49. A possible inspiration for the lyrics was a gig that The 101ers played at Wandsworth Prison in early 1976 (see Richard Dudanski: *Uncut* 2003).

The Rolling Stones' 'We Love You', the closing refrain was lifted wholesale from Toots and The Maytals' **54-46 That's My Number**.

One of the three people who get locked up in Jones' version of the song, seemingly for serious drugs offences, is called Keith. It's possible that this was a nasty swipe at former band member Keith Levene.

The song was recorded in September 1977 at CBS with Micky Foote. 'That funny noise at the beginning is the hi-hat, which was bent,' remembered Johnny Green. 'We amplified it right up and everybody loved it.' First performed live at Zurich in October 1977, 'Jail Guitar Doors' was a fixture in The Clash's live set for the next 18 months (often, after his own drug bust in July 1978, with an additional verse about Jones himself possibly suffering the same fate as his heroes). It was subsequently revived for the summer 1980 European dates. The song was covered in 2003, in a fine rockabilly style, by The Caravans.

JANIE JONES
[Strummer/Jones]
LP: *The Clash*

The longest-running song in The Clash's live act (first gig to last, with virtually no breaks in between), 'Janie Jones' was written by namesake Mick during the period just after Strummer joined The Clash. The tune and the chorus came to Jones while riding on a number 31 bus from Harrow Road to Chalk Farm. Strummer subsequently helped with the rest of the lyrics. They concern the soul-destroying monotony of office work, something Mick had briefly experienced for himself in his late teens (see **Career Opportunities**). The storyteller in 'Janie Jones' is bored with the dull, menial nature of his day and dreams of escape through rock 'n' roll, getting stoned or telling his boss where to shove the work in his in-tray.

The title character herself was a real-life vice queen who had enjoyed a brief spell of sensational tabloid notoriety when she was given a seven-year jail sentence in 1973 for running a brothel and perverting the course of justice by threatening witnesses. [50] 'Janie Jones was still Sunday paper material at the

50. A 60s cabaret performer, Janie Jones was more renowned in London for her swinging parties than her music and gained her biggest headlines in 1964 by attending a film premiere in a topless gown. She enjoyed a minor hit in 1965 with the Halloweenish novelty 'Witches Brew.' She remained on the periphery of the public eye with a marriage to songwriter John Christian Dee, but it was her prison sentence, in 1973, that brought her notoriety. After her release from jail, in 1977, around the time of *The Clash*'s release, she got in touch with the band and she and Strummer remained friends. He wrote her 1983 single 'House of the Ju-Ju Queen'. Jones published her memoirs, *The Devil and Miss Jones*, in 1993.

time,' noted Mick Jones. According to Strummer, her name was used because she was the sort of woman who would seem 'impossibly glamorous' to someone stuck in an office.

An of-the-era reference to a Ford Cortina and a possible allusion to the dreadful 1970s race-relations sitcom *Love Thy Neighbour* ('Fill her up, Jacko!') are juxtaposed with a nod in the direction of the 1950s rock 'n' roll scandal of payola. Musically, the most notable thing about this very simple song is Simonon's one-note bass-drone during the verses, which many have seen as a deliberate ploy by Jones to emphasise the boredom inherent in the lyrics. Alternatively, and more plausibly, the song was written at a stage when Simonon could hardly play a note. 'Janie Jones' was subsequently covered by Red London and The Farrell brothers.

JIMMY JAZZ
[Strummer/Jones]
LP: *London Calling*

The first of *London Calling*'s several songs concerning outsider/loner figures hassled by square society for their refusal to conform, 'Jimmy Jazz' concerns a young Rasta assassin who has cut off the ears (and head) of Jimmy Dread. Interestingly, however, the Jamaican patois – including references to The Abyssinians' *Satta Massa Gana* – isn't matched by an expected bluebeat backing. Rather, Strummer's interest in New Orleans jazz/blues, pricked by **Julie's Been Working for the Drug Squad**, is here given full rein. A tour de force for Jones (particularly his cunning bijoux acoustic opening, a beautiful pastiche in the style of 30s jazz genius Django Reinhardt), the song also features whistling by Clash roadie Barry Glare and a beautifully sleazy brass section courtesy of The Irish Horns.

First played live at Minneapolis, the opening date of The Clash Take The Fifth tour, the song became a regular encore throughout 1980 and featured during the New York and Paris residencies in 1981 and in Tokyo the next year. One of The Clash's most effortlessly classy numbers, 'Jimmy Jazz' was also, perversely, chosen as the opening number when The Clash first played the home of the blues, Chicago, in late 1979. It also appeared during the Busking tour. 'Jimmy Jazz' has been covered by Frantic Flintones and The C-Nuts.

JOHNNY TOO BAD
[Trevor Wilson/Winston Bailey/Hylton Beckford/Derrick Crooks]

Referenced in the lyrics of **The Prisoner** and briefly heard on the soundtrack of *Rude Boy*, The Slickers' 'Johnny Too Bad' was one of The Clash's, and particularly Simonon's, favourite songs. Simonon was familiar with it from the soundtrack to *The Harder They Come* (see also **Pressure Drop, 007 (Shanty Town), The Harder They Come**). 'Johnny Too Bad', with its sadly reproachful lyrics regarding rebellious youth ('you're just robbing and stabbing and looting and shooting'), was performed by The Clash on the Busking tour.

JULIE'S BEEN WORKING FOR THE DRUG SQUAD
[Strummer/Jones]
LP: *Give 'Em Enough Rope*

In early 1977 an elaborate police sting, Operation Julie, named after undercover policewoman Julie Taylor who was part of the team, netted a haul of some 1.5kg of LSD microdots. Some of the purest acid ever manufactured in Britain, it was produced mainly in a remote farmhouse in Wales. The conspirators included Cambridge chemistry students Richard Kemp, Christine Bott, Andrew Munro and Henry Todd. In all, 17 defendants pleaded guilty at Bristol Crown Court in March 1978 and were sentenced to a total of 130 years' imprisonment, with Kemp and Todd receiving 13 years each.

'The only way for the cops to bust them was to put in some hippies of their own, who had to take acid repeatedly to maintain cover,' noted Strummer in 1991. 'The song's about tripping policemen.' Featuring some of Strummer's most witty wordplay, 'Julie's Been Working for the Drug Squad' alludes to The Beatles' acid classic 'Lucy In The Sky With Diamonds' amid its sad shaking of heads at the wasted futures of those caught by the fuzz. Following *Julie*, the street price of acid in the UK skyrocketed, from approximately 50p to over £1 per tab.

In the studio, Headon's jazzy drum fills fitted in perfectly with the piano that was subsequently added by Blue Öyster Cult's Al Leiner. Only Jones' guitar work, full of ironic little exclamation marks, would have seemed out of place in a 1950s New Orleans nightclub. First performed live on the Sort It Out tour ('I think they call this R&B,' Strummer told the audience at Middlesbrough in November), early performances tended to be rather ramshackle, but The Clash eventually got to grips with its shuffle beat. (Once Mickey Gallagher was added to The Clash's live line-up, the addition of his keyboards helped to make performances much more organised.)

The song was a set regular during 1979 and appeared occasionally thereafter, wheeled out for special occasions like the LA Roxy show in 1980 or the London Lyceum dates in 1981.

JUNCO PARTNER
[Robert Ellen]
LP: *Sandinista!*

A traditional blues song[51] that Strummer had often performed with The 101ers.[52] The Clash's madly out-of-tune reggae version was recorded at Channel One studios in Jamaica during their infamously hasty visit to the island in April 1980. Although the song's lyrics concerned, largely, alcoholism and life on the streets, Strummer threw in a few personal touches, namechecking his girlfriend Gabriella, for instance.

Musically, 'Junco Partner' is the most extreme example of Mikey Dread's influence on The Clash, full of squeaky production tricks, dub-echo and the sound of the legendary Channel One piano (played by Strummer). Overdubs were carried out at Wessex, including the scratchy violin (some sources suggest this was played by Tymon Dogg, though this is unconfirmed). The band clearly enjoyed recording the song and it became a popular part of The Clash's live set in 1981-82 after debuting during the Spanish shows in May. The song was also performed on the Out of Control tour in 1984.

JUNKIE SLIP
[The Clash]
LP: *Sandinista!*

A loose, unadorned skiffle-style[53] tune of Strummer's that, with hindsight, can only have concerned Headon's escalating drug problems in early 1980. The horrible irony of the song is the prophetic way in which the lyrics' portrayal of helpless addiction predicted the depths to which Headon would sink as the decade wore on. 'You pawned your guitar and your saxophone/You're pawning everything in your mother's home,' anticipates a story, widely circulated in the music press at the time of his 1987 imprisonment, that Headon would regularly sell his gold records to fund his habit. Recorded in New York during the *Sandinista!* sessions, 'Junkie Slip' was

---

51. Bob Dylan used the song's lyric, *Knocked Out Loaded*, for the title of a 1986 LP.

52. A poor-quality version, recorded at the Roundhouse on 18 April 1976, appears on The 101ers LP *Elgin Avenue Breakdown* (see Keys To Your Heart).

53. Originally a synonym for American country 'jug band' music, skiffle was a light blend of R&B, Irish folk and traditional jazz. During the mid-1950s in Britain, as popularised by Lonnie Donegan, the style served as a poor man's rock 'n' roll for those who couldn't afford proper instruments. Among the, literally, hundreds of thousands of young men who embraced the form were just about everyone involved in the 1960s beat group explosion.

never played live by The Clash, perhaps because it was a little too close to home.

JUSTICE TONIGHT/KICK IT OVER
[W Williams/J Mittoo]
B-SIDE: 1/80

The Clash's first real experiment in the baroque splendour of dub, and one of their best. These two recordings are separate remix versions of **Armagideon Time** fused together into one eight-minute slab of mighty apocalyptic venom. Mixed by Bill Price and Jerry Green at Wessex in November 1979, this was included on The Clash's first 12-inch single, **London Calling**.

KEYS TO YOUR HEART
[Strummer]

A medium-paced soul number that bears more than a passing resemblance to Smokey Robinson's 'I Gotta Dance To Keep From Crying', the song was recorded by The 101ers in two sessions in March 1976 at Pathway studios. By the time 'Keys To Your Heart' was released as a single (Chiswick NS3) in July 1976, Strummer had already been a member of The Clash for two months. Clearly, however, the song had some personal meaning for him, the lines about being a teenage drug-taker suggesting an autobiographical edge. The Clash performed tidy, and quite soulful, versions of the song during the Acklam Hall gigs at Christmas 1979, and the shows in Birmingham and the Electric Ballroom in February 1980. [54]

KILL TIME
[The Clash]

Recorded at Electric Lady in late 1981 during the initial *Combat Rock* sessions. 'Kill Time', like the similar-sounding **The Beautiful People Are Ugly**, featured a calypso-style backing, and was ultimately excluded from the LP.

---

54. The 101ers' posthumous LP, *Elgin Avenue Breakdown*, was released in April 1981 (Andalucia AND101), with Strummer's blessing. A mixture of studio and (low-fi) live recordings, it features a couple of Strummer highlights – the searing rockers 'Motor Boys Motor' and 'Letsagetabitarockin' especially.

KING OF THE ROAD
[Roger Miller]

A hilariously odd version of the Roger Miller standard was recorded by Strummer, Simonon and Headon while larking around during rehearsals for the 16 Tons tour in January 1980 (see **Louie Louie**). Strummer was unable to remember many of the words so he supplied his own.

KINGSTON ADVICE
[The Clash]
LP: *Sandinista!*

Another Clash song concerning The Clash's near-farcical experiences in Jamaica in 1980 (see **Junco Partner**, **Washington Bullets**). Horrified by the increasing gun-use among the teenage population, Strummer turned in yet another state-of-the-nation address. Yet the pessimism and cynicism of many of his like-minded contemporary lyrics (**Corner Soul**, **Midnight Log**, **Junkie Slip**) is wholly missing here. Instead, what emerges is a melange of confusion ('the more I see, the more I'm destitute'). 'Kingston Advice', in common with many songs in the Clash's canon, offers observations on the iniquities of power ('in these days nations are militant/we have slavery under government'), but precious few actual solutions. The best that Strummer can offer is to look to the sky for signs of change.

Although Strummer's voice is drowned in echo and dub-effects, musically 'Kingston Advice' is extraordinarily simple, with an addictive two-chord reggae beat and Jones having a lot of fun throwing off a superbly 'down in one take' solo. A powerful and impressive performance, it's surprising, therefore, that 'Kingston Advice' was never played live by The Clash.

KNOW YOUR RIGHTS
[The Clash]
SINGLE: 4/82 **LP:** *Combat Rock*

A public service announcement with guitars! 'Know Your Rights' is The Clash's last great fanfare for the common man. The opening song on *Combat Rock*, with its heavy metallic drumming and rockabilly guitar breaks, it became one of the highlights of the band's live set during their later period after its introduction during the Paris residency in September 1981. Written a few weeks earlier at the Ear Studio rehearsals, 'Know Your Rights' was a shrewd attempt to shake its listeners from their inertia. A dogmatic litany of the basic human rights – all three of them, and each with their own provisos that castrate their usefulness – Strummer concludes that it has been suggested in certain quarters that these are insufficient. He then dismissively tells any complainers to 'get off the streets!' The lyrics concerning murder being a crime 'unless it is done by a policeman' was probably Strummer's comment on two recent cause célèbres: the deaths of Sunderland boxer Liddle Towers and New Zealand schoolteacher Blair Peach.[55]

A live favourite during 1982-84, a fantastic version of 'Know Your Rights', beginning with one of Strummer's warmest introductions ('it's nice to be here in a human kind of situation'), recorded in Boston in September 1982, features on *From Here to Eternity*. A very different arrangement was performed by The Clash at the Lochem Festival in May 1982, with a lengthy opening drum pattern by Headon that seems to belong to an entirely different song. The song has been covered by General Soup Kitchen and The Cowans.

KOKA KOLA
[Strummer/Jones]
LP: *London Calling*

Usually assumed by those only half-listening to be an indictment of capitalist multi-nationals, 'Koka Kola' is, in fact, The Clash's prophetic comment on the 1980s worst social malaise. 'It's about cocaine,' Strummer told Bill Flanagan in 1988. 'The other day I was thinking of *Wall Street* and I remembered that tune. It was all about yuppies and how they got into coke.' One of the best sets of lyrics that Strummer ever wrote, 'Koka Kola' satirises Yuppie cocaine culture and casts a jaundiced 'been there, done that' eye at New York's young executives and their exciting, yet paranoid, world of sex, drugs and money. 'Coke adds life' adapts a popular advertising slogan, but the police raid at the end of the song can, seemingly, only end in two ways for the snowflaked exec caught red-handed with a straw up his nose – death or jail.

First performed on The Clash Take The Fifth tour, 'Koka Kola' was a mainstay of The Clash's early 1980s live set, usually played in a flawlessly segued – and conceptually brilliant – medley with **I Fought the Law**. Even after it had been dropped, the song would still make occasional appearances in concert as late as 1984.

---

55. Towers died as a result of injuries sustained while being arrested outside Birtley's Key Club in late 1976. The subsequent coroner's verdict was 'misadventure'. Peach was hit on the head by a police radio while taking part in an anti-racist demonstration in Southall on 24 April 1979. See also The Angelic Upstarts' 'The Murder of Liddle Towers', The Jam's 'Time For Truth' and Ralph McTell's 'Water of Dreams'.

LAST GANG IN TOWN
[Strummer/Jones]
LP: *Give 'Em Enough Rope*

'Our music's violent, we're not,' Strummer told Mikal Gilmore in 1979 when asked about The Clash's ambiguous attitude towards aggression. 'If anything, songs like **Guns on the Roof** and 'Last Gang In Town' are supposed to take the piss out of violence. It's just that sometimes you have to put yourself in the place of the guy with the machine gun.'

Probably the first of the *Give 'Em Enough Rope* songs to be written, 'Last Gang In Town' had its genesis in the Teds-versus-Punks fights of the summer of '77. But Strummer's ambitions were greater than merely celebrating a minor subculture clash that earned a few tabloid column inches. By the following year, British youth culture was becoming more compartmentalised and warlike than at any time since the Mods and Rockers battles of the mid-60s. With the recent revival of Skinhead culture, an unexpected by-product of both punk and the rise of various far-right parties in British politics, and the emergence of The Casuals (crews of disco-music listening, sharply dressed football hooligans) there were a lot of kids on the street. And many were getting seriously chinned by other kids who happened to have different clothes, or a different haircut, and listen to different music. 'The Crops hit The Stiffs/And The Spikes whipped The Quiffs,' sang Strummer wearily. 'Last Gang In Town' also alludes to Dobie Gray's 'The In Crowd' and to two types of American folk music that Strummer had recently become interested in, Cajun and Rockabilly.

Musically, 'Last Gang In Town' sees Jones throwing in every Ronnie Wood and Mick Ronson lick in the book, and a few that aren't, during his two extended solos, whilst the bassline includes a rousing variant on The Move's 'Fire Brigade' riff (itself, a bastardisation of Duane Eddy's 'Peter Gunn Theme'). The song features the best bass playing on *Give 'Em Enough Rope*, although whether this was from the hands of Simonon or Jones remains the subject of considerable debate. First performed live in London in December 1977, 'Last Gang In Town' featured in the early 1978 gigs up to and including Victoria Park, whereafter it was dropped from The Clash's set. Live, the song was played much faster than its later recorded version, and with a significantly different ending.

THE LEADER
[The Clash]
LP: *Sandinista!*

A song about newspapers, and a fall from grace (all of the muck is raked because 'the people must have something good to read/On a Sunday'). 'We heard these great stories about Profumo,' remembered Kosmo Vinyl. 'I don't know how many were true, but we used to have a favourite featuring a prominent member of the Royal Family.'[56] With its rockabilly strut, and fabulous chugging guitars from Jones, 'The Leader' went into The Clash's live set for the Radio Clash tour in April 1981 and remained there for most of the next two years.

LET'S GO CRAZY
[The Clash]
LP: *Sandinista!*

Two incidents in August 1980 offer a tantalising glimpse into the heritage of 'Let's Go Crazy'. Firstly, Strummer was busted near Kings Cross station by the Metropolitan Police's notorious Special Patrol Group. Held under the controversial SUS laws, when Strummer's flat was searched, police found three ounces of homegrown weed. He was subsequently fined £100. Later that month, Strummer attended his first Notting Hill Carnival since the 1976 riot. Although his love for reggae remained undimmed, Strummer was also impressed by gentler Caribbean rhythms, like the calypso music performed by some Trinidadian steel bands.

A boisterous musical celebration of life, full of cajoling optimism, the lyrics nevertheless contain dark allusions to slavery ('400 years of dread') and to those in the black community (the teenage robbers known as sticks-men) whose actions, Strummer suggests, give the police an excuse 'To shut off the ganja and control the juice'.

---

56. Initially exposed by Peter Cook's satirical magazine *Private Eye*, the scandal concerned then Secretary of State for War, John Profumo, who was caught in a sexual liaison with a 22-year-old model, Christine Keeler. It was subsequently disclosed that another of Ms Keeler's circle of male friends was Vladimir Ivanov, a Naval attaché at the Soviet embassy in London. Questioned in Parliament, Profumo at first denied any impropriety. Faced with imminent press disclosures, he later admitted that he had misled the House. By midsummer 1963 Britain was awash with rumours concerning the sexual perversions of the Establishment. Allegations included High Court judges involved in a sex orgy and that one of the country's most eminent politicians had waited at table at a fashionable Knightsbridge party, naked and masked, with a placard around his neck reading 'If my services don't please you, whip me.' Strummer alludes directly to the latter rumour in 'The Leader''s second verse. 'The hypocrisy of it is what I'm trying to get at,' he told Paolo Hewitt. 'The way that people are jailed for this and that, and yet up on the top floor they're setting no example at all.'

A splendidly slapdash pseudo-samba, 'Let's Go Crazy' was performed live just once, as an encore at the opening show of the Radio Clash tour in Barcelona in April 1981.

LET THE GOOD TIMES ROLL
[Leonard Lee]

This rock 'n' roll classic, with its good-time lyrics, was performed by Strummer on the piano during *Rude Boy*. The song was almost certainly one that Strummer had played during his pub-rock days. He subsequently noted that he had 'probably' learned it from The Animals' 1965 recording.

LIFE IS WILD
[Strummer/Rhodes]
LP: *Cut the Crap*

Amid the lumpen disaster area of *Cut the Crap*'s painful political rhetoric at least 'Life Is Wild' has, in its favour, a certain joie de vivre – a celebratory fervour that stands in marked contrast to the other subject matter covered on the LP. That's about all it has going for it, however. Here is a celebration of freedom in which that freedom extends to bumming cigarettes and casually hanging out with your 'kindred souls'. A darker subtext threatens to arrive when Strummer sings that his girl 'has the dope', but, like so many one-liners on this LP, it ultimately goes nowhere. Like **Fingerpoppin'**, 'Life is Wild' is a song about freedom in relationships. Like **Cool Under Heat** it's a celebration of street-savvy. Like **Dirty Punk** it's about nonconformity. And, like all three, it's simplistic, banal drivel from a writer capable of much more. Musically, 'Life Is Wild' is almost the archetypal *Cut the Crap* song, drowning in a ham-fisted used of technology, badly overproduced, featuring samples that are buried in the mix (in this case, a series of excited football commentaries) and a gargantuan, raucous chorus that, whatever sentiments it's trying to express, sounds boorish and confused. 'Life Is Wild' was never played live by The Clash.

LIGHTNING STRIKES (NOT ONCE BUT TWICE)
[The Clash]
LP: *Sandinista!*

Essentially **The Magnificent Seven** part 2, 'Lightning Strikes' uses a similar Norman Watt-Roy bass-loop over which Strummer raps yet another ode to New York (see **Broadway, If Music Could Talk**). Subsequently, Strummer would suggest that the influence of the city on The Clash was inevitable given that there was a transit strike going on during March 1980 (it's actually mentioned in the present song). Strummer, Jones and Headon had, therefore, to walk several blocks from their hotel to the studio each day, thus being exposed to the sounds and smells of the streets whether they liked it or not. Another vehicle for Strummer's acerbic wordplay, 'Lightning Strikes' gives full rein to his love of bizarre characters ('Deli Joe, he ought to know/He runs the gangs on Pastrami Row'). Having taken a geographical tour of the city, namechecking everywhere from Harlem to Brooklyn via Christopher Street and the Bowery, Strummer suddenly gets an attack of homesickness (or, if his critics were correct, a pricked conscience). At which point the song finds itself back in London, for parochial references to the Westway and Hounslow.

Taken into The Clash's repertoire at the beginning of the Radio Clash tour in April 1981, 'Lightning Strikes' remained a fixture for the rest of the year. A version recorded during the New York residency in June 1981 was included on *Clash On Broadway*.

LIQUIDATOR
[Harry Johnson]

An organ-led rocksteady instrumental that was a UK hit in 1968 for Harry J's All Stars and still brings a fond smile to the face of 40-something ex-skinheads everywhere. Possibly inspired by The Specials' frantic reworking (part of the *Skinhead Symphony* on their *Too Much Too Young* EP, a number one hit in March 1980), The Clash reportedly played 'Liquidator' at several soundchecks during this period.

LISTEN
[Strummer/Jones]
B-SIDE: NME CL-1 4/77

One of the first tunes written after Strummer joined The Clash, 'Listen' was a chunky, bass-led instrumental which, according to Strummer, was included at their first gig in July 1976. Thereafter it doesn't appear to have featured in The Clash's set again, but it was still kicking around as late as April 1977 when they required a B-Side for the 'Capital Radio' *NME* mail-order single. Recorded, along with **Capital Radio One**, at CBS, 'Listen's use on the record was punctuated by fragments of Tony Parsons' interview with the band. Horribly out of tune in places, 'Listen' was obviously treated as a last-minute throwaway, and it shows. Strummer's guitar drops out completely at one point while the whole thing, although unprepossessing, sounds not unlike a Suzi Quatro backing track. The full version of 'Listen', without the interview segments, can be heard on *Super Black Market Clash*.

LIVING IN FAME
[Mikey Dread/The Clash]
LP: *Sandinista!*

Mikey Dread's rather mean-spirited, if very funny, put-down of the 1979-80 UK Ska revival, 'Living In Fame' suggests that a band should live up to their name, or they will surely 'die in shame'. If you call yourselves The Specials, Dread notes, then he wishes to see your potential. The Selecter, The Beat and Madness also cop some sharp critiques from Mikey before he runs out of Ska band names and turns his ire, instead, on The Blockheads and The Nipple Erectors. Thankfully, Dread decides at the conclusion that The Clash are 'ya ruler.' Damn right.

A fun recording, featuring Gary Barnacle's haunting sax riffs and Strummer's excited cries of '*Ey!*', 'Living In Fame' has been criticised for importing another, unwelcome, voice into The Clash's oeuvre. Yet, blessed with Jones' echo-treated guitar, the song sounds a hell of a lot more like The Clash than much of *Sandinista!* (see, for instance, **Shepherds Delight**). Recorded in New York in March 1980, the inclusion of 'Living In Fame' on *Sandinista!*, as with **Lose This Skin**, either suggests desperation to fill six sides of vinyl or, more charitably, a wish by The Clash to challenge the expectations of their audience. Heard today, as with so many of *Sandinista!*'s more ignored works, the song sounds just fine where it is.[57]

LONDON CALLING
[Strummer/Jones]
SINGLE: 12/79 **LP:** *London Calling*

Riding in a taxi one evening from The Clash's Pimlico rehearsal rooms to their flat at World's End, Strummer and his fiancée, Gaby Salter, began discussing the state of the world. 'There was a lot of Cold War nonsense going on,' Strummer told *Uncut*. 'We already knew that London was susceptible to flooding. She told me to write something about that. So I sat in the front room, looking out at Edith Grove. Years later, I found out I was looking right

---

57. Strummer's offhand comment as the song fades – 'Fuckin' 'ell, Mikey' – can, similarly, be heard as either reproach or praise depending on the listener's tolerance for dub-reggae on a Clash record sung by someone other than Strummer or Simonon.

onto the flat where the Stones lived when they started out, which seemed appropriate.' Indeed, this possibly subconscious serendipity may explain The Rolling Stones-like swagger of the resulting performance, a song which remains one of The Clash's best known to the general public.

Taking its title from the BBC World Service's call sign, the lyrics went through several drafts of polemic (Jones rejected at least one set concerning mobs in Soho) before arriving at the finished article. In 1988, Strummer described the song to *Melody Maker*, noting that 'I read about ten news reports in one day calling down all variety of plagues on us.' Written in the aftermath of the disaster at Three Mile Island in March 1979 (note the references to 'a nuclear error' and a meltdown – see also **Clampdown**), in 'London Calling' Strummer acts as an observer of the resultant winter-world of the apocalypse. The people, of course, are coming out of the cupboards and looking to pop music to save them from the horrors of everyday life, something that Strummer wants no part of ('don't look to us/Phoney Beatlemania has bitten the dust'). The song also includes several drug allusions, one of the main underlying themes of the *London Calling* LP. There's also a reference to Strummer's hepatitis scare of the previous year ('yellowy eyes'). The song's final line alludes to Guy Mitchell's 1956 hit, 'Singing the Blues', which would often be quoted from more directly in live performances.

Released as a showcase single from its attendant LP, 'London Calling' became The Clash's biggest hit in their homeland while they were still a functioning group (number 11). An integral part of the band's live set from its debut performance at Notre Dame Hall in July 1979 and for the rest of their career (usually as the opening call to arms), a great version, recorded at Boston's Orpheum Theater in September 1982, can be heard on *From Here to Eternity*.

Strummer and Jones' bank balances were no doubt swelled by the song's use on several movie soundtracks in recent years (*Ma Femme est une actrice*, *Intimacy*, *Billy Elliot*). Almost certainly the only Clash song you're ever likely to hear in a James Bond movie (2002's *Die Another Day*), one would have imagined that 'London Calling' was always as highly regarded as it is now. Not so. In *Smash Hits*, David Hepworth's contemporary review of the single considered that The Clash played too loud in the studio. 'Why won't Joe Strummer let us hear more than one word in every three?' he asked. 'Until they face these elementary facts, sides like 'London Calling' will always fail to condense all that fury and grandeur into a truly great record.'

The 'London Calling' video was filmed by Don Letts at Cadogan Pier, next to the Albert Bridge which leads into Battersea Park, on a cold and rainy night in December 1979. It featured the band wearing some of the coolest threads ever worn by a rock group and can be seen on *This Is Video Clash* and *The Essential Clash*. It remains one of a handful of definitive visual images of The Clash. 'London Calling' has been covered by One King Down, Stroh and The NC Thirteens. It was often performed live by The Pogues both during Strummer's tenure in the band, and afterwards.

London's Burning
[Strummer/Jones]
B-Side: 5/77 LP: *The Clash*

One of *The Clash*'s few overt drug songs, 'London's Burning' constituted Strummer's reflections, à la Lou Reed's 'White Light/White Heat', on the seductive power of amphetamine sulphate. Speed, because of its relative cheapness, was the punk scene's chemical of choice. 'I decided quite quickly,' noted Strummer, 'that the up wasn't worth the down.' Another verse was inspired by the view from the balcony of Jones' grandmother's flat. 'We'd hang out [at Wilmcote], lean on the rail and look down across where The Westway crosses Royal Oak,' Strummer told *Uncut*. 'I went home to our squat on Orsett Terrace and wrote it, whispering because my girlfriend was asleep.' Though the passage of time has distorted many people's memories of *The Clash* as being full of songs about tower-blocks, 'London's Burning' features the only direct reference to these architectural monstrosities on the LP. Possibly that was deliberate: 'Can you understand how much I hate this place?' Jones asked Tony Parsons angrily in 1977 concerning his home. In this regard, 'London's Burning' is the prime example of Parsons' stated opinion that The Clash's music dealt with urban alienation better than anyone before or since.

Interviewed by *Search and Destroy* in 1977, Strummer credited Jones with the line about television as the new religion.[58] The song's title, of course, was taken directly from the choral nursery rhyme about the great fire of London in 1666, although some commentators have suggested a link to The MC5's thematically similar 'Motor City Is Burning'. Certainly Strummer's song would prove a direct influence, itself, on The Ruts' 1979 hit 'Babylon's Burning.'

Recorded at CBS during *The Clash* sessions, 'London's Burning' featured Jones' most muso moment on the LP, a fearsome, feral guitar solo a million miles from punk's traditionally minimalist approach. Sonic naturalism

---

58. Further to the SF/futurist influence on *The Clash* – see also Remote Control – it's worth noting that the concept of control of the population via television is something of a recurring theme in British science fiction television – cf *1984*, *Quatermass*, *The Prisoner*, *The Year of the Sex Olympics*, certain episodes of *Doctor Who* and *The Changes*. The latter was a 1975 children's serial – a dramatisation of a Peter Dickinson novel – that also touched on environmental and social issues (like race) and had a Luddite attitude towards the sinister advance of technology.

occurred, too, in the squeal of feedback that ends the song, one of *The Clash*'s most exciting snapshots. A splendid 'live' version (taken from the April 1977 **White Riot** promo film in Dunstable) was released on the B-side of the **Remote Control** single (this performance can be seen on *The Essential Clash*). 'London's Burning' became one of The Clash's live highlights, and a perennial favourite of their set, first performed at The Screen On The Green in August 1976. A version (with some subsequent studio overdubs) recorded at the Victoria Park *Rock Against Racism* show in April 1978 can be seen in *Rude Boy* and heard on *From Here to Eternity*. The song often acquired subtly altered lyrics to make the town that was burning into wherever The Clash happened to be playing that particular night – a trend started in Birmingham in late 1976. 'London's Burning' was subsequently covered by Silverchair.

LONG TIME JERK
[The Clash]
B-SIDE: 6/82

Written mainly by Simonon, with some help from Strummer and Jones, 'Long Time Jerk' was recorded at Ear Studios in September 1981 (see **Midnight To Stevens**, **First Night Back In London**) and completed at Electric Lady in December. A harmonica-dominated, cajun-influenced skank with a hackneyed 'dance away your troubles' theme, the song is enlivened by various subnautical noises and Headon's precise snare-work. 'Long Time Jerk's lyrics probably concern Simonon's relationship with Pearl Harbour.

LOOK HERE
[Mose Allison]
LP: *Sandinista!*

Mose Allison was born in 1927 in Tippo, Mississippi. While still in his teens, he was performing with R&B bands on Memphis' famed Beale Street. Moving to New York, he became a jazz pianist and songwriter with a local cult following. It was in England, however, where Allison got most attention – The Yardbirds, John Mayall's Bluesbreakers and, most notably, The Who all covering his work. 'I've made a few bucks from some of my songs that the rockers have done,' Allison told *Blues Access* in 1998. 'But as far as my own records go, they've never paid out. I owe all the record companies money.' That sort of attitude must have *really* impressed The Clash.

Strummer was already familiar with Allison, having performed 'Young Man's Blues' with The Vultures. Something of a curate's egg in The Clash's discography, the basic track to 'Look Here' was recorded at Electric Lady. It developed into a frenzied jazz stomp featuring Mickey Gallagher's piano and Lew Lewis' wailing blues harp. Jones turned in one of his most concise performances, full of elegant flourishes and passing chords. And holding it all together was Headon, delighted, for once, to be completely in his own idiom. 'I'm hip!' shouted Strummer as the excitement in the studio reached fever pitch. Finished with various overdubs at Wessex, 'Look Here' is another example of the multi-angled worldview on offer in *Sandinista!* A blind grope in the dark towards a musical form many miles from **White Riot** that, by sheer force of effort and personality, neither outstays its welcome nor suggests a long-term departure from what The Clash were ultimately best at.

LOSE THIS SKIN
[Tymon Dogg]
LP: *Sandinista!*

Joe Strummer, then an art student going by the name of Woody Mellor, first met Tymon Dogg at a London flat the latter shared with one of Strummer's friends, Clive Timperley, in 1971. A folk songwriter and violinist, Dogg had briefly been contracted to Apple Publishing in the late 60s, and was already an experienced busker when he met young Woody. The pair busked together in Central London and went on a trip to France and Holland which ended with them being deported. They lost touch when Strummer moved to Wales in 1973, but on his return to London late the following year, Strummer found a room in Dogg's squat in Chippenham Road.

In March 1981, Dogg was in New York and, purely by chance, bumped into Jones, who invited him to Electric Lady. Delighted to see his old mate, Strummer persuaded the band to back Dogg on one of his own compositions, 'Lose This Skin', which was subsequently released as an independent single (Ghost Dance GHO1) in June. To give Dogg further exposure, the song was also included on *Sandinista!*

An oddly charismatic, Irish-sounding folk-jig with Dogg's violin to the fore, 'Lose This Skin' is a song about depersonalisation. It suggest that much of life is an act, especially for the lonely, and that skin is something people are 'imprisoned in.' With its biblical allusions to Lot's wife (turned to a pillar of salt for defying the word of the Lord in Genesis 19:26) and the search for inner freedom, the song fits in with many of the themes that The Clash were singing about during this period. An odd, but welcome, visiting voice to The Clash's canon, Dogg remained a close friend of Strummer and featured prominently on The Mescaleros' second CD, *Global A Go-Go*, adding his unique violin to songs like 'Johnny Appleseed', 'Shaktar Donetsk' and, especially, 'The Minstrel Boy'. The band Stubborn All-Stars produced an excellent cover of 'Lose This Skin' which appears on the *City Rockers* tribute LP.

LOST IN THE SUPERMARKET
[Strummer/Jones]
LP: *London Calling*

'I only saw my father once a year after being sent to boarding school,' Strummer told Robert Hilburn in 1984. 'He was a real disciplinarian, who was always giving me speeches about how he had pulled himself up by the sweat of his brow: a real guts and determination man. What he was really saying was, "If you play by the rules, you can end up like me." [But] I didn't want to ... I saw how the rules worked and I didn't like them.' 'Lost in the Supermarket' was not, as most people assume, written by Jones, who sings it. 'I gave him a present,' noted Strummer in 1990.

'Joe wrote the lyric, but I always thought he had me in mind. What he thought it was like for me living off Harrow Road,' remembered Jones. In fact, nothing could be further from the truth. The song opens with Strummer's clearly autobiographical memories of his parents' home in suburban Warlingham, with a hedge 'over which I never could see.'

A song that takes The Clash back to the theme of urban alienation (see **London's Burning**), 'Lost in the Supermarket' is one of Strummer's most sentimental and touching pieces, expressing regret, rather than anger, at his perceived abandonment by his parents at an early age. Using consumerism as a metaphor for depersonalisation, Strummer's words summon up a picture of a nation of lonely people desperately trying to find a connection in the harsh cacophony of the modern world. The song was actually conceived in a supermarket located under the block of flats Strummer was then sharing with Gaby Salter and her family. It should have been too small to get lost in but, as Strummer told Andrew Collins in 1999, 'It was 5.00am and the song occurred to me as I stumbled around dazed by the colours and the lights.'

'The night before we recorded that, I went to see Taj Mahal play,' remembered Headon in 1991. 'His drummer played a lot of snare beats on his floor tom. When I went in the next day I thought that sounded good last night, I'll use it on this song.' One of the most lush-sounding recordings on *London Calling* (particularly Simonon's layered neo-funk basslines), 'Lost in the Supermarket' was a tricky song to reproduce live. Except for a handful of performances in 1983, it was never attempted. The Afghan Whigs 1999 cover version featured Headon on drums. The song was also subsequently covered by Lady Luck and Battershell.

LOUIE LOUIE
[Richard Berry]

First recorded in 1957, and popularised by The Kingsmen's manic two-chord version in 1963, 'Louie Louie' has been performed by just about every garage-band. [59] The Clash played the song live, with Pete Townshend guesting on guitar, as an encore at Brighton Top Rank on 9 January 1980. A studio rehearsal, with Strummer improvising lyrics all over the place, was recorded around the same time. (See **King of the Road**, though some sources suggest that it may have been recorded with Guy Stevens in the early days of *London Calling*.)

LOVER'S ROCK
[Strummer/Jones]
LP: *London Calling*

It's somewhat ironic that a band as committed to outspoken attacks on racism (and rightly applauded for it) as The Clash should, at the same time, often suffer accusations of sexist gittery. 'Watch *Rude Boy* and read road manager Johnny Green's memoirs and you tap into the *Loaded* complex,' wrote Jon Savage in 1999. 'Men unable to transcend the inadequate social roles allotted by society and all too often relapsing into unthinking, occasionally misogynistic laddism.' At the risk of being a boorish apologist, this author considers such criticism to be, frankly, a right load of old middle-aged, middle-class pseudo-feminist bollocks. Nevertheless, if there's one song in The Clash's oeuvre that makes a rebuttal of such charges downright difficult, it's 'Lover's Rock'.

At first glance, the song's opening is lazily sexist. The initial verse concerns an unwanted pregnancy due to the singer's girl having neglected to take her contraceptive pill ('She forgot that thing/That she had to swallow'). The second verse makes it clear that the singer is, in fact, a Jamaican male who makes sarcastic references to Western men being free with their seed. This suggests that, as some in the black community are alleged to believe, whitey can't get it up with the same strength that yer average rude boy can. In this regard, at least, Strummer is clearly adopting a persona and attempting

---

59. It's estimated that 'Louie Louie' is the second most-covered song in history behind The Beatles' 'Yesterday', with over 1000 versions. It was also allegedly investigated by the FBI to discover whether its gobbledegook lyrics were, in fact, obscenities.

something ironic – spoofing a trend in contemporary reggae of sexual braggadocio that, much to the genre's detriment, remains there to this day (see, for instance, the 1990s output of Shabba Ranks). As the singer notes during the song's fade, 'ridiculous, innit?' The problem with irony, of course, is that it's something most people think their mum does with their shirts.

Sexist tendencies are inbred in most males, Strummer told *Creem*'s Susan Whitall in 1979. He used the interview to lambast heavy metal for its macho cockrock posturing, yet he could, he noted sadly, still find himself calling women 'chicks'. When *Search and Destroy*'s Annette Weatherman interviewed The Clash in 1977, there was a fascinating discussion on the punk movement's awkward attitude towards feminism and sexuality. Weatherman noted that 'there aren't enough girls coming out that share the idea. You've got 300 guys pogoing together.' Simonon mentioned that he'd recently read Germaine Greer, while Jones added, 'The fact is we don't go to bed with all that many women. Too much of the blatantly sexual gets boring.'

The present song was inspired by the term 'Lovers' Rock', previously used to describe a certain brand of sexually explicit pop-reggae, although after The Clash introduced the phrase into the white-rock fraternity, it took on a somewhat different meaning. Heavily criticised for exactly this conceit in Kevin Sampson's 1998 novel *Awaydays*, set in 1979 ('They'll be conquering America and doing jeans adverts next!'), the song never made it into the band's live set, although it was occasionally tried out during soundchecks.

THE MAGNIFICENT DANCE
[The Clash]
B-SIDE: 4/81

Filled with the sounds of ringing bells, furious handclaps and Headon's mamba-style percussion, 'The Magnificent Dance' is another 'Pepe Unidos' production (see **The Cool Out**).

This outstanding, mostly instrumental, remix of **The Magnificent Seven** was completed at Wessex in February 1981. When The Clash played their residency at Bond's in New York in June, this record was heavily featured on R&B radio stations like WBLS (who would often produce their own remixes by sampling in dialogue from movies like *Dirty Harry*). It became, as Strummer noted with both amusement and pride in *Westway to the World*, the sound of New York that summer. 'That was us,' he noted, 'weirdo-punk-rock-white-guys. Doin' the kit!'

THE MAGNIFICENT SEVEN
[The Clash]
SINGLE: 4/81

'Jonesy said, "We need something really funky cos Joe wants to do a rap,"' remembered Norman Watt-Roy in 1991. 'Joe wrote the words there and then, totally spontaneous. A couple of hours later it was in the can.' Strummer's lyrics are among his finest, an acerbic stream-of-consciousness delve into free-association that slips from one image to the next, suggesting the sound equivalent of TV channel-surfing. In this sense, although obviously influenced in musical terms by emergent rap, 'The Magnificent Seven', lyrically, has more in common with Chuck Berry's 'Too Much Monkey Business', Bob Dylan's 'Subterranean Homesick Blues' and 'A Hard Rain's Gonna Fall' and The Beatles' 'I Am The Walrus' and 'Come Together'. Along with Elvis Costello's 'Pump It Up', it thus provides a fascinating link in the chain of oblique poetic fancy in rock 'n' roll, a chain stretching forward, via REM's 'It's The End of the World As We Know It (And I Feel Fine)', to the 90s output of Underworld ('Born Slippy', 'Pearl's Girl').

'The Magnificent Seven's brilliant use of wordplay and linguistic games are a key element in its success. The title, of course, came from John Sturges' 1960 western. The opening verses concern the drudgery of the working day – a standard Clash theme – and, via namechecks for Honda and Sony, the rise of the soulless multinational corporations. Strummer is not, he notes, working for a pay-rise to improve himself, but rather to buy some nice consumer goods for his girlfriend, who has been seduced by gimmicky TV advertising.

Suddenly, at a cheeseburger lunch-break, the imagery changes to social observation. ('What do we have for entertainment?/Cops kickin' gypsies on the pavement.') Disconnected phrases flash by as Strummer's wordplay enters quasi-gobbledegook territory ('Italian mobster shoots a lobster'). Socialist visionaries Karl Marx (1818-83) and Friedrich Engels (1820-95) get stuck at a checkout in a 7-11 store, while pacifist icons Martin Luther King (1929-68) and Mahatma Gandhi (1869-1948) go to a football game. Their team, inevitably, gets murdered 50-0; so much for peace and harmony when there's a championship at stake.

Further references occur, to Greek philosophers Socrates (BC 470-399) and Plato (BC 427-347), disgraced US President Richard Milhous Nixon

(1913-94) and canine movie star Rin-Tin-Tin. 'Fuckin' long, innit?' mutters Strummer as the song reaches the five-minute mark with no end in sight. Then, coming over the wires, a final newsflash, one that sums up the sheer ludicrousness of modern existence and of taking *anything* too seriously: 'VACUUM CLEANER SUCKS UP BUDGIE was a *News of the World* headline,' remembered Strummer. 'I saw it when we were finishing the mix in England and I stuck it on the end. The budgie came out alive, too!'

Recorded at Electric Lady in March 1980, 'The Magnificent Seven' was a brave leap into alien territory for The Clash. No other white rock band had ever tried anything *remotely* like this (Blondie's similarly themed 'Rapture' wouldn't be recorded for another six months). Introduced into the band's live set on the European tour in April 1981, 'The Magnificent Seven' remained a mainstay for the rest of The Clash's career. A stunning six-minute-plus version, recorded in Boston in September 1982, features on *From Here to Eternity*. It's, as ever, a showcase for Strummer's ad-libbing ('I know this song is 20 minutes long'). It even brings out the best in cover versions, THC's 1999 effort being one of the finest ever rearrangements of a Clash song.

MARK ME ABSENT
[Jones]

A song about schooldays written by Jones, and sharing some thematic links to his later, superior **Stay Free**. 'Mark Me Absent's warm, chugging R&B feel is not a million miles away from what Strummer had been doing with The 101ers a few months earlier and, as such, the song sat awkwardly within The Clash's 1976 live sets. It was dropped by September.

MENSFORTH HILL
[The Clash]
LP: *Sandinista!*

Seemingly a sound collage in the style of The Beatles' 1968 experiment in musique concrète, 'Revolution 9', 'Mensforth Hill' is, in fact, nothing more than **Something About England** played backwards. (It does feature some additional haphazard instrumentation, synthesisers and voice-sample snippets supplied by Strummer.) Described in the *Sandinista!* sleevenotes as the 'title theme from a forthcoming serial', 'Mensforth Hill' is as disquieting and unsettling listening as its perceived template, if not half as imaginative. It's positioning on *Sandinista!*, however – between the politically tinged anger of **Charlie Don't Surf** and the sly band in-joke **Junkie Slip** – is a true masterstroke.

Once again, as with many of *Sandinista!*'s more subtle segues, it wasn't until the LP was released on CD in the late 80s that many listeners appreciated such clever switches in tone and mood throughout the 36-song collection. 'Mensforth Hill', needless to say, was never performed live by The Clash.

MIDNIGHT LOG
[The Clash]
LP: *Sandinista!*

Thanks to the success of revisionist rockers like Matchbox and The Stray Cats, the early 80s had seen a chart revival for this simplistic musical form – a merging of country and rock 'n' roll, inspired by the early Sun recordings of Elvis, Johnny Cash, Jerry Lee Lewis et al. Strummer had long been interested in rockabilly, mentioning the genre in the lyrics to **Last Gang In Town**. In musical terms, 'Midnight Log' is one of the highlights of *Sandinista!*, an excited and exciting performance, in which Simonon's slap-bass is prominent. It's perhaps surprising, then, that the song never appeared as part of The Clash's live set.

Lyrically, 'Midnight Log' is one of Strummer's most cynical and dismissive pieces; it sounds, frankly, like the words of a man who has abandoned any hope of redemption in a world full of corrupt police and multinational corporations. A world in which, to understand the difference between right and wrong, 'the lawyers work in shifts'. There are allusions to the Devil and to a flooding river that drowns the neighbourhood, making 'Midnight Log' a strange, yet conceptually valid, bedfellow to **The Sound of the Sinners**. But, unlike the latter song, wherein Strummer could at least see a form of natural justice in the sweeping-away of sin and filth by a tidal wave or an earthquake, in 'Midnight Log' you get the sense that even such acts of God would not shift the status quo. Strummer ends the song searching for answers in books that he doesn't believe in: 'For ciphers to the riddles/and reason to the rhymes.'

A hard song for hard times, 'Midnight Log's fatalistic, acquiescent attitude towards the more sordid aspects of the modern world is marbled with an apparent indifference. The message seems to be, there's only so much anger that one man can have.

MIDNIGHT TO STEVENS
[Strummer/Jones]
LP: *Clash On Broadway*

Strummer's touching tribute to The Clash's former producer, Guy Stevens, who had died a few weeks earlier, having 'finished the booze and run out of speed.' 'Midnight To Stevens' was recorded on 17 September 1981 on the Rolling Stones mobile unit at Ear Studios. It was then completely forgotten about (when the song was unearthed in 1991 for *Clash On Broadway*, Strummer admitted that he couldn't even remember writing it). The lyrics are a mixture of straight historical reportage (Stevens playing a CBS executive the master of *London Calling*) and rock 'n' roll fantasy (Guy providing the bail money to get Chuck Berry out of jail).

Jones' descending guitar lines, played on his new Gibson SG, are quite inventive – they wouldn't have been out of place on the theme tune of some late-1960s thriller series, for instance. But, otherwise, the song is nothing special and certainly didn't deserve its reputation as a suppressed masterpiece among Clash collectors in the late 80s.

Mona
[McDaniel]

A chugging Bo Diddley song, previously covered by The Rolling Stones. The Clash would have heard Diddley perform 'Mona' on the Pearl Harbour tour and recorded a one-take tribute with Guy Stevens during the early *London Calling* sessions.

Movers and Shakers
[Strummer/Rhodes]
LP: *Cut the Crap*

'Movers and Shakers' is an insulting and fatuous attempt to promote a do-it-yourself attitude among Britain's spiralling numbers of downtrodden youth, featuring a crass misquotation from Samuel Taylor Coleridge's *The Rime of the Ancient Mariner*.

What the cheesy, clumsily played, horribly mid-80s keyboard riff, that seems to have escaped from a nearby A Flock of Seagulls session, is doing on a Clash record is anyone's guess. The track's worst crime, however, is in its seeming to suggest that washing car windscreens is a worthwhile career move. In numerous Clash songs from **Career Opportunities** to **The Magnificent Seven**, Strummer had always poured scorn on the idea that people should take the first soul-destroying job that comes along just because society expected them to. As *Last Gang In Town* notes, it's alarmingly hypocritical to hear Joe Strummer, 'art school drop out, squat-dweller and dole-scrounger', promoting what is little short of theoretical Thatcherism in the form of 'self-reliance as represented by such menial and demeaning tasks.'

Perhaps the best thing that one can say about 'Movers and Shakers' is that, unlike the 1980s, it was over quite quickly. The song was subsequently performed acoustically by The Clash during the Busking tour.

MUSTAPHA DANCE
[The Clash]
B-SIDE: 6/82

A Jones-produced remix of **Rock the Casbah**, completed at the Power Station in New York in May 1982 and engineered by Bob Clearmountain. Stripping away Strummer's vocals helps to show off the ingenuity of Headon's arrangement to the full.

1977
[Strummer/Jones]
B-SIDE: 3/77

If a single lyric can be said to sum up the zeitgeist of punk's Year One then it's surely the chorus of this pre-emptive strike against the past: 'No Elvis, Beatles or The Rolling Stones/In 1977'. Out, by violence if necessary, with the old. In, at the point of a knife in West 11, with the new. Strummer (who was, of course, a big fan of all of the above) nevertheless approved of this quasi-Stalinist rejection of rock 'n' roll's past glories. How ironic, therefore, that the song's riff so obviously mirrors The Kinks' 'All Day And All Of The Night', though Jones' one-note solo is closer to Keith Richards in spirit than Dave Davies.

Strummer had initially thought the lyrics 'silly' and needed encouragement from his writing partner to include them. Wise choice. With references to dole queues, 'Sten guns in Knightsbridge', the Jubilee and George Orwell's *1984*, the song is a checklist of what would subsequently become – in lesser hands – punk's clichés of choice. Somehow, though, when The Clash used them, they sounded right.

Related, mainly by subject matter, to The Stooges '1969', the song quickly secured a prime place in The Clash's live set, usually as either the opening or closing song; its live debut occurred at the 100 Club in August 1976. A proto-version was one of the five songs demoed with Guy Stevens for Polydor in November. The single version was recorded, with Micky Foote, at CBS's Studios in Whitfield Street on 28 January.

'1977' was initially slated to appear on the LP (probably as the closing song). However, in keeping with punk's value-for-money ethic of not putting singles (or B-Sides) on LPs, it became one of the band's most quoted but least heard songs; it would not become available on CD in Britain until the release of *Clash On Broadway* in 1993. A tremendous version was filmed at Dunstable in April 1977 as part of the **White Riot** promo film and, subsequently, appeared on *The Essential Clash* DVD.

Performed at every gig during the year that it celebrated, '1977' was dropped from The Clash's set once the song itself became a part of the history that it wished to destroy. Frankenstein's cover version of the song features on *Backlash*.

NORTH AND SOUTH
[Strummer/Rhodes]
LP: *Cut the Crap*

An examination of life on the wrong side of Britain's geographical divide, 'North and South' begins with Strummer seeming to acknowledge the stereotypical nature of his own lyrics ('Don't want a cardboard cut-out'). This positive sign, however, isn't followed up and the song soon falls back on jaded clichés concerning 'the power of youth', marching through the streets to achieve political ends and 'diggin' a foundation, for a future to be made.' Like his contemporary Paul Weller, Strummer was a passionate and articulate man when it came to personal politics and social observation but, the second that anything resembling a manifesto needed to be drawn up, his powers of persuasion deserted him. [60]

Thankfully, although the lyrics are unremittingly poor, 'North and South' is one of the musical highlights of *Cut the Crap*. A rather pretty and soulful tune in which only an irritating keyboard riff detracts from the overall effect. Given the song's subject matter it was perhaps inevitable that 'North and South' received its first live performances during The Clash's miners' benefit gigs in December 1984. It was also played during the Busking tour.

---

60. cf several of Weller's more embarrassing lyrical moments with The Style Council during the 1984-85 period: 'A Gospel', 'Internationalists', 'A Stone's Throw Away', 'The Lodgers' et al.

007 (SHANTY TOWN)
[Desmond Dekker]

Another Desmond Dekker classic, and another song from the soundtrack of *The Harder They Come*. Like **The Israelites**, The Clash occasionally played '007' during rehearsals. Direct allusions to the song appear in the lyrics of both **Safe European Home** and **Rudie Can't Fail**.

ONE EMOTION
[Strummer/Jones]
LP: *Clash On Broadway*

A song inspired by that icon of punk, Roger Moore. 'We had an afternoon off,' remembered Jones. 'We used to nip to the cinema.' They ended up watching something starring the man with the hardest-working eyebrows in showbiz. Jones believes it was 'a really bad James Bond film' (probably *The Spy Who Loved Me*, which is actually quite a good one), though Strummer thought the genesis of the song came from TV repeats of Moore's 1960s series *The Saint*. Either way, 'it struck us how one-dimensional he was,' said Strummer in 1991. 'Then we wrote a serious song around it, trying to jib our way out of a hole.' A song about identity, the lyrics of 'One Emotion', while serviceable, seem rather forced by comparison to most of the other songs Strummer and Jones were writing during this period (see, for example, **Groovy Times**).

First recorded as a 4-track TEAC demo at Rehearsals in January 1978, the song was re-recorded at Basing Street during the *Give 'Em Enough Rope* sessions, but it remained unreleased until 1991 when this recording was included on *Clash On Broadway*.

ONE MORE DUB
[The Clash]
LP: *Sandinista!*

The Mikey Dread-produced dub version of **One More Time**. As with **The Crooked Beat**, this dub directly follows its template song on the LP. Unlike 'The Crooked Dub', 'One More Dub' is credited as a separate track in its own right.

ONE MORE TIME
[The Clash]
LP: *Sandinista!*

'One More Time' was a product of the Electric Lady *Sandinista!* sessions. A classy mid-paced reggae tune, the song refers to Marvin Gaye's 'Can I Get A Witness?' Meanwhile, Strummer's interest in the 1960s civil rights movement drew in allusions to Martin Luther King's segregated bus protests in Montgomery, Alabama and to the 1965 LA Watts riots. Filled with almost filmic imagery ('you don't need no silicone to calculate poverty') and to the violence inherent in the system (an old lady learning karate to enable her to walk safely on the streets), 'One More Time' is possibly The Clash's most extreme portrayal of ghettoism. As such, it walks a thin line between barbed social comment and outright parody, with its near-Dickensian descriptions. It's ironic that shortly after the song's release, in June 1981, several of Britain's inner cities exploded in exactly the kind of hate-driven fury suggested here. It was even more ironic that this was accompanied by some finger-wagging comments from Jones, who noted that 'destroying your own place, especially when the government ain't gonna give you a new one, seems really double dumb.'[61]

A popular song with The Clash's fans, 'One More Time' entered the band's concert set for the Radio Clash tour in April 1981. It was regularly performed during the next two years, occasionally being used as an opening number (at The Lyceum in October 1981, for instance). The song survived Jones' departure and made a dramatic return to the set during the London shows of December 1984.

1-2 CRUSH ON YOU
[Strummer/Jones]
B-SIDE: 1/79

One of Jones' earliest songs, predating The Clash by as much as a year and, like **I'm So Bored With You** and **Protex Blue**, rehearsed with The London SS. Although Bernard Rhodes had, as Strummer told Paul Du Noyer, instructed the band not to write love songs, 'Crush On You' obviously still had enough personal meaning for its author to survive well into The Clash. Sung onstage,

---

61. Asked, in a 1981 *NME* interview, about The Clash's attitude to rioting in light of songs like White Riot and One More Time, Jones seemed to suggest that the former was a song whose time had gone, and noted 'I don't think I'd make a good rioter. I'm not a street fighting man.' Interestingly, at the same time Rhodes declared that The Clash were 'interested in politics rather than revolution.'

initially by Strummer and usually as an encore, performances became erratic and somewhat campy and the song was dropped in early 1977. 'They used to do it at breakneck speed,' remembered Roadent in 1991. 'I liked it, but Joe thought it was dippy.' However, the song was revived in March 1978 at Marquee Studios, this time with Jones taking vocal duties. Subsequently, it also returned to The Clash's live set on a few occasions during the Sort It Out tour (notably at Middlesbrough in November). The song's opening was clearly inspired by The Beatles' cover of 'Twist And Shout' and also benefited from Gary Barnacle's blistering saxophone solo. Strummer's main contribution appears to have been the unusual jammed coda ('Why, shouldn't I ...?') which is missing from 1976 recordings of the song.

OOH, BABY, OOH (IT'S NOT OVER)
[Jones]

A 'look back in anger' tale in which the singer gets drunk while the object of his affections kisses other men, the song featured themes to be found in several of Mick's contemporary numbers. As Marcus Gray notes: 'The teenage life they depict – as defined by crushes, broken romances, school canteens, drunken parties and token rebellious gestures – is highly stylised.' Alleged to have been played at The Clash's first gig in July 1976, it disappeared soon afterwards, only to be revived as a TEAC demo in January 1978 prior to the *Give 'Em Enough Rope* sessions. Admiring the song's pseudo-soul groove, but unsure of the lyrics, Strummer and Jones remodelled it, later in the year, as **Gates of the West**.

OUTSIDE BROADCAST
[The Clash]
B-SIDE: 11/81

In August 1981 Jones went into AIR studios with Jeremy Green and provided three startling remixes of **This Is Radio Clash** (see also **Radio Clash**, **Radio 5**). 'Outside Broadcast' became much played on New York black radio.

OVERPOWERED BY FUNK
[The Clash]
LP: *Combat Rock*

Despite The Clash's occasional forays into dance music (specifically **The Magnificent Seven**), Strummer was less than keen on the genre's lyrical content – 'asinine, stupefying,' he noted in the present song, which first surfaced during the Ear Studios rehearsals in September 1981. Carrying this disappointment with the clone-like nature of the genre forward, funk becomes a fractured metaphor for the obese greed of capitalism feeding on itself ('don't you love our Western ways?'). Yet more references to Vietnam crop up in an LP full of them (**Car Jamming, Sean Flynn, Red Angel Dragnet**) and there's also an explicit critique of America's re-emergent debate on capital punishment. Namechecks for Edgar Rice Burroughs' king of the jungle, Tarzan, and jazz clarinettist Benny Goodman (1909-86) also occur.

The finished recording, completed at Electric Lady in December 1981, featured a rap by Futura 2000 (see **Escapades of Futura 2000**) and keyboards by Poly Mandell. A clever genre pastiche, the song is perhaps a caustic comment on sections of the contemporary UK music press and their somewhat arbitrary attempts to foist inappropriate significance on what was essentially a frivolous and pedantic musical form.

The standard subsequent critical line is that this is the point where The Clash were in danger of overdosing on their own dance-music pretensions and that 'Overpowered By Funk' was, and remains, a sadly prophetic title. As far as this author's concerned, that's the worst kind of inverted snobbery. Actually, taking into account the band's unfamiliarity with the territory, the song is a pretty fair stab at something alien to them. The structure, with Simonon's prominent bass and Headon's frantic hi-hat work to the fore, is a bold attempt and Jones' *shakashaka* guitars are fabulous and, more importantly, genre-correct. Nevertheless The Clash, like some of their critics, seem to have had their doubts about the song and, after it debuted during the Paris residency, it was dropped from their live set.

Paris Is Singing
[Strummer/Jones]

When The Clash played the Bataclan Theatre in Paris in September 1977, the show's final song was a make-it-up-as-we-go-along affair based (very) loosely on **London's Burning**. Usually referred to as 'Paris Is Singing', it was an interesting bit of self-indulgence from Strummer, in which he used similar stream-of-consciousness techniques to those which so frequently peppered live versions of **Police & Thieves** and **Capital Radio**. In this instance, he references the movie *The Asphalt Jungle, 1984* and (in a particularly well-received name-check) local punk favourites The Stinky Toys.

PIANO SONG
[Strummer]

This jaunty blues song, a variant (both musically and lyrically) of **Junco Partner**, copyrighted under the above title in 1979, was performed by Strummer in *Rude Boy* during a sequence in which Ray Gange's character makes overtly racist comments. The theme of the song is similar to **(White Man) In Hammersmith Palais**, particularly in the lines 'All the people down in Brixton town/Say "Hey White Boy, won't you lend me a pound?"' But, of course, Strummer doesn't have a pound. Or a dollar for that matter, a witty retort to those journalists who were already suggesting that The Clash were becoming obsessed with America.

PLAY TO WIN
[Strummer/Rhodes]
LP: *Cut the Crap*

An unusual song, structured in the form of a conversation between Strummer and Simonon over an electronica/percussion-heavy backing. The futuristic-sounding music promised a bold dive into unexplored territory. In fact, the song sounds not unlike some of experiments that Jones was attempting with BAD during this period. Sadly, the musical invention isn't matched by a similar inspirational vein in the lyrics. That Strummer, with his love of Americana, had longed to be an urban cowboy, riding 'the prairie of the wild frontier', had never been in doubt since he first experienced the US in 1978. Quite what that celebration of the pioneering spirit has to do with subsequent references to the space age, or a verse that discusses the traditional rivalry between England and Germany (and takes pride in the fact that, if it's hooligans you want, 'We British will tear up the streets') is anyone's guess. 'Play To Win' was never performed live by The Clash.

POLICE & THIEVES
[Lee Perry/Junior Murvin]
LP: *The Clash*

With its expansive biblical allusions to conflict, 'Police & Thieves' was written as a comment upon contemporary political events in Jamaica rather than as a call for the violent overthrow of Babylon.[62] By the time the single arrived in the UK, to become *the* reggae anthem of the oppressively hot summer of 1976, Junior Murvin's song had taken on a whole new meaning. In the aftermath of the Notting Hill riots (see **White Riot**), where Strummer and Simonon first heard 'Police & Thieves', it had become, rather than a redemptive spiritual musing on the problems of the world, a clarion call to violent revolution. To Jones, a cover version made perfect sense. 'In the way that 60s bands used to cover contemporary R&B classics, we covered the latest record from Jamaica,' he told the BBC in 1996.

'We had some brass neck to do that,' Strummer noted in *Westway to the World*. 'By rights they should have said "Ya heathen, mon, you ruined the works of Jah!" But they were hip enough to realise that we'd brought our own music to the party.' In 2002 he remembered that 'it wasn't like a slavish white man's Xerox of some riff. It was, like: "Give us your riff and we'll drive it around London."' Simonon had similar feelings. The Clash's idea, he told Eddie Izzard in 2003, was to take reggae music, 'put it on a number 31 bus and send it up to Camden.'

Tried out during *The Clash* sessions simply as an experiment, 'Police & Thieves' worked better than anyone dared to expect. Strummer told *Melody Maker* in 1978 that his initial reaction had been 'Great, a reggae tune, let's do it like Hawkwind! But Mick was more intelligent.'[63] Strummer subsequently took many opportunities to praise Jones' talent as an arranger, though in 1999 he still felt that 'It hasn't been said enough,' describing Jones' idea for twin guitars working both the off- and on-beats, against traditional rock practices, as 'genius'. 'Any other group would have played on the off-beat, trying to assimilate reggae,' Strummer told *Mojo*.

62. Recorded at more or less the same time as Bob Marley's *Rastman Vibration*, 'Police & Thieves' shared many lyrical themes with several of Marley's songs, notably 'Johnny Was' and 'Rat Race'. Jamaica was a political powder-keg during 1976, with open war existing between the two major parties: Michael Manley's socialist PNP government, whom Marley backed, and the conservative JPL opposition. In December, with an election due, Marley narrowly survived an assassination attempt and was forced to flee the country. He relocated to London, where he recorded the best-selling *Exodus* at Basing Street in early 1977 (featuring Junior Murvin on guitar), and didn't return to Jamaica for three years.

63. Like John Lydon, Pete Shelley and several others in the punk cognoscenti, Strummer was a great admirer of the psychedelic bikers, Hawkwind, best known for their spacey 1972 hit single 'Silver Machine'. Though they had long hair and their chemicals of choice veered towards hallucinogens rather than amphetamines, their political stance and lifestyle was most definitely punk. Indeed, much of The Clash's attitude as the self-styled 'People's Band' could have been applied to Hawkwind a few years earlier. Not that the feeling of kinship was entirely mutual. 'The Clash are the most orthodox band I've ever heard!' Hawkwind's poet/vocalist Robert Calvert told an apoplectic Julie Burchill in 1977. 'They just play three-minute pop songs and throw in a few slogans! They don't actually do any-thing to help anyone.' During the 1990s, when Strummer relocated to Somerset, he became friendly with the Hawks' main-man Dave Brock.

Simonon's tricky bassline dominates, while Jones backs up Strummer's growling scat-vocals by singing at the top of his range, à la Junior Murvin. The world's first – and for a long time only – six-minute Clash song, 'Police & Thieves' was introduced into the live set in April 1977. Often the vehicle for the band to improvise, Strummer always seemed to enjoy ad-libbing new lyrics and throwing in topical references[64], with live versions often lasting as much as ten minutes and segueing into other songs like **Blitzkrieg Bop** or **Hit the Road Jack**. The song, as a consequence, remained a Clash live fixture well into the 80s. Partly because of the exposure of The Clash's version, Murvin's original single was reissued in the UK in 1980 and became a Top 30 hit.

POLICE ON MY BACK
[Eddie Grant]
B-SIDE: 2/81 [US only] **LP:** *Sandinista!*

A furious cover version of a song by the multiracial North London band The Equals, best known for their infectious 1968 UK number one 'Baby Come Back'. The group contained Guayanan guitarist and songwriter Eddie Grant who, by the late 70s, became a reggae superstar in his own right. 'We recorded it at The Power Station, just the three of us, me, Mick and Topper, without bass,' Strummer remembered in 1991. 'Paul put his bit on later, in Wessex.'

'We used to play a tape of the Equals' version on the bus. Mick was the first one to play it to me,' noted Simonon. Kosmo Vinyl had to bring a copy of The Equals' *Explosion* LP over from London so that The Clash could make sure they got the lyrics right as they couldn't find a copy anywhere in New York. 'Police On My Back' is often said by those critics who don't like *Sandinista!* 'on principle' to be the most Clash-like song on the LP – the irony, of course, being that it's a cover version.

A powerful rocker with a ferocious minimalist guitar solo, the song became a live showcase for Jones, first introduced on the Far East tour in 1982 and a fixture throughout the following 18 months. (The version performed at Kingston, Jamaica in November 1982 opens with an urgent guitar riff that's a dead-ringer for U2's 'I Will Follow'.) Once Jones left the band, the song remained in The Clash's set, with Nick Sheppard handling the vocals during 1984-5.

64. A performance at Birmingham in early 1978, for example, developed into a provocative rant about 'the King of Finsbury Park' sitting in front of his TV being cynical, presumably a reference to Strummer's bête noire, John Lydon. During this period Strummer would often swop the latest punk gossip with the audience during live shows. More than once, this included barbed comments at Lydon's expense.

POP GOES THE WEASEL
[trad. arr. The Clash]

The sleevenotes for *Super Black Market Clash* suggest that this well-known nursery rhyme was a favourite soundcheck instrumental for the band. Whether this was meant as a joke or not is unknown.

PRESSURE DROP
[Frederick Hibbert]
B-SIDE: 2/79

A 24-carat reggae classic first recorded by Toots and The Maytals in 1970, 'Pressure Drop' was another bold cross-genre move for The Clash, who heard the song on the soundtrack LP from *The Harder They Come*. First played live on the White Riot tour, a studio version was recorded during the Lee Perry **Complete Control** sessions but was scrapped. A second attempt was made in the March 1978 Marquee Studio sessions that also produced **The Prisoner** and **1-2 Crush On You**. A blueprint for the subsequent 1979 UK ska explosion, especially the rhythm section, the recording was hampered by Strummer's sore throat, which is clearly evident on the finished vocal track. Live, the song was performed occasionally as an encore and was revived during the New York residency in 1981, on the UK leg of the Casbah Club tour, the subsequent US Combat Rock tour in 1982 and the Busking tour.

THE PRISONER
[Strummer/Jones]
B-SIDE: 6/78

Recorded at Marquee Studio, Richmond Mews in March 1978, Jones' 'The Prisoner' is one of the most depressing songs in The Clash's entire canon. It was named after Patrick McGoohan's surreal 1967 television series about the crisis of identity ('Do you get *The Prisoner* on TV?' asked Strummer introducing the song during the Get Out of Control tour). The song's specific inspiration came from the band's various brushes with authority during the summer of 1977. The lyrical references include a witty allusion to The Slickers' **Johnny Too Bad** and Chuck Berry's 'Johnny B Goode' meeting on Charing Cross Road, and also to *The Muppet Show* and *Coronation Street* (the day-to-day saga of working people). The song's angular double guitar break is one of the most thrilling moments in the whole of The Clash's recorded career.

Introduced to the live set at Mont de Marsen, 'The Prisoner' was performed in late 1977 but was soon dropped. 'It didn't have any real significance until Paul and Joe were in jail,' Jones noted in 1991, concerning the infamous night in June 1978 when arrested Clash fans sang 'The Prisoner' to Strummer and Simonon in the cells in Glasgow. 'About that time we started playing it live again.' A great performance from the Aberdeen Music Hall, filmed the night after the Glasgow fiasco, featured in *Rude Boy*.

PROTEX BLUE
[Strummer/Jones]
LP: *The Clash* [UK only]

With its references to adverts on the Bakerloo Line and the West End, 'Protex Blue' was a parochial London song in the best traditions of The Kinks and The Small Faces, two of Mick Jones' favourite bands. Another song from the latter days of The London SS, Simonon noted that 'Protex Blue' had been written before he first met Jones. 'It was the brand in all the pub condom machines,' added Jones, wryly. 'It was a valid subject for a song.'

'Protex Blue' is an anti-love song much in the subsequent punk tradition of The Sex Pistols' 'Bodies', Richard Hell's 'Love Comes In Spurts' and the disquieting output of bands like X-Ray Spex and The Slits. Sex, in punk generally, was something rather lurid that was usually performed without much emotion on either side of the bed. 'Two minutes of squelching noises,' as Johnny Rotten put it less than delicately. The language of 'Protex Blue' ('standing in a bog', 'that type of girl', 'skin flicks') is similarly matter-of-fact and blunt. The fact that Jones doesn't want to hold the object of his desire, he simply wants sex with her, is, however, juxtaposed with a much more positive statement: 'I don't want to *use* you.' By the time that 'Protex Blue' was recorded in February 1977, Jones was in his first long-term relationship, with Viv Albertine, and thus he may have amended the words from something less feminist-friendly in earlier versions.

On the musical side, the opening burst of chords suggest someone had overdosed on The Stooges' debut LP, though a close listen to the song actually reveals that the main riff is nothing less than (whisper it) a fast version of Led Zeppelin's 'Kashmir'. Featured at The Clash's first ever gig (possibly as the opening number, if Jones' comments at Sheffield Top Rank in November 1977 are accurate), the song dropped in and out of The Clash's repertoire at regular intervals. Nonetheless, it was a fine live number and made a welcome return to their set, with a radical rearrangement including an extended middle-section, on the 16 Tons tour in 1980.

RABIES (FROM THE DOG OF LOVE)
[The 101ers]

A nasty misogynistic song about sexually transmitted diseases, full of innuendo and bitter sleaze. In some ways 'Rabies' foreshadows The Sex Pistols' subsequent vitriolic exposé of back-street abortion, 'Bodies', particularly the verse concerning Crazy Daisy leaving something in a plastic bag down on Shepherd's Bush Green. However, the main theme of the song is summed up in its chorus, in which the singer finds himself down on his luck (and his knees) in the Praed Street Clinic. A staple of The 101ers' live set, a version was eventually released as the B-Side of the posthumous 1981 'Sweet Revenge' single (Chiswick NS63). Strummer took the song, along with **Jail Guitar Doors**, with him when he moved to The Clash.[65] 'Rabies' was certainly rehearsed during the summer of 1976 and is rumoured to have featured in their first live set in July.

RAF 1810
[Strummer]

The Red Army Faction, a German urban terrorist cell, first hit the headlines in April 1968 when student radical Andreas Baader and his girlfriend, Gudrun Ensslin, firebombed Frankfurt's Kaufhaus Schneider department store as a protest against capitalism. Members of Kommune 1, a leftist hippy collective, the pair were driven by their frustration with the counterculture and by hardened neo-Maoist beliefs. Baader was eventually imprisoned for the attack, but noted left-wing columnist Ulrike Meinhof helped him to escape custody and the myth of The Baader-Meinhof Gang was born. Unlike other terrorist organisations, the RAF's goals were ideological rather than political. They believed that violent protest would provoke the state into acting fascistically and that this, in turn, would mobilise the masses into armed revolution. Over the following three years the German authorities relentlessly pursued the movement's leaders and they went underground, including a period spent in Palestine where they received training from the PLO. They

---

65. First attempted by The 101ers at Pathway studios in March 1976, produced by Roger Armstrong, the released version was a Simon Jeffes-produced re-recording from a 10 April session at the BBC's Maida Vale studios.

would occasionally resurface to wreak havoc with a series of major terrorist offences. In the summer of 1972, Baader, Meinhof, Ensslin, Jan-Karle Raspe and Holgar Meins (the five core members of the group) were captured and imprisoned. On 18 October 1977, Baader, Ensslin and Raspe allegedly shot themselves while held in Stammheim high-security prison. Meinhof had already committed suicide by hanging the previous year and Meins had died on hunger strike in 1974.

Strummer's fascination with Baader-Meinhof had already been highlighted by his wearing an RAF T-shirt on-stage (and in several scenes in *Rude Boy*). And also via **Tommy Gun**, a song which was at once impressed with but frightened by terrorism. Mentioned in several contemporary interviews by its author, 'RAF 1810' was written around the same time. It remains unreleased, although it is rumoured to have been tried out during the *Give 'Em Enough Rope* sessions.

RADIO CLASH
[The Clash]
B-SIDE: 11/81

One of several Mick Jones remixes of **This Is Radio Clash** produced at AIR studios in August 1981. Basically a continuation of the main song, this version – which appeared on the B-Side of the single – included Strummer 'beaming from the mountain-top/using aural ammunition.' In other words, rapping a new set of lyrics that are, actually, far better than the first lot. These include allusions to *Apocalypse Now* ('with extreme prejudice on a terminator mission'), bureaucracy ('the Ministry of Whitewash'), Ewan MacColl's 'Dirty Old Town' and the Home Guard (a possible reference to the popular BBC wartime sitcom *Dad's Army*). When *The Essential Clash* was being put together, someone chose to include 'Radio Clash' on the CD, even though the track-listing has **This Is Radio Clash** instead. Whether this was a specific artistic decision, or a simple mistake, remains a mystery.

RADIO 5
[The Clash]
B-SIDE: 11/81

The third of Jones' **This Is Radio Clash** remixes (see also **Outside Broadcast**, **Radio Clash**), this is one of The Clash's more extreme sound experiments, complete with backward tapes, dub-echo and, for the only time on a Clash record, scratching.

RADIO ONE
[Dread]
B-SIDE: 1/81

Technically speaking not really a Clash recording at all (although Simonon may well have played bass on it), 'Radio One' is another of Mikey Dread's critiques of the contemporary music scene (see **Living In Fame, Rocker's Galore ..... UK Tour**).

REBEL WALTZ
[The Clash]
LP: *Sandinista!*

On this track Jones' Byrdsian jingle-jangle-morning guitars are cunningly interwoven with chiming bells and brass band flourishes (see **Something About England**). This flawed but interesting experiment (recorded at Wessex) was never attempted live by The Clash.

RED ANGEL DRAGNET
[The Clash]
LP: *Combat Rock*

Although 'Red Angel Dragnet' was sung by Simonon in what Jones subsequently described as the bassist's 'Jamaican Marlene Dietrich style,' it was actually written by Strummer. The initial inspiration came from the shooting, on New Year's Day 1982, of Frankie Melvin, a member of the New York subway vigilante group The Red Angels, by a policeman. 'I'd run out of writing paper and I only had Iroquois Hotel envelopes,' Strummer remembered in 1991. 'I wrote the lyrics down the middle [and] continued around the edge in a spiral. The next day, I said, "Paul, what do you think of these?" I remember him looking at me out of the corner of his eye, thinking has Joe flipped?'

Many of the song's images were inspired by Martin Scorsese's brutal 1976 exposé of urban paranoia, *Taxi Driver*, and specifically the dialogue of the central character Travis Bickle, played by The Clash's best-known celebrity fan, Robert De Niro. To such an extent that, with Scorsese's blessing, Strummer incorporated several lines directly from Paul Schrader's script and had Kosmo Vinyl attempt a De Niro impression to record them.[66] Musically lethargic, with

66. Chiefly for this reason, the song was impossible to play live without a major rearrangement.

its references to Jack The Ripper and Alcatraz prison and an allusion to Roger Miller's 'England Swings', the song's anger at injustice and conspiracy is reined-in by a geographical detachment that makes it unlike anything else in The Clash's discography. On the surface a cynical, vicious diatribe about the sick, venal underbelly of America, 'Red Angel Dragnet' is actually more about Hollywood's vision of the same subject. As such, it joins **Death is a Star** and **Sean Flynn** to form *Combat Rock*'s triad of myth-building songs, counteracting the myth-shattering sentiments of **Straight To Hell** and **Know Your Rights**.

REMOTE CONTROL
[Strummer/Jones]
SINGLE: 5/77 LP: *The Clash*

Written either during, or in the immediate aftermath, of the disastrous Anarchy tour, Jones' 'Remote Control' was a rant against oppression and conformity. Subsequently it has been virtually disowned by the band, mainly following CBS's decision to release it as a single without bothering to inform them. At the time, however, it was the source of some excitement within the group. 'Joe said, "Mick's written a mini-opera",' Terry Chimes remembered, referring to the fact that the song featured three changes of time-signature. In fact, 'Remote Control' is, lyrically, one of the best songs on *The Clash*, containing pointed observations about the faceless 'civic hall' nobodies who had cancelled gigs, the police and big business, especially record companies.

The first Clash song to mention punk by name, 'Remote Control' also alluded to the backslapping old-boy network of peerages to reward politicians who do what they're told. And, amid the 'repression' coda, yet more SF references (see **London's Burning**), specifically to the BBC's long-running *Doctor Who* ('gonna be a Dalek'). With its opening musical motif based on the popular football terrace chant 'You're Gonna Get Your Fuckin' Heads Kicked In' (trad. arr. The Hard Lads), 'Remote Control is the most musically ambitious piece on *The Clash*. This is particularly true of Chimes' interesting drum patterns and the sudden changes of time-signature (a prog-rock example of 'technique' that defied most of the established punk songbook rules).

Some sources suggest that the band's irate reaction to the release of 'Remote Control' wasn't so much because they didn't want a second single taken from *The Clash*, but because they didn't want *this* second single. The band themselves had told *Melody Maker* just a fortnight before 'Remote Control' was released that their next single was going to be **Janie Jones**. 'We've just been told this is our new single,' noted Strummer on stage in

Birmingham on 3 May. 'Let's hear it for artistic integrity. From now on we're The Sweet. Or maybe Chicory Tip!' For whatever reason, 'Remote Control' became a symbol of everything The Clash were fighting against. Though it was played regularly on the White Riot tour, and on odd occasions after this, by the end of 1977 it had been dropped from the set (only appearing subsequently at a one-off gig in July 1979). Thereafter, it was disowned by the band and wasn't used on most subsequent compilations; it's the only song on *The Clash* that doesn't appear on *Clash On Broadway*, for instance.

RETURN TO BRIXTON
[Simonon]

See THE GUNS OF BRIXTON

REVOLUTION ROCK
[J Edwards/D Ray]
LP: *London Calling*

Jackie Edwards' 1976 song 'Get Up' was the basis for The Clash's 'Revolution Rock'. The rewritten lyrics include references to Strummer being 'so pilled up that I rattle' and to the fans' favourite pastime ('smash up your seats and dance to a brand-new beat'). First recorded at Wessex in July 1979, an instrumental version features on the soundtrack of the *Rude Boy* movie. The song was re-recorded, with Guy Stevens, during the *London Calling* sessions. A live rave-up, 'Revolution Rock' entered The Clash's set during the Christmas 1979 London shows. A regular feature on the 16 Tons tour, the song was later dropped but made occasional live appearances in 1981.

THE RIGHT PROFILE
[Strummer/Jones]
LP: *London Calling*

One day at Wessex, Guy Stevens gave Strummer a copy of Patricia Bosworth's 1978 biography of the Method actor Montgomery Clift and suggested that Strummer write a song based on it. 'Here's a story of greatness and tragedy. It uplifts you through your tears,' he noted.

The subject appealed to Strummer. Born in 1920, Clift was the son of a successful New York stockbroker who was ruined in The Wall Street Crash. A Broadway star in his late teens, Clift signed to United Artists and had a string of hit movies in the 40s and 50s. 'The Right Profile' names four of his finest films: *Red River, A Place in the Sun, From Here to Eternity* and *The Misfits*. He also worked with Hitchcock on *I Confess* and appeared in *Judgment At Nuremberg*. In May 1957, leaving a Hollywood dinner party thrown by his friend Liz Taylor, Clift's car veered off the road and collided with a telephone pole. The accident left the actor with a broken jaw (which required extensive plastic surgery) and partially paralysed the left side of his face. He returned to acting within months, requesting directors to shoot his right profile, but his career never recovered its momentum and he subsequently became addicted to booze and the barbiturate Nembutol. Clift suffered a heart attack and died in July 1966. Stevens perhaps recognised parallels to his own alcohol addiction and Johnny Green, for one, believes that 'The Right Profile' was as much Strummer's tribute to The Clash's producer as it was to Clift.

Featuring the best use of brass of any of the band's records, 'The Right Profile' is the closest The Clash ever got to becoming a genuine soul band, the song's infectious swing and passionate vocals coming directly from the heart. Of particular note is Jones' subtle guitar framework which takes the song to an entirely new level. Sadly, without dragging The Irish Horns out on tour with them, there was no way the song could be performed live without a massive rearrangement and 'The Right Profile' remains a hidden gem in The Clash's canon.

ROADRUNNER ONCE
[Jonathan Richman]

This Jonathan Richman two-chord classic was a staple of many punk groups' repertoires. The Sex Pistols' hilariously incompetent version can be heard on *The Great Rock 'n' Roll Swindle*, for instance. The Clash often played 'Roadrunner' in rehearsals and soundchecks (*Last Gang In Town* mentions a version being rehearsed prior to the March 1977 Harlesden Coliseum show). A rough, mainly instrumental version was recorded at the soundcheck before the New York Palladium show on 21 September 1979. See also **Baby Please Don't Go**.

ROBBER DUB
[Strummer/Jones]
LP: *Black Market Clash*

The 'Dread at the Controls' dub version of **Bankrobber**, mixed for release on a proposed 12-inch single which was subsequently cancelled. This version finally saw the light of day in 1993 on the *Super Black Market Clash* CD.

ROCK THE CASBAH
[The Clash]
SINGLE: 6/82 **LP:** *Combat Rock*

Almost certainly the only Clash song to be referenced in the cult TV show *Buffy The Vampire Slayer*,[67] 'Rock the Casbah' was the band's biggest hit in America.[68] It remains, along with **London Calling** and **Should I Stay Or Should I Go**, The Clash song best known by the general public.

Topper Headon wasn't just a great drummer. He was also a more than useful bassist and, although he had no formal training, he could play a bit of jazz piano too. 'The true genius of 'Rock the Casbah' is Topper,' Strummer told Richard Cromelin in 1988 during the blackest hour of Headon's life. 'He banged down the drum track. Then ran over to the piano and then the bass. This is, like, within 25 minutes and 'Rock the Casbah' is there. And now he's serving 15 months in jail.' The piano riff was one that Headon had toyed with for a while. 'Every time we would go into a studio and there was a piano, he would always play this riff,' remembered Barry Glare in 1991.

'I told the engineer to put the tape on. I only played it twice around the houses. They said [to] leave it,' Headon himself recalled in the *Clash On Broadway* booklet. 'I said we can't, there's only two verses and a middle bit, there should be four verses. So they spliced the tape and doubled the length of the song.' With the addition of Jones' industrial-sounding guitars, the backing track was completed. Headon's funky basslines and boogie piano were a perfectly formed slice of rock-disco and had 'hit single' written all over them. Now all they needed were a decent set of lyrics. Enter, stage left, Joe Strummer, stand-up comedian.

'We found that whenever we played a tune on the *Combat Rock* sessions, it would be six minutes minimum,' Strummer noted years later. 'Bernie heard **'Sean Flynn'** and said "Does everything have to be as long as a raga?" I got back to the Iroquois and wrote "The King told the boogiemen, you have to let that raga drop." For some reason I started to think about what someone had told me, that you got lashed for owning a disco album in Iran.' Tickled by the

67. Episode 69, 'The I In Team' (first US broadcast 8 February 2000). Spike: 'I don't care if it's playing 'Rockin' the Casbah' on the bloody Jew's harp, get it out of me!' James Marsters, the actor who plays Spike, is a huge Clash fan. During a recent online interview he fondly remembered attending a gig in Los Angeles (probably during the Combat Rock tour). He smuggled a bottle of tequila past security and, mid-set, handed it to Strummer, who promptly passed it round the rest of the band. In 2002, Marsters formed his own punk-influenced band, Ghost of the Robot.

68. The single was actually a remix, produced by Mick Jones and engineered by Bob Clearmountain at New York's Power Station in May 1982.

The last gang in town –
Topper Headon, Mick Jones,
Joe Strummer and Paul
Simonon pictured in 1978.

Mick Jones – 'You're my guitar hero!'

Topper Headon – 'the human drum machine'.

Paul Simonon – a portrait of the artist as a young man.

'Coke adds life where
there isn't any.'

'Razor-edged poets of a
lost generation.'

Working for the
Clampdown in 1980.

Mick takes flight:
Combat Rock in the US, 1982.

Simonon, Jones, Headon and Strummer at the Ivor Novello Awards on 24 May 2001.

Terry Chimes, Mick Jones and Paul Simonon accept their awards
as The Clash enter the Rock & Roll Hall of Fame in March 2003.

A selection of 7" picture sleeves:

White Riot (1977)
Complete Control (1977)
Clash City Rockers (1978)
Tommy Gun (1978)
London Calling (1979)
Bankrobber (1980)
Know Your Rights (1982)
Should I Stay or Should I Go (US version, 1982)
This Is England (1985)

'That heart of his always worked too
hard.' Joe Strummer leads The
Mescaleros at one of his final gigs, in
Hastings on 20 November 2002.

unharmonious images that this Middle Eastern train of thought had triggered – oil wells, prophets, Sheikhs in Cadillacs, jet-fighters dropping their bombs 'between the minarets', Bedouin nomads defying the local Shariff – Strummer was inspired to one of his most inventive and funny lyrics.[69] A celebration of the power of music to get right up some snooty noses, a damning indictment of fundamentalism and a pithy series of observations about the complexities of the region, the song's greatness lies in its ability to comment on serious ethical issues with humour but *without* racism. Of course, not everyone got the joke. In 1991, during Operation Desert Storm, Strummer was dismayed to discover that 'Rock the Casbah' had become one of the most requested songs on US radio, mostly from people who assumed that it referred to bombing Iraqis (a fate that 'Rock the Casbah' shared with The Cure's 'Killing An Arab').

First performed on the Down The Casbah Club tour, 'Rock the Casbah' was a key song in The Clash's live set, 1982-85. Stripped of its trademark piano riff, the song became much heavier when played live. Indeed, the version The Clash played in Jamaica in November 1982 sounds rather like an out-take from *Give 'Em Enough Rope*. Strummer remained proud of the song and, subsequently, often performed it with The Mescaleros.

Don Letts' inventive video, filmed in Texas in June 1982, is one of The Clash's most memorable – and definitely the only one in which the band are almost outperformed by an armadillo. Broadcast approximately once a day for the next decade on MTV, it can be seen on *This Is Video Clash* and *The Essential Clash*. The irony, of course, is that it's Terry Chimes behind the drum kit (and sitting beside the swimming pool) on the video, the song's composer having been fired from the band a month earlier. 'Rock the Casbah' has since been covered by Demonspeed, Sollar Twins and The NC Thirteens.

ROCKERS GALORE ..... UK TOUR
[Strummer/Jones/Campbell]
B-SIDE: 6/80

The B-Side of **Bankrobber**, this recording used the stripped-down instrumental track of he single, over which Mikey Dread toasted his impressions of the UK 16 Tons tour in early 1980. Quite amusing they are too, as the singer sees 'places and faces I'm-a never see'd before.' With completely uncoded

---

69. Strummer may have been inspired by Hawkwind's 1977 song 'Hassan I Sahba (Assassins of Allah)', which deals with similar subjects in a correspondingly humorous way.

references to marijuana smoking back at the hotel and Mikey's various exhortations ('*SKANK IT!*'), 'Rockers Galore' amounts to an act of friendship by The Clash to a man who would, in the next year, help to move the band in a radical new direction.

RUDIE CAN'T FAIL
[Strummer/Jones]
LP: *London Calling*

In Caribbean parlance, a Rude Boy is a teenage thug, one of those lager-drinking youths seen in *The Harder They Come*, hanging out in the Government Yard in Trenchtown spoiling for a fight. The Rudies had been a popular part of ska and reggae culture for decades, cropping up in the lyrics of many Jamaican songs, their lives being either celebrated as a rebellious expression of freedom or castigated for their wicked and sinful ways.

'We'd had a good summer going to West Indian blues dances and drinking Special Brew for breakfast,' Strummer fondly remembered about the short (and rather wet) summer of 1978. Taking its inspiration from the scat lines that Strummer sang on **Safe European Home**, the present song was evolved during rehearsals at Vanilla Studios in Pimlico during the spring of 1979. Strummer even included an autobiographical note concerning the location via his reference to a number 19 bus, the very one that took him from his new home near Chelsea's King's Road to Vanilla each day.

'When we went into Vanilla it was a matter of knocking up the songs from scratch,' noted The Clash's roadie Barry Glare. 'They'd come in early, jam for a few hours, go over the road and play football, then come back and jam again.' The song's title phrase actually has its origins in Desmond Dekker's 1967 hit **007 (Shanty Town)**. The lyrics also include a reference to another reggae classic, Dr Alimantado's 'Born For A Purpose'. The choppy guitar riff was an obvious tribute to Bo Diddley, with whom the band had just toured America, but this was beautifully juxtaposed with Simonon's bone-shaking ska bassline as a countermelody and Headon's rhythmic rim-shots. 'Sing, Michael, sing!' urges Strummer, and Jones does – turning in his most successful solo vocal to date, throwing off the cod-Jamaican stop-your-messing-around lyrics with some aplomb.

The summer of 1979 would see the extraordinary rise of Two Tone, an independent record label formed around the Coventry band The Specials AKA, whose energetic brand of social-comment ska-punk struck a chord with the record-buying public. The Specials' first single, 'Gangsters', concerned, in part, their dealings with The Clash's manager when they provided support during the On Parole tour. [70] The follow-up, a cover of Danny Livingstone's 'A Message To You Rudy' – a Top 10 UK hit in October – proved that the influence was cutting both ways. Aided by a somewhat contrived, but massively popular, Mod revival around the release of the movie *Quadrophenia*, long-time Clash rivals The Jam had suddenly jumped into the big league – 'The Eton Rifles' was a number three hit in November. [71] For the first time since the break-up of The Pistols, The Clash were facing serious competition as Britain's best band. It must have pissed them off royally to see relative newcomers like The Specials, Madness and The Selector suddenly having bigger hits than them while, essentially, working in the same cross-generic areas. 'You think you're pretty hot/In your pork pie hat' is, in this context, not merely a spiteful put-down, it's little short of a declaration of war.

Recorded at Wessex Studios in July 1979 and used as the closing song in *Rude Boy*, 'Rudie Can't Fail' is, in many ways, a continuation of the outsider/loner theme that runs though most of the songs on *London Calling*. But with references to Rudie realising his soul and searching for a saviour, there is a gentle pathos in this lonely figure standing on the outside of society looking in. And in a song that alludes to *Doctor Who* (see also **Remote Control**), there's more than a hint that escape from 'living in service' is often the stuff of fantasies.

The song, one of the band's brightest and poppiest, first appeared in The Clash's live set during their London dates in July 1979 but was only used occasionally thereafter (on some dates on the UK and US legs of the 16 Tons tour in 1980). This is odd in view of the song's undoubted popularity with Clash fans. Like **Armagideon Time**, 'Rudie Can't Fail' was subsequently used in the Strummer-compiled score for John Cusack's movie *Grosse Pointe Blank* and it was subjected to one of the best-ever cover versions of a Clash song, by The Mighty Mighty Bosstones, for the *Burning London* project.

Footnote: 'Rudie Can't Fail' enjoyed a surprise revival in the late 1990s when Newcastle United football fans used it as a chant concerning their then-manager Ruud Gullitt. Sadly for all Toonies, Ruudi did fail, being sacked after just one season.

---

70. According to Adrian Thrills, Jerry Dammers wrote 'Gangsters' – a cunning reworking of Prince Buster's 1967 hit 'Al Capone' – on a guitar that Strummer loaned him. It's alleged that the seven-piece Specials were hired for the Sort It Out tour at a fee of £25 per gig – not each, that's between them. When The Clash found out, they were appalled and forced Rhodes to double the fee. Certainly 'Gangsters' opens with Neville Staples' indignant shout of 'Bernie Rhodes knows "Don't argue"!'

71. Despite some opportunist coat-tail hangers, the 1979-80 Mod scene did produce a couple of terrific, and very underrated, bands – particularly The Chords.

SAFE EUROPEAN HOME
[Strummer/Jones]
LP: *Give 'Em Enough Rope*

'It was Bernie's idea,' Jones noted, concerning the decision to dispatch himself and Strummer to Kingston, Jamaica for two weeks in December 1977. The reason for the trip was to write songs for the upcoming second LP, sessions for which were, at that stage, planned for March. But Jamaica wasn't exactly what they had expected. 'We must have looked like a strange pair to the locals,' noted Jones. Strummer, in particular, seems to have found the experience very unsettling: 'We only knew Lee Perry but, of course, we couldn't find him ... We just walked around in our punk gear. I'm surprised we weren't filleted and served on a plate of chips. We went down the docks and I think we only survived because they mistook us for sailors.' However, the trip did influence both the sound and the lyrics of many of the songs on *Give 'Em Enough Rope*.

'Safe European Home' was written in The Pegasus Hotel in Kingston (many fans assume, because it's mentioned in the lyrics, that Joe and Mick stayed at the Sheraton). 'We went to the pictures a lot. It was like *The Harder They Come*. Not on the screen but in the audience,' Strummer remembered in 1990. '[They] were much more fun than the films.' The conceptual dislocation of two white boys with guitars, far from home and trying to stay alive in a harsh alien environment, finds its best outlet in the bemused confusion of 'Safe European Home'. On arrival, they are mistaken for Martians by the local Johnnies who, of course, want to sell them some drugs. 'Went to the place where every white face/Is an invitation to robbery' sang Strummer. 'The Jamaican Tourist Board gave me and Mick a fiver for this one,' he noted when introducing the song on stage in 1979.

Paul Simonon's bitter anger that he hadn't been invited to join his mates' trip to what he considered to be his spiritual home of Jamaica may have subsided by the time recording took place at Basing Street. But only a little, as his agitated, spiky bassline clearly proves. (In *Westway to the World*, over 20 years after the event, he still seemed upset.) Again, though, the real star here is Headon, who underpins Jones' powerful, Mick Ronson-style, heavily tracked riffing with staccato bursts of machine-gun fire. 'Sandy [Pearlman] called me 'The Human Drum Machine' because I didn't make one mistake on the album,' noted Headon proudly in 1990. 'It was a buzz to get a producer who got such a great drum sound.'

With its 'They got the sun/And they got the palm trees' message (subtext: let 'em keep it), 'Safe European Home' features Jones' finest backing vocals since **Complete Control**, and amid Strummer's scat vocalising at the climax, some exquisite harmonies – a much-overlooked part of The Clash's oeuvre. Used as the explosive set-opener on the Sort It Out tour, the song remained a live favourite for much of the rest of the band's career. 'Safe European Home' reflects the final, and most pointed, isolationist tirade from a group who, even by the song's release, were already making rapid strides towards true, and lasting, internationalism. By the time of their next LP, The Clash were no longer bored with the USA. Soon thereafter, they'd be busy conquering it.

SCRAWL ON THE BATHROOM WALL

A title mentioned in several contemporary press reports during 1978 as a song recorded during the *Give 'Em Enough Rope* sessions.

SEAN FLYNN
[The Clash]
LP: *Combat Rock*

On 6 April 1970 American photojournalists Sean Flynn and Dana Stone left Phnom Penh on rented Honda motorbikes to find the front lines of fighting in Cambodia. Travelling south-east, the two were stopped at a checkpoint in Svay Rieng Province and led away by elements of either the Vietcong or the Khmer Rouge (sources vary). Information subsequently obtained by the CIA from indigenous sources indicated that Flynn and Stone were executed by their captors in mid-1971.

A decade later, Strummer was becoming fascinated with this era, via movies like Francis Coppola's *Apocalypse Now* (see **Charlie Don't Surf**, **This Is Radio Clash**) and Michael Cimino's *The Deer Hunter*. These seemed to have exposed America's collective guilt complex over having (a) been in Vietnam in the first place but, more importantly, (b) having once got there, *lost* the damn war. Written at Vanilla during rehearsals for the 1981 European tour, and recorded at Marcus Music in April, Strummer's ruminative, absorbed narrative sees Flynn lost in his own literal heart of darkness. One in which the past is a closing door and, allegedly, 'each man knows what he's looking for.' Or not, as the case may be. According to Gary Barnacle, Headon was largely responsible for the oriental and gong-like clangour of the backing track.

One of The Clash's most spectacular-sounding recordings – you can almost feel the clammy heat of the Cambodian jungle in the LP's grooves – 'Sean Flynn' nevertheless received an icy reception in some parts of The Clash camp. Notably from Bernard Rhodes, who described it uncharitably as 'a raga' (see **Rock the Casbah**). Cut almost in half by Glyn Johns during the mixing of *Combat Rock*, the released version of 'Sean Flynn' is still a fierce piece of musical experimentation, but it only tells half the story.

Not exactly the kind of thing to have them pogoing in Row Z, 'Sean Flynn', predictably, was never attempted live by The Clash.

SEX MACHINE
[James Brown/Bobby Byrd]

Recorded by The Lash (Strummer, Jones, Simonon, Mickey Gallagher and Charley Charles) on 28 December 1982 for the B-Side of Janie Jones' **House of the Ju-Ju Queen** single.

SEX MAD ROAR
[The Clash]
B-SIDE: 10/85

An anti-pornographic rockabilly diatribe, played regularly live during 1984 as **Sex Mad War**. A version was recorded at the tail-end of the *Cut the Crap* sessions in January 1985 and the song, under its new title, appeared on the B-Side of the 12-inch **This Is England** single. It's notable for Simonon's attacking bassline and Peter Howard's staccato drum fills.

SEX MAD WAR

See SEX MAD ROAR

SHENANDOAH
[trad. arr. The Clash]

On 5 February 1982 The Clash were interviewed on the New Zealand TV show *Shazam*. Jones, messing around with a ukulele that Strummer had recently bought, began plucking out the chords to this famous American capstan worksong, and Strummer followed him with a rather dubious remembering of the lyrics. Mercifully, it didn't last very long.

SHEPHERDS DELIGHT
[Mikey Dread/The Clash]
LP: *Sandinista!*

A piano and acoustic guitar-led instrumental, recorded with Mikey Dread at Pluto Studios in February 1980 during the **Bankrobber** sessions. Sounding not unlike the incidental music from some anonymous BBC2 documentary about homelessness, the disturbing wailing noises that punctuate the recording were created by Dread playing with a squeaky toy and then manipulating the tape-speed. There are also various train and aircraft noises, taken from stock tape and treated with heavy dub-echo.

It's all interesting enough as an experiment in musique concrète, although it sounds as unlike The Clash as it's physically possible to. A strange choice to be the final word on *Sandinista!*, 'Shepherds Delight' is a slightly sinister and downbeat end to a remarkable, under-appreciated work.

SHOULD I STAY OR SHOULD I GO
[The Clash]
SINGLE: 9/82 **LP:** *Combat Rock*

Written in the autumn of 1981 and first rehearsed by The Clash in September at Ear Studios, Jones' retro-sounding rock stomp was 'Our attempt at writing a classic,' according to its author. The song would end up far outdistancing its intended station as *Combat Rock*'s most Clash-like song to become, in the 1990s, a million-selling advertisement for Levi jeans.

It's inevitable, with hindsight, that the lyrics – hollered with gusto by Jones – can be viewed as a possible comment on his position within the band. Indeed, this is a position that Strummer took on more than one occasion after Jones' departure from The Clash. Jones himself didn't wholly discount the theory. 'Maybe it *was* pre-empting my leaving,' he told Stuart Bailie in 1991, although he added that the song mostly concerned 'a personal situation' which most commentators take to be self-flagellatory references to his soon-to-implode relationship with Ellen Foley.

'On the spur of the moment I said "I'm going to do the backing vocals in Spanish,"' Strummer remembered in 1991. 'We needed a translator so Eddie Garcia, the tape operator, called his mother in Brooklyn Heights and read her the lyrics over the phone and she translated them. But Eddie and his mum are Ecuadorian, so it's Ecuadorian Spanish that me and Joe Ely are singing on the backing vocals.'

'I ran into them in New York,' remembered Ely in 2000. 'When you listen, there's a place in the song where Mick says, "Split!" Me and Strummer had snuck up behind and jumped out at him in the middle of singing, and scared the shit out of him. He looks over and gives us the dirtiest look. They kept that in the final version.' Jones' original lyrics had included the very suggestive line 'on your front or on your back'. During Glyn Johns' remixing sessions in April 1982, Jones re-recorded his vocals and changed this to 'if you want me off your back', it having been pointed out that the former was unlikely to get much US radio airplay.

Introduced to the live set at Paris in September 1981, 'Should I Stay Or Should I Go' remained in The Clash's repertoire until Jones' departure and for some time thereafter, when it was sung by Nick Sheppard. [72] A chugging version, recorded on 8 September 1982 in Boston, features on *From Here to Eternity*. Don Letts' video for the single was a live performance filmed at Shea Stadium in October 1982. This can be seen on *This is Video Clash* and *The Essential Clash*. Jones subsequently used a vocal sample from 'Should I Stay Our Should I Go' on his BAD II song 'The Globe'. *Burning London* includes a rap cover version by Ice Cube and Mack 10, while the song was also covered by Error Type 11, The Long Tall Texans, Spastic Vibrations, Die Toten Hosen, Bai Bang, Super Green and, memorably, Kylie Minogue.

SHOUTING STREET
[Strummer]

The last song written while The Clash still existed as a going concern. In 1999 Simonon remembered Strummer telling him that he had written the song, in late 1985, and suggesting that the two of them get together and work on it. 'I said "Fine" but I didn't get another call.' The song, a classic slice of 1950s rockabilly about Portobello Road, would eventually be recorded by Strummer in 1989 for his solo debut *Earthquake Weather*.

SILICONE ON SAPPHIRE
[The Clash]
LP: *Sandinista!*

Another of the Wessex *Sandinista!* sessions' more radical experiments was to take the backing track to **Washington Bullets**, treat it with some volatile

---

72. During the European leg of the Out of Control tour, 'Should I Stay Or Should I Go' developed into a heavy metal thrash with Sheppard aggressively bellowing the lyrics.

phasing effects and then plaster over the top a shimmering Strummer spoken-word vocal in the manner of **If Music Could Talk**. With a few futuristic lyrics discernible through the swirling mists of the instrumental track ('hardwired logic/machine language'), 'Silicone On Sapphire' suggests that Strummer had been listening to the pretentious 'machine rock' of the Kraftwerk- and Bowie-influenced Gary Numan. Or possibly to the sci-fi inspired early work of The Human League, both of whom were experiencing huge popularity in Britain during 1980. Actually, much more likely he'd been reacquainting himself with the 'space-rock' of Hawkwind (cf 1977's 'Spirit of the Age', a Robert Calvert song about cryogenics which shares the rather aloof qualities of 'Silicone On Sapphire').

There's actually something quite unnerving about 'Silicone On Sapphire', in which the song's cold metallic surface reflects the rhapsodic and the eerie tangled together. Listening to the track, it's possible to experience something perilously close to an out-of-body experience, momentarily carried away by an involuntary flood of mental images: out-of-focus concrete walkways and electricity pylons; allotments shrouded in the morning mist. It all adds up to a sort of mysticism of mundanity.

Again, as with so much of *Sandinista!*, it's necessary to hear 'Silicone On Sapphire' in the context of its neighbours. Taken in isolation, the song sounds like nothing more than the soundtrack to an undistinguished science fiction movie. Placed on side six of *Sandinista!* between similarly brave and wilfully left-field recordings, **Living In Fame** and **Version Pardner**, 'Silicone On Sapphire' furthers the song-cycle thematic of the LP (see, also, **If Music Could Talk**'s debt to **Shepherds Delight** and **Mensforth Hill**'s to **Something About England**).

SITTING AT MY PARTY
[Jones]

A fast, raging diatribe about an unwanted (female) party guest, this rather slight Jones song was left over from his previous band, The London SS. Played occasionally by The Clash in 1976, it was soon dropped when better material was written. Sometimes referred to on Clash live recordings as 'Work'.

SOMEBODY GOT MURDERED
[The Clash]
LP: *Sandinista!*

During early 1980 Strummer had been approached by Jack Nitzsche, who was scoring *Cruising*, a movie starring Al Pacino set in New York's gay S&M scene.

Asked to provide a heavy rock song, Strummer went home that evening to discover that the car park attendant at the flats where he was living in World's End had been 'stabbed over five pounds.' Strummer's lyric of sadness at such a pointless crime ('I've been very hungry, but not enough to kill') inspired Jones – who also sings the song – to one of his most complex and unusual tunes. A synthesiser provides the ostentatious swooshing noises heard throughout and the song was recorded, in some excitement, at Electric Lady before being completed at Wessex later in the year. 'We wanted a guard dog sound,' remembered Headon. 'My dog, Battersea, wouldn't let anybody hit me, so we went into the studio, I held onto him and every time we wanted him to bark, Joe would thump me!' Sadly, Strummer never heard back from Nitzsche, so the song was used on *Sandinista!*

The first of the *Sandinista!* songs introduced to The Clash's set (at The Roxy in Los Angeles in April 1980), 'Somebody Got Murdered' remained a live fixture for the next three years until Jones' departure. Libertine's late-1990s cover features on *Backlash*.

SOMETHING ABOUT ENGLAND
[The Clash]
LP: *Sandinista!*

The Clash tried their collective hand at some radically un-punk musical styles, but 'Something About England' is their only stab at one of the most archly conservative yet most quintessentially English of all genres, music hall.

The influence of music hall on British rock 'n' roll is as vital and organic to it as the influence of country and blues is on its American equivalent. The first recognisably populist working-class music that people had to pay to listen to, elements of vaudeville and comedy songs had been an important part of British songwriting and performance since the 1870s when, in London alone, there were around 300 music halls and palaces of variety.[73] The format was based on simple, usually amusing, songs about working-class experience, lives and loves, often including a dose of double entendre aimed at both the common people in the stalls and the toffs in the circle. Variations on this form continued after the Great War and achieved even wider popularity via the advent of radio and films – in the process making stars of acts like Lancastrian ukulele player George Formby, social satirists Michael Flanders and Donald Swann and cockney duo Bud Flanagan and Chesney Allen.

---

73. The best known performers of the Victorian and Edwardian music hall included Marie Lloyd, Vesta Tilley, George Robey, Harry Champion, George Formby Sr and Harry Lauder.

In the 1950s, songwriter Lionel Bart and singers like Tommy Steele, Lonnie Donegan, Anthony Newley and Joe Brown all combined the excitement of the emergent rock 'n' roll sounds from America with elements of English (specifically cockney) music hall. As Ian MacDonald notes in *Revolution in the Head*, during the 1950s British parents would still sing music hall songs to their children and, as a consequence, this tradition permeated English pop throughout the next decade and beyond. Examples of music hall whimsy infiltrated the works of The Beatles, The Small Faces, Syd Barrett, The Bonzo Dog Doo Dah Band and, especially, The Kinks, among others. The style, in fact, was a cornerstone of the British brand of psychedelia circa 1966-7.[74] Via his interest in mime, David Bowie's theatrical brand of what would subsequently become glam rock included many vaudeville elements too, and this aspect of Bowie's influence on groups like Cockney Rebel shouldn't be underestimated.

Punk may seem an odd resting place for a form so deeply rooted in the past, but there's little doubting Johnny Rotten's assimilation of numerous elements of music hall's 'comedy of the absurd' into his stage performances (something Rotten himself has been surprisingly open about). Via this, and superb London bands like Ian Dury and The Blockheads, Madness and Squeeze, elements of music hall continued to appear in the 1980s, in the music of Manchester's irreverently miserablist The Smiths, and the 90s output of the Kinks-influenced Blur and the Bowie-influenced Pulp.

A fascinating counterpoint to **Broadway**, 'Something About England' allows a UK equivalent ('whom time could not erode') of the New York tramp in the former song the opportunity to testify himself. It has been suggested that, during the later songs recorded for *Sandinista!* (like this one, at Wessex, in August 1980), Strummer was deliberately attempting to nullify some of the American influences on the New York material by writing his lyrics about deliberately parochial English subjects. That may be true, although the poetic language and social vision of 'Something About England' is, surely, universal. The song is patriotic without being xenophobic and wistful and nostalgic without becoming mawkish or trite.

Jones begins 'Something About England' with a sentimental, if valid, rejection of crass racism (concerning the ignorant belief that immigrants steal hubcaps and that all would be wine and roses if 'England were for Englishmen again'). Strummer specifically alludes to the 1936 'Hunger

---

74. See, for example, Keith West's 'Excerpt from *A Teenage Opera*', Blossom Toes' 'We Are Ever So Clean', The New Vaudeville Band's 'Winchester Cathedral', Scaffold's 'Thank U Very Much', David McWilliams' 'Days of Pearly Spencer', The Small Faces' 'Lazy Sunday', The Kinks' 'Dead End Street', The Who's 'Dogs', The New Animals' 'Good Times' etc.

March' from Jarrow to London, which attempted to highlight the poverty caused by the economic depression of the era. The song hurtles through the decades, casting a cynical eye at the human cost of war and reconstruction ('the architects couldn't care').

A sad, downbeat song, 'Something About England' effortlessly slips into the trenches of the First World War for a snippet of 'It's a Long Way to Tipperary' (with its familiar references to Piccadilly and Leicester Square). Musically, it's mini-opera with several segments, held together by Jones' piano, Headon's quotation-mark percussion and a brass section (played by Headon's friend Gary Barnacle, his father Bill, a noted jazz musician, and military bandsman David Yates). Because of the song's complexity (and, possibly, the risk of the opening verse being misunderstood by some of the boneheads on the fringes of their audience), The Clash never performed the song live.

THE SOUND OF THE SINNERS
[The Clash]
LP: *Sandinista!*

Christianity, it's fair to say, has produced many great contrasts: at one extreme the teachings of Jesus Christ, the Sistine Chapel and Aretha Franklin; at the other, the Crusades, the Spanish Inquisition and Cliff Richard. 'The Sound of the Sinners' is the least likely gospel song since The Rolling Stones' 'I Just Wanna See His Face'. 'That's not a piss-take,' Strummer assured Bill Flanagan. 'I was thinking of LA and the great earthquake. I had, "After all these years to believe in Jesus." Topper said, "How about drugs?" [I thought about] all those people who take too much LSD and end up in sanatoriums. Lots of them think they're Jesus.'

The twin themes of sin and temptation drive this infectious pseudo-gospel jam, which, seemingly with reasonable affection, lampoons its religious subject matter. Yet there is also some real conviction in the song's evocation of the forthcoming tidal wave of Armageddon. Biblical allusions include the destruction of Jericho (Joshua 2-3), while the song also makes a pointed attack on the church's need to raise its own funds. Strummer was probably thinking of the discontinuity between commercialism and faith, although, in the 1980s, a series of financial and sexual scandals would shake even the most agnostic view of Christian piety, particularly in the US.[75] 'The Sound of

---

75. cf James' 'God Only Knows' and, particularly, U2's 'Bullet the Blue Sky' ('The God I believe in isn't short of cash').

the Sinners' does exactly what it says on the collecting tin, pray that someone, *somewhere*, knows what's going on with regard to the end of the world. Amen.

The song's amusing voice-over coda drags the listener's perception of Christian faith back from the naked joy of the American deep south to more comfortable (and, therefore, boring) home counties Church of England surroundings. 'The Sound of the Sinners' baffled many of The Clash's audience, though the song was popular enough to find a place in the band's live set during 1983. Strummer noted that this is Elvis Costello's favourite Clash song.

SPANISH BOMBS
[Strummer/Jones]
LP: *London Calling*

'Spanish Bombs' had a similar origin to **London Calling**. Travelling home from Wessex Studios late one evening, Strummer and Gaby Salter were talking about the Basque separatists in Spain who were currently engaged in a bombing campaign against various holiday resorts on the Costa Del Sol. 'There should be a song called 'Spanish Bombs',' noted Strummer. So he wrote one.

In it, he drew parallels between the current situation in Spain and the Spanish Civil War of the late 1930s. This was sparked by a chance remark from Johnny Green concerning George Orwell's *A Homage To Catalonia*. Green, fascinated by this period of history, loaned Strummer some books on the subject, which helped to pepper 'Spanish Bombs' with allusions to dramatist Federico García Lorca (1899-1936), the *Guardia Civil*, 'The Red Flag', Vaughn Horton's 'Mockingbird Hill' and trenches full of a ragged army of poets. The evocation of the Civil War was sumptuously romantic but, as with other songs on *London Calling*, heroic deeds of the past were not evoked simply for the sake of nostalgia. Instead, Strummer clearly hoped that the lessons of history could be used to provide solutions to the problems of the present (cf **The Card Cheat**).

Containing some of Strummer's most beautiful imagery (the colours of red and black run through the song like rivers), 'Spanish Bombs' is ripped out of time and transported to the present day with references to DC10s, disco casinos, shattered hotels and burning buses. Another fabulous band performance, 'Spanish Bombs' was one of the highlights of *London Calling*, an ambitious song with, as Tom Carson noted in *Rolling Stone*, 'jangling flamenco guitars and a lilting vocal meshing in a swirling kaleidoscope of courage and disillusionment, old wars and new corruption.' Of particular note is yet another superb piece of elegant guitar work by Jones, his delicate passing chords and descending phrases recalling Django Reinhardt (see also **Jimmy Jazz**).

Debuted at Atlanta in October 1979, the song featured occasionally in The Clash's live set in 1980 and was regularly performed thereafter. It proved to be particularly popular when the band played several gigs in Spain in 1981. On the 1980 US tour, Jones' reliance on guitar effects pedals often led to a rather disorganised and shrill climax to the song in concert.

Stay Free
[Strummer/Jones]
LP: *Give 'Em Enough Rope*

Soppy sentimental ballads about male bonding and the strength of friendship aren't something one naturally associates with The Clash. Except for Jones' 'Stay Free', of course. 'Even the skinheads cry,' Mick told *Trouser Press* in 1979. 'It really moves them.'

'Stay Free' is Jones' paean to his school friend Robin Crocker. 'He was a wild one, everybody used to get him to do the things they wished they could do themselves,' remembered Jones. 'But it wasn't totally about him, that was a starting place. What happened to him happened to a lot of people.' Jones and Crocker had first met in a maths class at Strand School in 1969, Crocker having been held back a year because of his disruptive behaviour. According to Clash legend, he and Jones fought that first day over whether Bo Diddley was better than Chuck Berry. Their mutual love of music conquered their differences, however, and the pair became friends, hanging out together, doing a bit of minor-league thievery and spending their evenings going to gigs with their gang 'down Streatham on the bus.' Crocker was eventually expelled from school and, in March 1970, he was arrested for his part in a bungled armed robbery on John Parry Ltd, a betting shop in South London. He was sentenced to three years in prison.[76] After his release, he and Jones resumed their friendship and Crocker became an important part of The Clash's entourage, firstly as Jones' guitar roadie, then as a journalist with *ZigZag* under the nom de plume Robin Banks.

With its bass-heavy mix, 'Stay Free' tends to highlight the limitations of Jones' voice, although his personal involvement in the song is abundantly clear; even in the obviously staged reconstruction of the song's recording in *Rude Boy* there is real emotion in Jones' voice. The song also features some almost imperceptible

---

76. In reality, it wasn't Brixton where Crocker served his time, but rather Wormwood Scrubs and Albany on the Isle of Wight.

acoustic guitar and Booker T-style organ (played by Bob Andrews of The Rumour) to thicken the texture beneath yet another powerhouse performance from Headon. First performed during the On Parole tour, 'Stay Free' was a live favourite for much of the rest of Jones' time in The Clash – being his main show-case on successive tours in 1979, '80 and '81. Jones was often forced to explain some of the song's English allusions to overseas audiences: 'This is the appen-dix. Butlins means *the nick*. The nick means *the penitentiary!*' he told the crowd at Chicago in 1979. In 2003, Pete Wylie recorded a cover version of 'Stay Free.'

STEPPING STONE (I'M NOT YOUR)
[Boyce/Hart]

A much-covered 1960s classic most associated with The Monkees' 1966 version. The Sex Pistols recorded the song in 1976. 'Stepping Stone' was performed by The Clash on the Busking tour.

STOP THE WORLD
[The Clash]
B-SIDE: 11/80

Recorded as a backing track at Electric Lady in March 1980 as part of the *Sandinista!* sessions, and completed at Wessex in September, 'Stop the World' was initially intended to be The Clash's contribution to a compilation LP to raise money for the Campaign For Nuclear Disarmament. 'I was messing around on the organ trying to play [Booker T's] 'Green Onions',' remembered Strummer. 'I got Topper to play along and I put down this thing because it sounded interesting. I put the lyrics to it at Wessex just before it became a B-Side.' With the song's radio samples and discordant guitars, the lyrics concern a post-nuclear holocaust nightmare and include one of Strummer's most poetic couplets: 'Shaking with mystery tears/One lonely night in Ladbroke Grove.'

THE STREET PARADE
[The Clash]
LP: *Sandinista!*

One of the most underrated songs on *Sandinista!*, 'The Street Parade' appears at first glance to concern itself with broken relationships. On closer inspection, however, the lyrics are a celebration of one's ability to lose oneself in a crowd. Strummer, like his contemporary Paul Weller (who covered similar themes in 'Away From the Numbers' and, specifically, 'In the Crowd') was numbed by the idea of becoming detached from reality by the trappings of stardom. The opportunity to disappear into the street parade was clearly an enticing one for Strummer and his haunting, poetic lyrics speak of a man desperate for an occasional escape route from being who he is ('it's hard not to cry, in these crying times').

The lyrics are matched by a gorgeous syncopated band arrangement, with Jones' graffiti-like guitars playing off a sweet, floating horn section and stabs of Caribbean marimbas (see also **Washington Bullets**). The Clash clearly thought a lot of the song – it's the uncredited extra track on the final side of the *Clash On Broadway* compilation, for example. 'The Street Parade' was a key part of The Clash's 1981 stage set, featuring in the Radio Clash Europe tour, the New York and Paris residencies and the UK tour late in the year.

STRAIGHT TO HELL
[The Clash]
SINGLE: 9/82 LP: *Combat Rock*

A 'Desolation Row' for the 1980s, 'Straight To Hell' contains many of Joe Strummer's finest lyrical images with an austere clarity that haunts the listener. The song, a harrowing series of snapshots of debased humanity, begins in England, a country that in late 1981 was split down the middle between those who spoke the King's English 'in quotations' and those who lived in decaying, rusted steel-towns, suffering the harshness of winter. In a single line of brutal poetry – 'water froze, in the generations' – Strummer says more about the reality of working-class Britain of the era than any number of *Play For Today*s. In the blink of an eye, the listener is then transported half a world away, to Vietnam where the bamboo kids, the children of American GI's sperm-donation programme, straddle the cultural divide between Coca-Cola and rice. Next, we're down in the sewers of 'International Junkiedom, USA', observing the emergent crack culture that would rip America apart over the following decades.

'Straight To Hell' is full of such prophetic observations, a stunning example of cartoon grotesquerie in which there are many victims and no one is innocent, but some are more guilty than others. The final verse offers a dismissive world-view, a no man's land of drugs, cold and misery, where the immigrants downstairs want to play their incessant bongo-bongo music all night. It could, as Strummer tells his listeners, be anywhere ('any frontier, any hemisphere'). It could be your street. And in this Hell on earth, there is no escape, no asylum ('King Solomon he never lived round here'). Just more of the same.

The backing track was recorded at Electric Lady on 30 December 1981. The song began as a vague Jones guitar doodle that had been tried in several different styles. 'You couldn't play rock 'n' roll to it,' noted Headon. 'I started messing around on the snare. Basically it's a Bossa Nova.'[77]

'Just before the take, Topper said to me "I want you to play this," and he handed me an R Whites lemonade bottle wrapped in a towel,' remembered Strummer. 'He said, "I want you to beat the front of the bass drum with it."' It's only really when one listens to live recordings of 'Straight To Hell' from the period after Headon had been replaced by Terry Chimes that you appreciate quite how much Headon's instinctive genius brought to the song.

The lyrics were written by Strummer on New Year's Eve and were recorded immediately, the session finishing shortly before midnight. 'We took the E train from the village up to Times Square,' noted Strummer. 'I'll never forget coming out of the subway exit, into a hundred billion people, and I knew we had just done something great.' During *Combat Rock*'s mixing, Glyn Johns shortened 'Straight To Hell' by almost a minute, removing a verse concerning New York's Latino drug dealers ('from alphabet city all the way A to Z, dead head'). The unedited 6.50 version was included on *Clash On Broadway*.

Introduced live on the Down the Casbah Club tour, [78] 'Straight To Hell' was a fixture of The Clash's set 1982-84 and made a welcome, stripped-down reappearance on the Busking tour. Strummer, subsequently, performed the song live with both The Pogues and The Mescaleros. A wonderfully moody version, recorded in Boston in September 1982, appears on *From Here to Eternity*. Moby's 1999 cover, featuring Heather Nova, is the final track on *Burning London*. The song was also covered by Skinnerbox.

THIS IS ENGLAND
[Strummer/Rhodes] [79]
SINGLE: 10/85 **LP:** *Cut the Crap*

Subsequently described by Strummer as his 'last great Clash song', 'This Is England' was written during early 1984. In essence, it's another variant on the

77. A Brazilian variant on samba and baiao.

78. Some sources suggest that 'Straight To Hell' was performed during The Clash's September 1981 Paris residency. This seems unlikely given that it was, according to its author, not written for another three months. The fact that 'Straight To Hell' *didn't* feature on the band's early 1982 Far East tour – particularly given the relevancy of its lyrics to South East Asia – clearly suggests that The Clash were still working on a live arrangement at this time.

79. 'This Is England' was credited to The Clash on the single, but to Strummer/Rhodes on *Cut the Crap*.

divisionist politics of **Straight To Hell** (see also **North and South, Three Card Trick**), yet 'This Is England' is a surprisingly compassionate identification with the life of the unemployed. The song's images, of decaying council estates and sinister police oppression, were both standard Clash themes, and are used in several other songs on *Cut the Crap* to little effect. Yet here, somehow, they work majestically.

The song's opening verse is couched in a series of weak couplets of the kind that blight the rest of the LP, but as soon as the first chorus is reached, with its emotional call for a national identity that doesn't involve violence, 'This is England' clicks into place effortlessly. Strummer's imagination is fired by the metaphor of the dying British motorcycle production industry, the harsh South Atlantic winter that hundreds of young Britons recently died in ('Ice from a dying creed') and the pompous jingoism that accompanied the Falklands War ('I see no glory'). The song is filled with loathing for the passionless, plastic 1980s and the 'me generation' ('who cares to protest?'), and includes a misquotation from Wilson Pickett's 'Land of a Thousand Dances' which leads into the biggest question of all: 'When will we be free?'

A beautiful, mid-paced tune strapped onto the back of an epic, multi-layered guitar riff, the song features the best use of sampling on any Clash record – these include loops of a child's voice and an ethereal-sounding football crowd. If there is a musical criticism of 'This Is England', it's only in the dumbed-down Fairlight-programmed drum patterns. Yet that's a small complaint when compared to the ingenuity of the rest of the song's construction. 'I remember playing bass on that and Joe being ecstatic,' noted Nick Sheppard. 'He said "That's the only bit of the record with any bollocks to it!"'

Not everyone was impressed; indeed, Gavin Martin's review of the single in *NME* was brutal: 'Still determined to slay the totems, bare the social ills, attend the wake of our crumbling banana republic, Strummer's rant bears all the signs of agit rocker well into advance [sic] senility.' Debuted live during the Out of Control tour, 'This Is England' was performed periodically throughout 1984. Played faster, and without the soul of the recorded version, it stands in marked contrast to most of the *Cut the Crap* songs which actually improved in a live context.

This Is Radio Clash
[Strummer/Jones/Headon/Simonon]
SINGLE: 11/81

First recorded at Marcus Music in Kensington in April 1981, then re-attempted at Electric Lady in November, the idea for 'This Is Radio Clash' came from a conversation between Strummer, Kosmo Vinyl and Bernard Rhodes about The Clash setting up their own radio station. Strummer admitted to *Melody Maker* in 1988 that he had ripped off the bassline from Queen's 'Another One Bites The Dust' (although that, in itself, had been derived from Chic's 'Good Times', one of music's most imitated bass patterns). Having recently read Michael Herr's *Dispatches*, a book which partly inspired *Apocalypse Now*, Strummer had the line 'ghettology as an urban Vietnam' looking for a song to go with it.

The rest of the lyrics were fleshed out later and these would include a series of witty images depicting the Clash as satellite pirates 'orbiting your living room'. The words are clearly for the most part directed at American ears, with references to the Bill of Rights and napalm. There are, however, some prosaic allusions, to Radio Free Europe and the American Armed Forces network, not to mention a heartfelt plea from the band to 'save us, not the whales!' The sinister laugh that begins the song was inspired by Grandmaster Flash and The Furious Five's 'The Message'.

Gavin Martin, traditionally one of The Clash's biggest supporters, gave the single a bitch of a review in *NME*, describing the song as 'another rag-bag of musical clichés and political simplifications ... a sprawling, splintered fantasy which presents the zombified vision of would-be guerrillas with rampant hysteria.' The song was subsequently covered by The Urge.

Don Letts' video for the single was drawn from footage taken from the unreleased *Clash On Broadway* film. It features on *This Is Video Clash* and *The Essential Clash*.

THREE CARD TRICK
[Strummer/Rhodes]
LP: *Cut the Crap*

One of Strummer's best songs from the period after Jones left The Clash, 'Three Card Trick' is a concerned series of observations on the UK's geographical and political divide – it covers the same kind of ground as **North and South**, but does so with infinitely more style.

A classic opening line is followed by Strummer bemoaning the breakdown of morality and compassion in a society that, as Margaret Thatcher would famously declare a year later, no longer existed. However, Strummer clearly believed that Britain's youth wouldn't fall for this outrage 'like your mummy and your daddy did.' With its descriptions of blood 'inside the fountain pen', the lyrics take on an almost Shelley-like (Percy, not Pete) edge. The song's reggae rhythm is a flashback to The Clash of old and although, like most of the *Cut the Crap* material, it suffers from a poor vocal arrangement (those ubiquitous 'all-the-gang-together' backing chants), 'Three Card Trick' is one of only two moments on the LP (the other is **This Is England**) where The Clash actually sound like The Clash.

Introduced to the band's live set on the Out of Control tour in early 1984, 'Three Card Trick' was the only post-Jones song to survive in The Clash's repertoire all the way to their final performances in the summer of 1985.

TIME IS TIGHT
[Booker T Jones]
LP: *Black Market Clash*

The Clash's version of Booker T And The MGs' soul classic 'Time Is Tight' (which had already influenced half a dozen of their songs) is rather charming. Jones not only duplicates Steve Cropper's delicate slide-guitar lines on the original recording, but also provides an ingenious replacement for Booker T's seminal organ solo by, basically, ignoring it and letting Simonon and saxophonist Gary Barnacle carry the riff. The Clash never sounded more like a surf band than on this. The Attractions' Steve Nieve contributes some piano lines to the second half of the song.

Recorded at Marquee Studios in March 1978, the song was remixed by Bill Price at Wessex in August 1979 during the *London Calling* sessions for inclusion on the American compilation LP, *Black Market Clash*. Often performed at soundchecks (Lester Bangs heard The Clash playing it in 1977, for example), the band's only known live performance of 'Time is Tight' was as the set opener of their April 1980 show at the Roxy Club in LA.

TOMMY GUN
[Strummer/Jones]
SINGLE: 11/78 **LP:** *Give 'Em Enough Rope*

Strummer was often accused of political naïveté. His ambiguous comments in early 1978 on the subject of terrorism – in the shape of the Italian Red Brigades and the German Red Army Faction (whose stated agenda was the very punk 'Don't talk, *DESTROY!*'; see **RAF 1810**) – seem in retrospect like incredibly one-dimensional shock tactics designed to get up as many noses as possible. As some Irish Clash fans loudly noted in *NME*, wearing an 'H Block' T-shirt to show solidarity with some of the IRA murderers held there was unlikely to go down well with the families of people killed on the Falls Road. 'One is never sure just which side [The Clash] is supposed to be taking,' wrote

Nick Kent in *NME*. 'The Clash use incidents ... as fodder for songs without caring.'

To be fair, Strummer's adoption of terrorist chic as part of his belief system actually represented something of a natural progression for him. The social rhetoric that had first fired The Clash was largely drawn, via Bernard Rhodes, from the American and French underground movements of 1968.

When Strummer sang 'you can be a hero in an age of none', his listeners implicitly understood the dichotomy in such a contradictory statement. The sentiments of 'Tommy Gun' may be contrived, but the song acts as a didactic – a pointed debunking of arrogant elitism juxtaposed with Strummer's insight into the mind of the murderously obsessive. 'Tommy Gun', like all great works of contradiction, succeeds chiefly because it exposes the confusion that is inherent in almost everyone's attitude to violence. In its own roundabout way, 'Tommy Gun' is actually a pacifist song – Strummer's updating of the sentiments of John Lennon's 'Revolution' (he, too, wanted to see the plan). But, mixed in with that, is a degree of posturing that brings to mind Alex in *A Clockwork Orange*, asking the rival gang to 'show us your yarbles, if you have any yarbles to show.' It was noticeable, however, that Jones had less time for such preoccupations as Strummer, interrupting an interview with *Record Mirror*'s Ronnie Gurr to observe pointedly that 'I don't support this killing stuff.'

'Really, I was saying that us rock'n'rollers are all posers and egomaniacs,' Strummer told Gavin Martin. 'But we know that terrorists are as bad, or worse than we are. They definitely love to read their own press ... I know they dedicate their life to a cause, but they're always posing for pictures.' In this regard, Strummer was probably thinking of the notorious Venezuelan terrorist assassin Ilich Ramirez Sanchez (Carlos the Jackal), whose wanted photograph featured him wearing shades. This had, by the late 1970s, acquired an iconic status almost the equal of Alberto Korda's art poster of Che Guevara that decorated every self-respecting student radical's bedroom wall.

With its machine-gun drum fills (suggested by Headon, who played them, magnificently, both in the studio and subsequently on stage) and awkward start-stop structure, 'Tommy Gun' was The Clash's first significant foray into sonic assault. A cacophony of controlled feedback, containing Jones' morse-code guitar solo and Headon's finest hour, beating out a military tattoo on his skins, this was The Clash at their most vicious.

The Clash's first Top 20 hit (number 19), a video for 'Tommy Gun' was filmed by Don Letts, his first with the band, at the soundcheck to the Harlesden Roxy show on 25 October 1978. First played live at The Rainbow in December 1977, 'Tommy Gunn' remained one of The Clash's most popular stage numbers. Dropped from the set in late 1979, it was subsequently revived in 1980, and appeared again in 1982 and 1984. The Mob's 1999 cover features on *City Rockers* and the song was also covered by Special Duties.

TRAIN IN VAIN
[Strummer/Jones]
SINGLE: 12/80 [US only] **LP:** *London Calling*

The Clash's first American hit (listen to the Beatlesque screams that accompany Jones singing the opening line on the version recorded at Bond's in June 1981 and featured on *From Here to Eternity*), 'Train In Vain' only existed because *NME* asked The Clash for a song to be used on a flexi-disc. The subsequent falling-through of the flexi left Jones' hastily composed song of regret at the break-up of a relationship with no home. Tacked onto *London Calling* as its unheralded final song, 'Train In Vain' was a last-minute triumph, a caustic PS to all those who had written off The Clash as having lost their way. As such, it forms an interesting counterpoint to **I'm Not Down**, written a few months previously. The references to needing new clothes and somewhere to stay reinforces the point that the song at least partly concerned Jones' feelings of depression in early 1979, after his flat was burgled.

One of The Clash's most painful songs of rejection, it was written, rehearsed and recorded in less than 24 hours. A US Top 30 hit in April 1980, the song was introduced to The Clash's live set during the Christmas 1979 gigs in London. Thereafter, it remained a fixture of live performances until Jones' departure. The video, a live version filmed by Don Letts at the Lewisham Odeon on 18 February 1980, features on *This Is Video Clash* and *Essential Clash*. It's notable for Strummer's amusing introduction 'We'd like to take the soul train from platform one... if you don't want to come, there's always a toilet.'

'Train In Vain' is easily the most covered song The Clash wrote, being subsequently recorded by Third Eye Blind, Ill Rapture, Dr. Haze and DJ X-Cel, The Sabrejets, Dwight Yoakam, Annie Lennox, The Manic Street Preachers and Jones Crusher. Kirsty MacColl also performed 'Train in Vain' on stage and the song features in the 2001 movie *Someone Like You*.

THE TRAIN KEPT A' ROLLIN'
[Bradshaw/Main/Kay]

A rock 'n' roll classic, best known from Johnny Burnette & His Rock and Roll Trio's 1956 recording and subsequently covered by bands as diverse as The

Yardbirds and Motörhead. This was one of Strummer's favourite songs and contemporary reports suggest that The Clash rehearsed a version immediately prior to the *Give 'Em Enough Rope* sessions.

TWIST AND SHOUT
[Medley/Russell] [80]

A 24-carat standard, first recorded by The Isley Brothers and, famously, covered by The Beatles in 1963. The Clash performed a rough and ready version on the Busking tour.

UP IN HEAVEN (NOT ONLY HERE)
[The Clash]
LP: *Sandinista!*

A visit to his grandmother's council flat after the opulence of his stay in flash New York hotels inspired Jones to write this scathing attack on 'These crumbling blocks/Reality estates that the heroes got.' The opening lyric may have been suggested by the similarly themed 'Towers Of London' by XTC, recorded in June 1980, two months before 'Up In Heaven'. The first verse, with its references to piss-stinking lifts and the invisibility of inhabitants to the outside world, suggests a return to the urban alienation discussions of songs like **London's Burning**. But the text here is more personal to Jones – it's clear that he's speaking from direct experience when he sings of wives hating husbands and children who 'daub slogans to prove they lived there.' The 'bourgeois clerks' responsible enrage Jones, who is compelled to ask 'How can anyone exist in such misery?' The song also quotes from 'United Fruit' by Phil Ochs, a Greenwich village folk-singer contemporary of Bob Dylan.

The composer's anger in his lyrics is matched by the strikingly ringing tones of his guitar, highly reminiscent of the sound created by post-punk bands like Gang of Four, Joy Division and Echo & The Bunnymen. Perhaps surprisingly, given the song's undoubted social relevance, it was never performed live.

80. A pseudonym for New York songwriter Bert Berns.

UPTOWN TOP RANKING
[Althia Forrest/Donna Reid]

Jamaican schoolgirls Althia and Donna recorded their Joe Gibbs-produced single in early 1977 and it was an underground smash with London's punk community during the summer. The song was on the jukebox at Rehearsal Rehearsals and, according to Strummer, The Clash messed about with a **Police & Thieves**-style cover for a few weeks, before wisely dropping the idea. Six months later, the rest of the country caught up when the original single knocked Wings' 'Mull of Kintyre' off the top of the UK charts.

VERSION CITY
[The Clash]
LP: *Sandinista!*

All the great bluesmen have jumped the soul train which, Strummer notes, can 'pull you through to better days'. So it's not likely to be something run by British Rail then. The train in question may be the 'Midnight Special' or the 'Mystery Train' that Elvis sang of. Strummer's allusions to a lonely soul at a crossroads were inspired by one of the great delta blues legends, Robert Johnson, and his 1936 song 'Cross Roads Blues', which tells of the singer selling his soul to the Devil for fame and fortune. Complete with allusions to Gibson and Fender, and its imagery of time and distance passing, the excitement surrounding 'Version City' is self-evident.

Headon's chugging, train-rhythm drums and Jones' wailing harmonica drive forward this addition to the long line of British impressions of American train songs ('Freight Train', 'Rock Island Line', 'The One After 909' etc). Mickey Gallagher's piano flourishes are an added touch of subtlety. With the backing track recorded in New York, the song was finished at Wessex. Surprisingly, this powerful song was never a part of The Clash's live set.

VERSION PARDNER
[Robert Ellen]
LP: *Sandinista!*

A somewhat pointless dub of **Junco Partner**, completed at Wessex during the later stages of *Sandinista!* The differences between the two versions lie largely in the excessive use of squeaky sound effects, put through an echo-box, on 'Version Pardner' by Mikey Dread. Nevertheless, contextually, 'Version Pardner' is one of the cornerstones of the *Sandinista!* song-cycle theme (see **Silicone On Sapphire**). And, like most of the reggae recordings on the LP, when all's said and done, it's pretty good to dance to at a party.

War in a Babylon
[Max Romeo/Lee Perry]

Yet another record on the Rehearsal Rehearsals jukebox was Max Romeo & The Upsetters' militant Lee Perry-produced single from 1976, 'War in a Babylon'. Part of an incredibly prolific collaboration between singer and producer during this period (including singles like 'Chase The Devil' and 'Norman'), the song uses the same basic rhythm as Bob Marley's 'Three Little Birds' but with a decidedly more in-your-face lyric. The Clash rehearsed the song, briefly, in late 1976.

Washington Bullets
[The Clash]
LP: *Sandinista!*

The key song to understanding the concept of *Sandinista!*, 'Washington Bullets' took a jaundiced view of America's influence on the outside world that was, in terms of popular awareness, a decade ahead of its time. While it suited the contemporary UK music press to portray The Clash's relationship with America as sycophantic, when they first toured the US Strummer, in particular, made a serious effort to talk to activists and members of various underground political groups. And to learn as much as he could about the reality behind the American Dream. One of the first people that he befriended was Mo Armstrong, a former Vietnam veteran who ran a second-hand record store in San Francisco. Armstrong supplied Strummer with literature about the Sandinistas and their revolution in Nicaragua which was, at the time, virtually unknown to the outside world. For The Clash to call their subsequent album *Sandinista!* in order to draw attention to this sinister saga of covert American Imperialism, and to its *defeat*, showed considerable courage.

It's easy to forget in a post 9/11 world but, for most of the last 50 years, and certainly since Fidel Castro's Marxist revolution in Cuba in 1959, the CIA's interest in foreign affairs hasn't been in the Middle East. Rather the Agency has been more concerned with propping up a collection of extremely dodgy right-wing dictatorships in Central and South America. To be fair, some of these administrations were democratically elected (though one can validly question the legality of at least a portion of such elections). Far more, however, were placed in power via coups with active CIA-aid. Consider Augusto Pinochet's murderous military overthrow of the Socialist Popular Front government of Salvador Allende in Chile in 1971 and the subsequent decades of torture and political oppression. Or Alberto Fujimori's war with the Maoist Shining Path in Peru. Or over 10,000 desaparecidos in a succession of ultra-right Argentinean regimes. Or the junta death-squads in El Salvador.[81] The list is a fairly sobering one.

In 1979 the Anastasio Somoza dynasty, which had held power in Nicaragua since 1936, was toppled by the revolutionary forces of FSLN, the Sandinistas, after US President Jimmy Carter denied Somoza military aid. Having waged a guerrilla war on Somoza for over a decade, the rebels' cause was aided by a popular uprising over the cold-blooded assassination of newspaper publisher Pedro Joaquín Chamorro by government forces in 1978. Once in power, the Sandinistas put in motion a genuine social revolution, but, with their Communist affiliations and strong links with Cuba, they antagonised the new US government under Ronald Reagan. Within a year, and with active CIA support, opponents to the new regime had formed an alleged 'liberation army', known as The Contras, in neighbouring Honduras. The fact that this force contained many former members of Somoza's notorious secret police bullyboys didn't seem to bother the Reagan administration, which, from its inauguration in 1980, had Nicaragua high on its hit-list in the region.

For the next decade The Contras, firing Washington's bullet, fought running battles against the Sandinistas, who were further hampered by stringent US sanctions. Yet they held onto power and, by the late 1980s, via the notorious Iran-Contra affair, America was being perceived, internationally, as the aggressors in this squalid little conflict in its backyard. Long-promised free elections were finally held in 1990 and, although the Sandinistas emerged as the largest party, they lost power to a liberal coalition led by Pedro Chamorro's widow, Violeta. To the surprise of those who had been numbed by a

---

81. During The Clash's 1981 New York residency, Strummer regularly shouted 'El Salvador' during performances of 'Washington Bullets'. 'The US is limbering up for *another* Vietnam,' he noted in a contemporary interview. 'It's only films like *Apocalypse Now* that are gonna save El Salvador.' (See also Charlie Don't Surf.)

decade-long US propaganda offensive, the Sandinistas abided by the democratic process and their leader, Daniel Ortega, handed over the presidency with good grace. Thus democracy achieved what the US had spent so much money, effort and lives trying to do by non-democratic means.

'Washington Bullets' features a litany of references to these events, and to others in the region like the brutal torture and murder of Chilean folk songwriter Victor Jara (1932-73), a supporter of Allende, by Pinochet's goons in the Santiago Stadium. The song also balances this rhetoric with a vicious indictment of Communism, specifically referring to the Russian invasion of Afghanistan in 1980 and to Mao's suppression of Tibet two decades earlier ('Ask the Dalai Lama in the hills of Tibet/How many monks did the Chinese get?').

There's also a bit of homegrown guilt concerning Britain's insatiable appetite for supplying both mercenaries and arms to some of the world's worst trouble spots. Other lyrics hit closer to home. When The Clash were in Kingston recording at Channel One, ten minutes after they had driven past a notorious trouble spot, Hope Road, a 14-year-old youth was shot in a drug deal, a haunting image that inspired Strummer's opening verse.

Musically, 'Washington Bullets' began – as many songs on *Sandinista!* did – via simple experimentation. 'Topper used to be first in every day,' remembered Bill Price. 'He'd wander round and find something interesting to play, like a marimba, and start jamming on it. We'd record some. Then the rest of the band would arrive, listen to it, and start overdubbing. That would form the basis for another track. Pretty soon we were up to track 35!'

A popular song on the live circuit, 'Washington Bullets' made its debut on the Radio Clash European tour in April 1981, and remained a fixture of the band's set for the rest of the year and the Far East tour in early 1982.

WE ARE THE CLASH
[Strummer/Rhodes]
LP: *Cut the Crap*

The lyrics to this track begin with a bugle-call to all the punk rockers, hip-hoppers, Brit-poppers and hair-droppers to come and pay their respects to The Clash, a band who 'ain't gonna be treated like trash.' It's pretty much all downhill from there.

Drowned in cacophonous vocals and jerry-built polystyrene-wall-of-sound guitars (some of which seem to belong in an entirely different song – for example, the oriental-sounding middle-section), 'We Are The Clash' is **Clash City Rockers** rebuilt with bionic legs but with a lobotomy having also taken place. Underneath its macho posturing, the song is all riff and no substance. 'We Are The Clash' was a regular part of the band's 1984 live set.

WHAT'S MY NAME
[Strummer/Jones/Levene]
LP: *The Clash*

How much Keith Levene contributed to The Clash's songs during his period with the band remains the source of some debate. His claim to have had 'a good hand' in all the songs on *The Clash* is unproven, although it's certainly true that his influence on The Clash's general sound was not inconsiderable. Levene's 2001 statement that 'I was contributing to the helter-skelter factor, to the velocity of how the songs were played,' almost certainly has some merit. [82] In *The Boy Looked at Johnny*, Parsons and Burchill wrote that 'Levene was soon too involved with heroin to devote any time to playing guitar, and quit The Clash, leaving behind only one song,' an allegation that Levene has always strenuously denied. Strummer's version was marginally different. 'Keith was doing a lot of speed. His weekend would go on till Tuesday and he wouldn't show up for rehearsals, so he kind of walked out by himself. I thought Keith was brilliant, but I realised [he] had other eggs to fry.'

Most sources suggest that 'What's My Name' was principally written by Jones and Levene around May 1976 at Riverside Studios, which The Clash were using before Rehearsal Rehearsals became available. Levene himself stated this in a 1999 interview, though three years later he remembered things slightly differently, saying that he wrote the bulk of the song in Sheffield in July during The Clash's first gig. He also noted that he showed the song first to John Lydon, with whom he would form Public Image Ltd. 'The only parts the song had when it came to me was, "What's my name?"' Strummer remembered in 2002. 'That's all the song was. I put in a couple of verses to keep the choruses apart.'

The song went through several different sets of lyrics judging from various 1976-77 live recordings before arriving at the final version – a howling catalogue of rejection, brutality and domestic violence ('dad got pissed so I got clocked'). The overall theme is the singer's inability to fit into conventional society – he couldn't even make it into the ping-pong club. His sense of identity crisis, a major theme of much 70s media, is such that, by the end of

---

82. Levene's major influence was Can's Michael Karoli. Levene's subsequent work with Public Image Ltd (specifically on 1979's avant-garde classic *Metal Box*) is a long way, both musically and conceptually, from The Clash. There are, however, interesting crossover points – PIL's experiments in dub-reggae, for instance.

the song, he is breaking and entering just to find out who he really is. (Earlier versions of the song featured a much more chilling coda, with the singer round the back of your house with a flick-knife rather than a celluloid strip. The suggestion being that society's depersonalisation had mutated into homicidal psychosis.) The recording was relatively straightforward, although it's much tidier than most previous (and, indeed, many future) live performances, highlighted by Jones' dramatic introduction. It also featured Simonon's best moments on the LP, a solid and sinister rising bassline that summons up the impression of urgency and fear.

Always an extraordinary number when performed live – see, for instance, the manic version filmed by Granada for *So It Goes* in 1977 – 'What's My Name' was introduced at The Screen On The Green in 1976. It remained a permanent fixture in The Clash's set until 1980 and was revived in 1984 with Simonon on vocals. A version recorded (with radically different lyrics and subsequent studio overdubs) at The Music Machine in July 1978, and featured in *Rude Boy*, can be heard on *From Here to Eternity*. Jones Crusher produced a straightforward cover of the song in 1999 and Charles Napier an instrumental version in 2003.

(WHITE MAN) IN HAMMERSMITH PALAIS
[Strummer/Jones]
SINGLE: 6/78 LP: *The Clash* [US only]

'We were a big-fat-riff-group,' Strummer noted in 1999 concerning his favourite self-written song. 'We weren't supposed to do something like that.' The song in question was a three-minute slice of perfectly formed white-reggae before the term, or even its creative limits, had been properly defined. Another building block in The Clash's attempts to incorporate the celebratory power and righteous anger of dub into their music, the song's importance lies in the fact that, unlike **Police & Thieves**, this was reggae not just played, but also written, by a white man. 'Strummer adopts a somewhat disillusioned worm's-eye view of how rapidly the aims and rhetoric of '77 have disintegrated into apathy [and] commercialised transient fashion,' wrote *NME*'s Roy Carr, in a fairly accurate reading of the song. How this came about is a story in itself.

On 5 June 1977 Strummer and Roadent went to the Hammersmith Palias on Shepherd's Bush Road for an all-night reggae show headlined by Jamaican toasters Dillinger, Leroy Smart and Delroy Wilson. What they found horrified them. 'It was all very *Vegas*. The audience were hardcore and I felt that they were looking for something different than a showbiz spectacle.' But, that wasn't all. 'A lot of black sticksmen were trying to snatch these white girls' handbags, and I intervened,' Strummer told Sean O'Hagan in 1988. He got some aggro for his trouble. It was another clear example of the complexity of the cultural mix that Strummer longed for, but was sussed enough to realise wasn't going to happen overnight (see also **White Riot**). 'I was getting at the division between white and black rebels,' he told *Melody Maker* some years later. 'And the fact that we gotta have some unity or we're just gonna get stomped on.'[83] Articulating his wish to hear roots-music instead of pop-reggae of the kind popularised by Ken Boothe ('Everything I Own'), or watch Four Tops-style dance routines, Strummer then turned his attention to the punk movement. There, he found a scene split by in-fighting and posing. Pausing only for a spiteful dig at The Jam (wearing Burton suits, changing their votes, 'turning rebellion into money'), and namechecks for Robin Hood and Adolf Hitler, Strummer ended with the confession that he was 'the all night drug-prowling wolf/who looks so sick in the sun.'

A hard, bitter, disgruntled song about lost ideals, '(White Man) In Hammersmith Palais' was The Clash's first radical departure from their established sound. It had already been part of the band's live set for six months (and had gone through several changes of lyric [84]) when it was recorded in February 1978 at CBS in The Clash's first self-produced session. The result was probably their finest studio recording to date, an effortless group performance in which each individual was given an opportunity to shine. This was particularly true of Simonon, who played, in effect, lead bass. A marginally different recording of 'White Man', produced by Sandy Pearlman during the *Give 'Em Enough Rope* sessions at Basing Street, was included on the various artists compilation LP *Rock Against Racism's Greatest Hits* (Virgin RAR1) in 1980.

The song entered The Clash's repertoire just weeks after it was written, in August 1977 at Mont de Marsen. It was to remain a virtual permanent fixture until The Clash's demise in 1985. A version recorded in September 1982 in Boston, and including lyrical quotations from The Ethiopians' 1966 rock-steady classic 'Train to Skaville', was included on *From Here to Eternity*. The song was subsequently covered by 311.

Footnote: The Palais occupied its site for 82 years until its closure in 1999. To mark its demise, the management presented Strummer with the sign from the venue's entrance. 'I guess I'll have to send a man with a van round to pick it up,' he told the *Independent*.

83. Strummer remained fascinated by the dream of a truly multicultural Britain and this marbled the lyrics of many of his songs. This trend reached its apex with his final LP, 2001's *Global A Go-Go*, and particularly 'Bhindi Bhagee'.

84. Originally the 'turning rebellion into money' line was 'millions of Yen down Japan-way.'

WHITE RIOT
[Strummer/Jones]
SINGLE: 3/77 **LP:** *The Clash*

On 30 August 1976 the Notting Hill Carnival, an annual Bank Holiday event in London's West Indian community since the late 1950s, exploded in an orgy of pent-up violence and aggression. The summer of 1976 had been the hottest in almost a century and, in the months leading up to the event, there had been unusually heavy police pressure on the black community. 'We were there at the very first throw of the very first brick,' Strummer would note proudly. The day had begun peacefully until, as Strummer remembered in 1999, 'Paul, Bernie and I [saw] this conga-line of policemen come through the crowd, under The Westway, up by Ladbroke Grove. Someone threw a brick at them, then another, [then] all hell broke loose. Obviously, that affects you.' While Rhodes cowered in the background and Simonon gleefully joined in with the brick-throwing, Strummer, along with some rastas, attempted a bit of arson on an abandoned car. With somewhat disappointing results. 'The Notting Hill riot was a black riot. It was a spontaneous expression of "We ain't taking this anymore." 'White Riot', in its clumsy way, was saying that white people had to become activists too or else they'd get plastered over in society,' Strummer told *Mojo*.

Not everyone in the band found the idea so appealing. 'I felt when you have a carnival you sometimes have a bit of aggro and it's no big deal,' Terry Chimes remembered in 2002. 'They were talking about it like it's some major event in world history. In fact it was just a few punch-ups, which happens all the time.'

In essence, 'White Riot' was Strummer's rewrite of The Rolling Stones' 1968 agitprop sermon, 'Street Fighting Man.' As Simon Frith noted in 1980, a song called 'White Riot' had appeared in *The Weathermen Songbook* (1969). 'The Weathermen, the guerrilla remnants of the 1960s' anti-racist, anti-war movements, had their own punk politics and their own theory of white devilry,' wrote Frith. The song's riff distantly alludes to The Who's 'Baba O'Riley'.

Recorded at both the Polydor demo sessions, and at Beaconsfield, the latter version of 'White Riot' is the one which appears on the UK *The Clash* LP. The subsequent single version, recorded at CBS on 28 January 1977, and complete with sound effects of a police siren, smashing glass and a burglar alarm, was included on the US version of the band's debut LP. Another effect was the 'stomping overdub', the sound of the band and a few friends like Roadent, Mark Helfont and Sebastian Conran [85] stamping up and down

---

85. The son of Habitat guru Terence and author Shirley Conran, Sebastian was an art student who came into the Clash circle via Micky Foote, whose girlfriend lived in a 15-bedroom property that Conran owned at 31 Albany Street in Regent's Park. Conran helped the Clash with their (cont. overleaf)

around a microphone. The main difference between the two versions is that the single has a much more organised guitar solo.

Both these recordings, however, are much slower than the one-thousand-miles-per-hour attack that the song was normally given in live performances, which began with the song's debut at The 100 Club in September 1976. 'Maybe when you're in a studio, you're less jazzed-up than when you're in front of a pulsating crowd,' Strummer suggested in 2002. An idea of the sheer psychodrama that was The Clash playing 'White Riot' on stage in 1977-78 can be glimpsed in the various performances of the song seen in *The Punk Rock Movie*, *Rude Boy* and the Dunstable promo presented on *The Essential Clash*.

Always a favourite with their audience, 'White Riot' was nevertheless a source of some conflict in the band, particularly to Jones, who soon tired of playing it. Consequently, after 1979, the song appeared live only occasionally – usually as a second or third encore after a particularly exciting gig. Sometimes, 'White Riot' would be prefixed by a lengthy drum solo and Strummer counting down from ten into the song (as at, for example, Atlanta in October 1979). During the post-Jones period, the song returned as a regular feature of the set and Strummer was still playing it (now rechristened 'Riot Riot') at his final live show in 2002. Cracker and Fang both produced rather uninteresting cover versions in 1999. The Angelic Upstarts also recorded it, while Alternative TV were still playing 'White Riot' live in 2003.

WRONG 'EM BOYO
[C Alphanso]
LP: *London Calling*

Like **The Israelites**, The Rulers' Jamaican rocksteady hit 'Wrong 'Em Boyo' was one of the records on the jukebox at Rehearsal Rehearsals and a particular favourite of Simonon. The song is a variant on the true story of the murder of Billy Lyons by Lee Sheldon on Christmas Day 1895 in St Louis. Lyons and Sheldon had spent the day drinking in Bill Curtis' saloon and were in high spirits. However, when the discussion turned to politics, they began arguing, the conclusion of which was that Lyons snatched Sheldon's Stetson from his head. The latter indignantly demanded its return ('Give me back my

---

85. (cont.) gear and designed posters for them, and Strummer soon moved into Albany Street. However, Sebastian's association with The Clash ended virtually overnight when rumours that Strummer was living in a millionaire's home reached the music press in early 1978. Strummer immediately returned to squatting in a house in Daventry Street, Marylebone.

hat, nigger' was the reported command). When he didn't get it, Sheldon produced his revolver and fired. As his victim fell to the floor, Sheldon took back his hat and coolly walked away. He was arrested at his lodging house soon afterwards. Lyons subsequently died. Sheldon, also known as Stag Lee, was later tried for murder. The first trial ended in a hung jury amidst major political controversy when Sheldon was defended by the celebrated lawyer Colonel Nat Dryden. However, Sheldon was convicted at a second trial, served his time and was eventually released in 1909, three years before his death from tuberculosis.

This incident soon became legendary in the American South, and moved into song – and down the Mississippi to the New Orleans delta, where the killer's name became, variously, Stagolee, Stagger Lee or Stack-A-Lee in a series of ballads. As early as 1911 Guy B Johnson published the first version in the prestigious *Journal of American Folklore*. The latter was the spelling on one of the earliest recorded versions, by Frank Hutchison in 1927. This was also the name of an R&B hit in 1950, performed by New Orleans singer Archibald in Professor Longhair style. Meanwhile, both Duke Ellington and Woody Guthrie had recorded songs inspired by the story, which also became the basis for such blues classics as Howlin' Wolf's 'Back Door Man'. Korean War veteran Lloyd Price wrote the pop classic 'Stagger Lee' in 1958 and had a huge hit with it (the song was subsequently covered by, among others, Jerry Lee Lewis and James Brown). This was the first version of the legend in which Stagger and Billy's fight was over gambling (in this case, a card game). Subsequently, several different songs with the same basic story have been recorded – including those by Fats Domino ('Stack and Billy'), The Isley Brothers and Nick Cave & The Bad Seeds.

Strummer, who had performed Price's version in The 101ers, chose to incorporate a few lines of this as an introduction. A live favourite following its debut performance in Boston in September 1979, the song, with its infectious skanking beat, was regularly played in concert during the next four years. On the Clash Take The Fifth tour, Strummer would often dramatically introduce the song with variations on the legend. At San Francisco, for example, this began: 'Deep in the jungle of rhythm and blues lurks a ghost, undiscovered by the future, forgotten by the past. On my left Mr Stagger Lee and on my right Mr Billy Liar. So make sure this is a fair contest ... no kicks below the cock line and no punch up the poop-chute and let's *rock it*.'

YMCA
[Jacques Morali/Henri Belolo/Victor Willis]

After The Clash's gig at Boston's Orpheum Theater on 19 September 1979, the band did an entertaining phone-in on the local WBCN radio station, at which they fielded a few sensible questions and several downright weird ones. One of the records they chose to play was the Village People's camp disco-classic 'YMCA'. They also sang along to it live on air. The ensuing, heavily bootlegged, racket simply has to be heard to be believed. The band were seemingly big fans of the song – in October 1978, when they visited Le Palace nightclub in Paris, they were infamously spotted shaking their funky stuff to 'YMCA', much to the disgust of local punks.

YOU CAN'T JUDGE A BOOK (BY LOOKING AT THE COVER)
[Willie Dixon]

Recorded by The Clash at Wessex in the first, frantic three days of activity during the *London Calling* sessions. Strummer, amusingly, retitled the song 'You Can't Judge A Woman (By Looking At Her Mother)'. Strummer's pseudonymous sleevenotes for *The Story of The Clash, Vol. 1* note that the song was performed at the soundcheck before a show in Detroit on the 16 Tons tour in 1980.

YOUR ROCKIN' MAMA
[Carl Mann]

A cover version rehearsed by The Clash in the spring of 1978, prior to the *Give 'Em Enough Rope* sessions.

THE ALBUMS

THE CLASH

UK: CBS 82000, 8 April 1977 [12] (LP/Cassette).
CBS 40 32232, November 1984 (LP/Cassette).
Columbia 468733-2, August 1991 (CD).
Columbia 495344-2, October 1999 (CD).

US: Epic 36060, 26 July 1979 [126].
Columbia 495345-2, October 1999.

UK: 'Janie Jones', 'Remote Control', 'I'm So Bored With The USA', 'White Riot',
'Hate & War', 'What's My Name', 'Deny', 'London's Burning', 'Career Opportunities',
'Cheat', 'Protex Blue', 'Police & Thieves', '48 Hours', 'Garageland'.

US: 'Clash City Rockers', 'I'm So Bored With The USA', 'Remote Control',
'Complete Control', 'White Riot', '(White Man) In Hammersmith Palais',
'London's Burning', 'I Fought the Law', 'Janie Jones', 'Career Opportunities',
'What's My Name', 'Hate & War', 'Police & Thieves', 'Jail Guitar Doors', 'Garageland'.

Mick Jones (guitar, harmonica, vocals), Joe Strummer (guitar, vocals),
Paul Simonon (bass), 'Tory Crimes' (drums).

RECORDED: CBS Studio 3, Whitfield Street, London. 10-27 February 1977.
Except 'White Riot', National Film and Television School 8-track studio, Station Road,
Beaconsfield. January 1977.
PRODUCED: Micky Foote.
ENGINEERED: Simon Humphrey.

NOTE: Early UK copies of *The Clash* came with a red sticker which, together
with two coupons collected from subsequent issues of *NME*, entitled
purchasers to send for a free single (NME CL-1), containing 'Capital Radio',
'Listen' and a Tony Parsons interview with The Clash.[86]
Initial copies of the US release featured a free single (Epic AE7 1178):
'Groovy Times'/'Gates of the West'.

The Clash first entered a recording studio in November 1976 when Polydor
A&R man Chris Perry, keen to sign the band, offered them the opportunity to
cut some demos. With 60s maverick Guy Stevens as their chosen producer

---

86. This was carried out on 21 March 1977 on the London Underground. 'I had to be at a tube
station at a certain time,' recalled Parsons in 1999. 'It was like *Help!* or *A Hard Day's Night*: suddenly
these heads popped out the door, I jumped on and we went round the Circle Line shovelling
amphetamine sulphate up our noses and talking.'

and house engineer Vic Smith at the controls, the band recorded primitive versions of 'Career Opportunities', 'Janie Jones', 'White Riot', '1977' and 'London's Burning' at Stratford Place Studios near Oxford Street. The first two of these recordings would subsequently appear on *Clash On Broadway*. 'We all had a lot of regard for Guy Stevens,' Terry Chimes remembered.[87] 'It was evident that the A&R man and the engineer didn't.' The results were, therefore, somewhat disappointing. Chimes also recalled that the studio had a nylon carpet which caused him a series of static electric shocks from his drums. Vic Smith had insisted that Strummer try to pronounce his words, feeling that the lyrics were a vital part of The Clash's raison d'être. Strummer did, and the results, he told Tony Parsons, 'sounded like Matt Monroe. I thought "I'm never doing that again."' Chris Perry, who had narrowly missed signing The Sex Pistols the previous year, would also have The Clash snatched away from him when they signed for CBS. It was, however, to be third time lucky for Perry who, on Shane MacGowan's recommendation, signed The Jam to Polydor in March. He would subsequently create Fiction records and launch The Cure.

Next, The Clash tried a do-it-yourself approach, recording six songs (the five from the Polydor sessions plus 'I'm So Bored With The USA') with their soundman Micky Foote at the National Film And Television School in Beaconsfield, which they used free of charge due to Julien Temple's connections there. The raw, feral version of 'White Riot' on *The Clash* comes from this source.

Once the band signed with CBS, it was quickly arranged for The Clash to begin recording at the company's Whitfield Street Studio 3, a tiny room at the top of the building. They discovered on arrival that this was the same studio where The Stooges had recorded *Raw Power* with David Bowie in 1973. 'It was the shittiest room in London,' remembered Strummer, 'but when I found that out I kissed the floor.' He also recalled that the studio was 'very sparse, like a long oblong.' 'Hessian wallpaper and drab 50s decor,' is how it was described in the *Clash On Broadway* booklet. The Clash maintained their combative attitude even, perhaps especially, now. 'They wouldn't shake my hand because I was a hippy,' recording engineer Simon Humphrey told *Mojo*'s Pat Gilbert. 'The first time I met Joe Strummer he was setting up with his Twin Reverb [amplifier] next to the drum kit. I said you can't put it there. He asked why. I said, because it's going to affect the drums, it needs a bit of separation.' Strummer's reply was reportedly, 'I don't know what separation is. And I don't like it!'[88]

87. This wasn't a view shared by everyone. 'I was afraid of Guy, because I'd had dealings with him in the past,' noted Jones in 1991. 'I was in a band [Little Queenie, later Violent Luck] auditioning for him and he said "I love the band but the guitarist ain't cutting it."'

88. It was during this period, February 1977, that Strummer had been beaten up by a 'psychotic teddy boy' in the toilets at the Speakeasy club, which probably didn't improve his sociability.

Humphrey, then 21, had previously worked on sessions with Gary Glitter, Smokie, Hot Chocolate, Mud and ABBA. 'I think I got [the job] cos I was the youngest. I can't think of any other reason,' he told *Uncut*. Humphrey also admits that nobody within CBS had any idea of what to do with The Clash other than to get them into the studio quickly and record something in case the punk bubble burst. Thus, just three days after The Clash signed with CBS, on Friday 28 January 1977 they were in Whitfield Street recording 'White Riot' and '1977', the two sides of their first single. Temporarily without a drummer, the band persuaded Terry Chimes to guest on the sessions and those of the subsequent LP.

They also elected to use Micky Foote – who had no previous studio experience – as producer. 'It was a matter of set up and keep the overdubs to a minimum,' remembered Foote in 1991. 'The album couldn't have been done any other way.' A friend of Strummer's since his days in Newport, Foote had been The 101ers' soundman and had joined Strummer in defecting to The Clash the previous summer. 'One of the things that they were absolutely adamant about was that they didn't want to use anybody who was part of the old school,' Humphrey remembered in 2002. A possible reason for this was their experiences with Guy Stevens who, according to Strummer in 1977, had been 'too pissed to work' during the November sessions. 'I think [Foote] was fairly honest. I don't think he pretended to be something he wasn't,' Humphrey told *Uncut*.

The album was recorded in just 12 days, over three consecutive Thursday-to-Sunday sessions starting on 10 February. 'No one else is booking the studio so why not let these idiots have the downtime, [that way] we're not losing any money,' was what Strummer believed CBS's attitude was towards them. Nevertheless, the band, and Jones in particular, used the time wisely. 'Mick was the first person to clock that there was potential [in] double-tracking, overdubbing, etc,' remembered Humphrey. 'I like the first album best,' noted Jones in 1999, despite having often claimed in the past that, because of his outrageous speed-intake at the time, he couldn't even remember the sessions for it. 'Mick picked up the studio-vibe very quickly,' Humphrey noted. 'He was the one running the show, teaching Paul what to play. Mick had three different guitars, including his Les Paul Junior which was really classy. One day it fell over and the neck snapped. He was absolutely devastated, so upset that he had to go home.' Terry Chimes, too, had definite ideas on how he wanted to be recorded. 'I insisted, right at the start, on a live drum sound. I remember saying if we had a 'deadened' sound, it would be like The Eagles.'

As far as Strummer was concerned 'any guitar of note on the record is Jonesy. I'm in there, chundering away with the bass drum and the snare, but

88. It was during this period, February 1977, that Strummer had been beaten up by a 'psychotic teddy boy' in the toilets at the Speakeasy club, which probably didn't improve his sociability.

I'd say anything you can actually discern must be Jonesy.' In contrast to some of the studio experimentation on the record – the phased guitars on 'Cheat' for instance – the recording of 'Janie Jones' couldn't have been simpler. 'It was recorded almost live,' noted Simon Humphrey. 'I seem to remember that being a very raw track. Only one guitar.'

Although Terry Chimes was only sitting in with the band when he recorded the LP, he was still disappointed to find himself credited under his band nickname, Tory Crimes, on the cover. In Sean Egan's 2001 *Mojo* article, Strummer described Keith Levene's subsequent claims to have co-written most of the songs on *The Clash* as the 'demented outpouring of an overexcited mind.' The front cover featured a fearsomely moody shot of Strummer, Jones and Simonon by American photographer Kate Simon – a friend of the band. It had been taken, in late 1976, in an alley opposite Rehearsal Rehearsals. The extraordinary back-cover photo of the police charge at the Notting Hill riot was the work of another band associate, Rocco Macauley. 'Everybody at the record company was shocked when *The Clash* went straight into the charts,' Simon Humphrey confirmed. 'They hadn't realised the extent of what was happening.'

Reviews of *The Clash* were, in the hostile landscape of the 1977 music scene, predictably polarised. 'Membrane-scorching tension, a natural feel for dynamics ... a mirror reflection of 1977 working-class experiences that only seem like a cliché to those people who haven't lived through them,' wrote Tony Parsons in *NME*. '[The Clash] chronicle our lives and what it is to be young in the Stinking Seventies better than any other band, and they do it with style, flash and excitement.' *Sniffin' Glue*'s Mark Perry and *ZigZag*'s Kris Needs were Clash camp followers anyway so their reviews, describing the LP as 'the most important album ever released' and 'one of the most important records ever made' respectively, should surprise no one (though Needs' colleague, John Tobler, merely commented that the LP was 'all right'). Representatives of older voices in the rock community were considerably harder to please. Hence the curt dismissal of *The Clash* by critics such as *Melody Maker*'s Michael Oldfield, who considered it to be 'a tuneless repetition of chords at breakneck speed. [It] should go down well with the Blank Generation. Thank God I'm "Too Old" to have enjoyed it.' In *Sounds*, Pete Silverton wrote that 'The Clash are the essentials of street London personified' and gave the LP five stars.

Although, by today's standards, the production sounds thin and weedy (and the songs oddly slow in the context of what are now considered punk's accepted rules), *The Clash* has arguably aged far better than many of its contemporaries. The freshness and power it had in 1977 may have dissipated slightly, but thematically it's still an absolute barometer of its time. And, perhaps, of other times too. Pete Silverton's review included a comment about 'Remote Control' and 'London's Burning' containing 'SF/Fantasy phraseology', and several commentators have subsequently noted a distinct futurist edge that marbles the proto-realism of *The Clash*'s landscape of piss-stinking tower-blocks and urban ghettos. This is certainly Marcus Gray's view, citing the possible influence of David Bowie's mid-70s LPs like *Diamond Dogs*, as well as the 'bleak dystopias' of Anthony's Burgess' *A Clockwork Orange* and the works of George Orwell and J G Ballard.

Epic, the US branch of CBS, were so appalled by the crude sound quality of *The Clash* that they dithered for two years over whether to grant the LP a US release. Eventually, with *The Clash* having sold a reported 100,000 copies on import, they finally put out a version in July 1979. This dropped 'Deny', 'Cheat', 'Protex Blue', '48 Hours' and the Beaconsfield version of 'White Riot' in favour of various 1977-78 singles and B-Sides (plus the 1979 recording of 'I Fought the Law'). Strummer actually rather liked the US version. 'It makes a good collection,' he told *Uncut* in one of his final interviews. 'If you've never heard the group before, it's a good bunch of tunes.'

Despite Epic's indecision, those American critics who heard *The Clash* were entranced. 'I hate gushing about a new band, but The Clash have produced such a strange and wonderful blend of pop, metal, aggro and politics that I keep playing the sucker,' wrote *Trouser Press*'s Ira Robbins. Tom Carson in *Rolling Stone* added that 'Perhaps more than any album ever made, *The Clash* dramatised rock 'n' roll as a last, defiantly cheerful grab for life, something scrawled on the run, on subway walls. Here was a record that defined rock's risks and its pleasures, and told us, once again, that this music was worth fighting for.' In 1979, Robert Christgau described *The Clash* as 'the greatest rock 'n' roll album ever manufactured anywhere.'

Give 'Em Enough Rope

UK: CBS 40 82431, 10 November 1978, [2] (LP/Cassette).
CBS 40 32444, November 1984 (LP/Cassette).
Columbia 40 32444, April 1989 (CD).
Columbia 495346 2, October 1999 (CD).

US: Epic 35543, 17 November 1978.

'Safe European Home', 'English Civil War', 'Tommy Gun', 'Julie's Been Working for the Drug Squad', 'Last Gang In Town', 'Guns on the Roof', 'Drug-Stabbing Time', 'Stay Free', 'All the Young Punks (New Boots and Contracts)'.

Mick Jones (guitar, piano, vocals), Joe Strummer (guitar, piano, vocals), Paul Simonon (bass, vocals), Topper Headon (drums), Gloves Glover (piano), Al Fields (piano), Al Lainer (piano), Bob Andrews (keyboards), Stan Bronstein (saxophone).

RECORDED: Utopia Studio, Fitzroy Road, London; Basing Street Studios, London; The Automatt, Folsom Street, San Francisco; The Record Plant, West 44th Street, New York. May-September 1978.
PRODUCED: Sandy Pearlman for K.P. Productions Inc.
ENGINEERED: Corky Stasiak, Dennis Ferranti, Gregg Caruso, Kevin Dalimore, Chris Mingo.

Is *Give 'Em Enough Rope*, as Pat Gilbert suggests, 'the 'difficult second album' blown up to epic proportions, that never could or would replicate the zeitgeisty thrill and naïve brilliance of its legendary predecessor'? Or is it a great rock 'n' roll album, under-appreciated at the time of its release and only now finding its voice? Bit of both, actually. 'We weren't ready to make a second album,' Strummer remembered. 'It took so much out of us to make the first one.'

How Sandy Pearlman came to produce the record has never been fully explained. 'The first time I heard of Pearlman was in Bernie's Renault,' Strummer said in 1991. 'Bernie was checking out Blue Öyster Cult. I thought he'd gone bonkers.' With his shoulder-length hair, baseball cap and interest in the occult, Pearlman was certainly an unlikely choice to work with The Clash. Unlikely, but not completely off the map; Pearlman's CV also included producing the New York punk band The Dictators, of whom Jones, in particular, was fond. Pearlman himself told *Mojo* in 2003 that when he first met The Clash they told him that they loved the sound of his Blue Öyster Cult productions. Jones remembered that 'we weren't concerned who did it, because it was going to be great whatever.'

With recording scheduled to begin in March 1978, Rhodes paid for Jones and Strummer to fly to Jamaica in December 1977 for a two-week writing trip. The holiday was something of a nightmare, but at least they came back with a couple of great songs, 'Safe European Home' and 'Drug-Stabbing Time'. However, Simonon, pissed off that he hadn't been invited, decamped for an 'educational' trip to Leningrad and Moscow with Caroline Coon. He still hadn't come back by early January when Strummer, Jones and Headon began rehearsals and demoed some of the new songs on 4-track. Headon's friend Gary Barnacle contributed to these, playing saxophone on 'Drug-Stabbing Time'. When Simonon eventually returned, he was banished to an upstairs room with tapes of the new songs to learn the basslines.

The band played several shows in January to try out some of the new material, and to let Pearlman see them in action. At one of these, there was a nasty altercation between Robin Crocker and the new producer, although Pearlman himself says that the subsequent retelling of the story has been grossly exaggerated. 'He took a swing at me, I took a swing at him. He cut my cheek ... My nose was not broken and they were incredibly apologetic,' Pearlman told *Mojo*. There was a further delay when Strummer had to enter hospital in late

January to recover from his phlegm-induced hepatitis. This meant that the proposed March sessions at CBS were postponed. The band went back to Rehearsals to work on further new material, while Pearlman returned to the US.

When Pearlman returned, he found that, because of the pigeon-shooting incident, Headon and Simonon were required to report daily to Kentish Town police station. He booked the band into the nearby Utopia Studios but, after just a few days, they were asked to leave. 'The engineer, Corky Stasiak, was a surfer dude who introduced them to American-grade ganja, which they weren't used to,' remembered Pearlman. 'One night I heard noises coming from outside the studio. I opened the door and saw that Simonon had upturned a pot plant and he and Topper had created a track for his trials bike in the lobby.'

Pearlman subsequently took The Clash into Island's state-of-the-art Basing Street studio off Portobello Road. There, he made them do multiple takes of each song until they got the backing tracks note-perfect. As an example of Pearlman's perfectionism, his team took three days just to get the drums set up in a satisfactory position – remember that the entire *The Clash* LP had been recorded in 12 days. Only Headon was proficient enough to get his parts right every time (much to Pearlman's delight), and – not being a natural musician – Simonon was more prone to mistakes than everyone else. This made for a lot of studio time and some bad tempers all round. It is often alleged (though, interestingly, not by Pearlman) that Jones replaced many of Simonon's bass parts after Paul had gone home.

For Simonon, recording *Give 'Em Enough Rope* was 'the most boring situation ever ... It was such a contrast to the first album and it ruined any spontaneity.' Brassed off with the interminable retakes, Simonon asked Dave Mingay, who was filming some of the sessions for *Rude Boy*, if it would be possible to have films running in the studio – suggesting some of his favourite war movies. Mingay came up, instead, with hundreds of reels of documentary footage from The Imperial War Museum from the likes of Stalingrad and El Alamein. A projector and screen were set up and the band spent many hours' downtime drinking beer and watching films of Stukkas dive-bombing. There was even some suggestion that they might be more inspired if they played while the films were running, but the noise of the projector ruled this out.

Strummer had acquired a new guitar for the recordings, a Gibson semi-acoustic as played by Chuck Berry, and when *Sounds'* Pete Silverton attended the sessions he found Strummer in a relatively benign mood, albeit constantly referring to Pearlman and Stasiak as 'the General' and 'the Captain' respectively. Silverton was more surprised to find Jones almost permanently stoned. Nevertheless, it's generally agreed by all involved that Jones worked harder on these sessions than the rest of the band put together. 'I think they realised it was a learning experience, though it was never expressed as succinctly as that,' remembered Johnny Green. 'Mick was right over [Pearlman's] shoulder all the time, watching what he was doing.' Despite the time they took, the sessions were very productive; in addition to the ten songs on the LP, The Clash also recorded early versions of 'Groovy Times', 'Gates of the West' and 'One Emotion', several covers and a reworking of 'White Man' which was subsequently used on a compilation LP.

Pearlman was something of a gourmet. He often ordered Indian takeaways from three different Notting Hill curry houses – typically, noted Johnny Green, a dahl from one, the sag aloo from another and nan bread from somewhere else. He and Stasiak were subsequently dubbed The Glutton Twins by The Clash's crew. By contrast, the band's diet usually involved a take-away from the local McDonald's.

It has been well documented that Jones became heavily involved with cocaine during this period. The band's hard-line punk ideology was, thus, in danger of imploding. 'Mick's hair was getting longer,' noted Simonon curtly. 'Mine and Joe's were getting shorter.' Pearlman remembers being told, during this period, that Jones was about to be sacked and replaced with ex-Sex Pistol Steve Jones. Certainly during July 1978, while the band were touring the UK, Steve Jones did appear at several dates as a guest. Johnny Green, however, suggests that 'there were a lot of games being played back then.'

CBS didn't like the results of the Basing Street sessions and, at one stage, threatened to take the mixing of the LP – provisionally entitled *Rent-A-Riot*, then *Take No Prisoners*, then *All the Peacemakers* – not only out of The Clash's hands, but out of Pearlman's too. That situation was averted when Pearlman insisted that Jones and Strummer fly to America to finish the album during August in better-equipped studios in San Francisco and New York. The experience changed both men's lives. 'We were based in Chinatown,' remembered Jones. 'We made friends with people like Mo Armstrong. We had a lovely time.' Attending the cinema one afternoon before their nightly session, Jones and Strummer found themselves watching one of the worst examples of bloated 70s extravagance, Robert Stigwood's disastrous *Sgt. Pepper's Lonely Hearts Club Band*. 'It was unbelievable,' Jones noted. 'They had every ligger in LA! Everyone with no better place to go.'

Having spent three weeks in The Automatt, the songs finally started to take shape in Jones and Strummer's mind. Greil Marcus heard some of the tracks and noted that Pearlman had broadened the band's sound – 'There are more guitars per square-inch on this record than on anything in the history of Western civilization,' the producer proudly told him. But, Marcus continued, Pearlman hadn't compromised The Clash's darkness or their force. 'He couldn't,' noted Strummer. 'He's been trying for six months to turn us into Fleetwood Mac. I think he gave up last night.' It's often stated that the guitar sound Pearlman produced was the antithesis of punk's minimalist approach. However, it must be said that Jones' work on this LP isn't a million miles away from what several of his contemporaries were doing at exactly the same time – especially The Jam's Paul Weller. [89]

Before the final stage of recording in New York, Jones and Strummer got a week off. The former decamped to LA, where he stayed at the Tropicana and became a visiting God to the emergent US West Coast punk scene. Strummer, meanwhile, headed off, Jack Kerouac-style, for a roadtrip across the country with a couple of friends in a Chevy pickup. The final touches of an LP begun in a dingy London rehearsal room eight months previously were recorded in a studio with a panoramic view of downtown Manhattan. The boogie piano on 'Julie's Been Working for the Drug Squad' was initially played by The Living Legends, blues pianists Al Fields and Gloves Glover, but later, to Jones and Strummer's bemusement, it was re-recorded by Blue Öyster Cult's Al Lainer. The saxophone on 'Drug-Stabbing Time' was provided by Stan Bronstein of Elephant's Memory, who had previously worked with John Lennon. Jones would later note: 'We had lots of fun watching our album being recorded by session musicians.'

During this period Jones also played with Sid Vicious' pick-up band at a gig at Max's Kansas City. 'People there were as out-of-it as you can be without actually being dead,' the guitarist said later. In September, Simonon and Headon were flown out to New York to hear the final mixes. The record they heard was big, brash and furious. The Clash were no longer a band who sang Strummer's parochial little Westway vignettes about tower blocks and dead-end jobs. Now they were dealing with prophetic visions of international terrorism, the rise of the far right and pan-continental culture shock. It had been hard work ('it was 98 days in Hell' remembered Jones; 'we came out like zombies,' added Strummer), but at last it was finished.

Give 'Em Enough Rope was released in November 1978, the cover poached by New York designer Gene Grief from a Chinese Communist postcard showing a dead cowboy being scavenged by vultures. 'When *Give 'Em Enough Rope* came out in England, it was considered the greatest thing ever recorded,' Sandy Pearlman wrote in 2002. 'It was given five stars by *Sounds*. It was on

---

89. Compare, for instance, the solo on 'Stay Free' to Weller's playing on several songs on The Jam's highly regarded 1978 LP *All Mod Cons* – notably 'In the Crowd', 'To Be Someone' and 'Down in the Tube Station at Midnight'. *All Mod Cons* was the first Jam LP to be exclusively produced by Vic Coppersmith-Heaven, the man who had engineered The Clash's Polydor demos in 1976. Like Pearlman, Coppersmith-Heaven's approach was to multi-track Weller's guitars into 'a punk wall-of-sound', a far cry from the 'no overdubs' ethic of 1977.

the front page of music papers, went into the charts at number two, and was universally greeted as the second coming of French bread. Even though I, actually, don't think it was the best record I ever made, it was the best reaction I had ever got.' To an extent this is true. Dave McCullough in *Sounds* did, indeed, rave about the LP. *NME*'s Nick Kent was more cautious, suggesting that it highlighted as many Clash weaknesses as it did strengths. Hailing 'Safe European Home' as their 'finest moment', he nevertheless derided the band's 'facile concept of shock-politics.'

In *Melody Maker*, one-time Clash champion Jon Savage's review bore the taint of a man who felt seriously betrayed. 'The Clash's view of the human condition,' wrote Savage, 'while imprecisely expressed, isn't very sanguine this time out.' He concluded that 'It's as though they see their function in terms of 'the modern outlaw' ... So do they squander their greatness.' In America, by contrast, the LP got a fantastic reception. Greil Marcus in *Rolling Stone* ('The Clash rain fire and brimstone, with a laugh. *Give 'Em Enough Rope* is a rocker's assault on the Real World in the grand tradition of *Beggar's Banquet* and *Let It Bleed*') and Lester Bangs in *Village Voice* were especially enthusiastic.

The standard line for most retrospective reviewers is that *Give 'Em Enough Rope* was the point at which The Clash almost overdosed on rock 'n' roll excess and that we all had one hell of a lucky escape. Unfortunately, such opinions completelyignore the influence the LP subsequently had. For most young Americans who got into the band, it was *Give 'Em Enough Rope* and not *The Clash* that was the soundtrack to their lives. As Pete Doggart noted in *Record Collector*, 'Like Chris Thomas with the Sex Pistols, Pearlman beefed-up The Clash by overdubbing guitars. In 1978, his booming, three-dimensional land-scape seemed the stuff of American AOR stations; in 1999, ironically, it sounds more 'punk' (aggressive, confrontational, in-yer-face) than the band's debut.' Listen to the ballistic fury of 1990s US groups like Rage Against the Machine, Nirvana, Green Day, Rancid, Offspring, Four Star Mary et al and you'll hear bands who absorbed and digested *Give 'Em Enough Rope* in all its ragged, pompous, overblown, magnificent glory.[90]

In need of a major re-evaluation, *Give 'Em Enough Rope* is the sound of a band spreading its wings, not having them clipped.

LONDON CALLING

UK: CBS CLASH 3, December 1979 [9] (LP/Cassette).
Columbia 460114-1, February 1988 (LP/Cassette).
Columbia 460114-2, April 1989 (CD).
Columbia 495347 2, October 1999 (CD).

US: Epic 36328, January 1980, [27].

'London Calling', 'Brand New Cadillac', 'Jimmy Jazz', 'Hateful', 'Rudie Can't Fail',
'Spanish Bombs', 'The Right Profile', 'Lost in the Supermarket', 'Clampdown',
'The Guns of Brixton', 'Wrong 'Em Boyo', 'Death Or Glory', 'Koka Kola', 'The Card Cheat',
'Lover's Rock', 'Four Horsemen', 'I'm Not Down', 'Revolution Rock', 'Train In Vain'.

Mick Jones (guitar, vocals, piano), Joe Strummer (vocals, rhythm guitar, 'pianner'),
Paul Simonon (bass, vocals), Topper Headon (drums, percussion),
Micky Gallagher (organ), The Irish Horns (brass), Barry Glare (whistling).

RECORDED: Wessex Studios, London July-November 1979.
PRODUCED: Guy Stevens.
ENGINEERED: Bill Price, Jerry Green.

Having been effectively homeless since sacking Bernard Rhodes in October 1978, The Clash needed a new base of operations to replace Rehearsal Rehearsals. Johnny Green and Barry Glare found it in the shape of Vanilla, a small rehearsal studio on Causton Street near Vauxhall Bridge. 'It had the advantage of not looking like a studio,' wrote Green. 'Out front was a garage. We left instructions: "We ain't here." We were not disturbed.' Apart from a brief trip to Newcastle for the *Alright Now* TV show in March, the band were in Vanilla daily throughout the spring of 1979, working on new material. They would occasionally run through old songs for their forthcoming live shows ('Protex Blue' never sounded fresher, according to Green), but mainly it was the new material that would form the basis of *London Calling* that was concentrated on.

Jones and Headon worked tirelessly trying different rhythms and musical styles. All the band were heavily involved in the development of the songs. 'The Guns of Brixton' came about when Simonon realised that 'You got money for writing songs. I was doing the artwork and clothing but not getting paid for it. I thought, Sod that, I'm going to get involved in the music.' Any guests who showed up were usually taken across the road for a game of five-a-side football (The Clash's individual football styles are lovingly described by Johnny Green in *A Riot Of Our Own*) and then sent round the corner to the pub till the day's work had finished. 'People from the record company came down and we played them,' remembered Jones. 'They got quite into it. I don't think anybody was hospitalised.' Everyone agreed that a classic was in the making.

After a few weeks, the band decided to record some demos. With the help of The Who's soundman, Bob Pridden, Green and Glare hired a TEAC 4-track portastudio and, once they learned how to balance the sound, recordings began. These included a bunch of cover versions like The Rulers' 'Wrong 'Em Boyo' and the Edwards/Ray composition 'Get Up', which they turned into 'Revolution Rock'. Three of the new songs – 'London Calling', 'Hateful' and

90. The movie *High Fidelity* features a sequence in which two characters discuss The Clash as one of the two obvious inspirations for Green Day (Stiff Little Fingers being the other).

'Koka Kola' – specifically dealt with the problem of drugs, something very much on the band's mind at the time following the death of Sid Vicious in February. Other songs like 'Death Or Glory' and 'Four Horsemen' were wry and funny statements from a group that, if you believed certain sections of the music press, didn't have a humorous bone in their bodies. The recordings sounded fantastic. In fact, Strummer told Charles Shaar Murray that he wanted to record the entire LP there, thus bypassing expensive studio time. CBS would have none of it, so Jones suggested reproducing the intimacy of the Vanilla recordings at Wessex, a small studio that The Clash had used earlier in the year for *The Cost of Living* EP and the *Rude Boy* soundtrack overdubs. CBS agreed but wanted a name producer. Top of Strummer's list was Guy Stevens. [91]

A DJ-turned-producer who had first got The Who listening to R&B, christened Procul Harum, wrote the sleevenotes for a Chuck Berry EP (the first record Joe Strummer ever bought) and had been the ideas man behind Mott The Hoople, Stevens had worked with The Clash before, in 1976, recording their Polydor demos. By 1979, he was, according to Pat Gilbert, 'on the skids, crippled by a drink problem.' Strummer found him in a bar in Soho. Stevens was interested, but wanted to hear the material before committing himself. Unfortunately, he didn't have a tape recorder. Johnny Green was dispatched on two missions. Firstly to buy a tape deck in Tottenham Court Road for the producer. And, secondly, to buy another tape deck after Green got drunk and left the first one on the tube. Stevens loved the songs and said he was in. 'He made me feel really at ease,' remembered Simonon. 'If I played a wrong note, he didn't care.'

In Wessex, the band set up with Stevens and engineers Bill Price and Jeremy Green. The first song they recorded was a cover of Vince Taylor's 'Brand New Cadillac'. After a searing run-through, Stevens announced 'It's a take!' Headon pointed out that the performance had sped up halfway through. 'So what?' asked Stevens, not unreasonably, 'all great rock 'n' roll songs speed up!' It was going to be that sort of LP. The sessions went remarkably well from the off; indeed, while The Clash were in Finland for the Rusrock Festival, Stevens told *NME*'s Roy Carr that an entire LP's worth of material had been recorded in just three days.

Legends have been created around Stevens' behaviour during the *London Calling* sessions. He had a ritual of getting a taxi from his home to the studio via Highbury, Arsenal's ground, for inspiration. Finding that there was a Clash fan working in the Arsenal office, for a few T-shirts Guy was allowed into the ground each day to kneel in the centre circle. There was also the memorable occasion when Stevens poured red wine into the studio's piano to 'improve the

---

91. The band had recently returned to Wessex, in July, to record 'Revolution Rock' and 'Rudie Can't Fail' with Bill Price for the *Rude Boy* soundtrack.

sound.'[92] 'We were doing 'Death Or Glory',' remembered Simonon. '[Guy] just lost it. He ran into the room, picking up chairs and throwing them against the wall.' On another occasion, Stevens lay down in front of Maurice Oberstein's car until the executive agreed that the recordings he had heard were magnificent.

'I remember Mick strumming country songs, Paul reggae, Topper disco,' Johnny Green told *Mojo* in 1999. 'They started swapping instruments; Mick would play drums ... There was a high level of communication.' The rhythm tracks were recorded first, followed by a guide vocal. When Jones fretted over perfecting a solo, Stevens would tell him, 'For fuck's sake, Jerry Lee Lewis would have this in the can and be round the boozer by now.' Later, when a guitar rep called at the studio with a selection of new models for Mick, Stevens noted that they were all very nice 'but *you* could do it on *that*,' pointing to Strummer's battered old Telecaster.

After a while, however, Stevens' antics started to become something of a liability to the music and he was effectively sidelined. On some occasions the band would tell him not to turn up. Often, when he did, Johnny Green was given the job of keeping him out of the way while recording was taking place. Essentially, Jones and Price became *London Calling*'s uncredited producers.

'We'd spent five months rehearsing *London Calling* and banged it off in four weeks,' remembered Strummer. 'The horn parts were all done in one day by The Irish Horns, who made up their own arrangements on the spot. We'd suggest the way it should go, they'd fill it out. They hit five tunes from scratch.' There was also another new face in the studio. 'I was asked to do the session,' Mickey Gallagher remembered. 'I got sent a copy of *Give 'Em Enough Rope*, had a listen and thought, my God, what do they want *me* to do?' Gallagher's untamed organ riffs added a vital missing ingredient to The Clash's sound and, for the next two years, both in the studio and on stage, he became, to all intents and purposes, the band's fifth member.

'We're still digging reggae,' Strummer told Adrian Thrills, 'what we've added is Motown, but as a simple four-piece group plus two tablespoons of organ and half-a-pint of horns. To me, music is feeling, the best there is. Every time Bob Geldof comes out with that emotionless eunuch's voice, it boosts me ten miles in the soul, just for the irritation.' 'We're stepping into a few areas that we've left untouched, like sexuality, urban psychosis, plumbing the depths,' Strummer told Paul Morley.

By September, the band had recorded 18 songs – including reworkings of 'Revolution Rock' and 'Rudie Can't Fail' from the pre-Stevens sessions. They

92. Although Stevens emerged from *London Calling* with his critical standing rehabilitated, sadly he didn't live to enjoy the fruits of this renaissance. On 29 August 1981, he overdosed on a drug prescribed by his doctor to help reduce his alcohol dependency.

were, therefore, able to tour the US in complete confidence. 'The album was mixed by Bill Price while we were in America,' Strummer told Bill Flanagan. 'Mick changed one or two tracks, but in the main it's Price's mix.' The band briefly toyed with calling the LP *The New Testament* but, ultimately, settled on naming it after one of the songs. Back at Wessex after the US tour, they did further mixing (also recording 'Armagideon Time' for the single's B-Side). Still annoyed over CBS charging £1.49 for *The Cost of Living* EP, Strummer suggested making *London Calling* a double-LP. CBS refused point-blank. The Clash then asked if they could include a free single with a one-disc LP. CBS agreed to this, and also to it being a 12-inch single. It was at this point that The Clash insisted that this 12-inch single should play at 33rpm and contain eight songs. Soon, this became nine songs. In November, *NME* asked The Clash to record something for them to be released as a flexi-disc. Jones wrote 'Train In Vain' overnight and the band recorded it the next day, only for IPC, the paper's publisher, to suddenly decide that they couldn't afford to produce the flexi. Thus, the song was used as the final cherry on the cake of *London Calling*. It was too late to amend the sleeve or the label (although the song's title was carved into the run-out groove of the fourth side). Outmanoeuvred, CBS agreed to what was, to all intent and purposes, a double-LP retailing at the cost of a single. 'It was our first victory over CBS,' Strummer told *Sounds'* Chris Bohn in December.

Photographer Pennie Smith accompanied the band on The Clash Take the Fifth tour with the intention of getting a photo to be used for the *London Calling* cover. She described the experience as 'like being on a commando raid with the Bash Street Kids.' At the New York Palladium on 21 September, Pennie got her shot. Simonon decided that what was needed was a bit of The Who-style auto-destruction. He began repeatedly smashing his bass on the ground. Smith saw him coming straight towards her and moved back as she took the photo, explaining why it's slightly out of focus. It didn't matter – in one single image Smith, the band's favourite photographer, had captured everything there was to say about The Clash. She then spent the rest of the night trying to persuade Strummer that the photo wouldn't make a good cover. 'I was wrong,' she gladly admitted in *Westway to the World*. 'The sound of that bass hitting the stage is probably the best we ever made,' Strummer sarcastically told MTV in 1989. Ray Lowry designed the cover as a parody of the first Elvis Presley LP, with the same pink and green lettering and its iconic central photo.

To promote the forthcoming LP, on 7 December 1979 Jones and Simonon were interviewed by John Tobler for Radio 1's *The Friday Rock Show*. A strange forum, perhaps, given the show's usual heavy metal bias, but maybe that was the whole point. Was The Clash's new style a reaction against the Americanisation of the last LP, they were asked? Jones agreed that it probably was and said the double-LP's price tag was 'at great personal expense. To us.' He answered questions on his writing partnership with Strummer and noted that 'I get certain types of song to sing. Weedy ones!' What, Tobler wondered, were they going to say to those who claimed that *London Calling* didn't sound like The Clash? Both Jones and Simonon replied that it sounded like The Clash to them. 'People can't expect us to stay the same – that *thing* from 1977. We like music too much. Staying the same kills your love of music,' concluded Jones. 'I'm so glad they got rid of Sandy Pearlman,' added presenter Tommy Vance after premiering 'The Right Profile' and 'The Guns of Brixton'. 'It was getting far too American ... They're back into good old British rock. The Clash. *Great!*'

On the LP's release, *NME*'s Charles Shaar Murray, having presumably forgotten his 1976 desire to gas The Clash in their own garage, wrote that this was 'the first of The Clash's albums [that is] truly equal in stature to their legend,' and yet it was one that 'for the most part disposes of the more indigestible portions of that legend.' *London Calling*, he continued, made up for 'all the bad rock 'n' roll played in the last decade.' At *Melody Maker*, James Truman was also impressed. 'The Clash have discovered America, and by the same process, themselves,' he noted. Garry Bushell of *Sounds*, on the other hand, gave the LP only two stars and titled his review *Give 'Em Enough Dope*. 'Unable to go forward, they've clutched at straws, ending up retrogressing via Strummer's R&B past and Jones' Keith Richards fixation, to the outlaw imagery of The Stones and tired old rock clichés.'

In the US, it was universal praise all round; Robert Christgau described *London Calling* as 'the greatest double album since *Exile On Main Street*.' In *Rolling Stone*, Tom Carson considered the LP 'passionate and large-spirited. *London Calling* celebrates the romance of rock 'n' roll rebellion in grand, epic terms.' It didn't merely reaffirm The Clash's own commitment to rock-as-revolution, Carson continued. 'Instead, the record ranges across the whole of rock's past and digs deeply into legend, history, politics and myth for its images and themes. Everything has been brought together into a single, vast, stirring story – one that, as The Clash tell it, seems not only theirs but *ours*.' A decade later, the magazine would award *London Calling* the epitaph 'album of the 80s'. [93] Long-time fan Lester Bangs wrote a frankly relieved review for *Soho Weekly News*, which concluded: 'They pulled it off – a double album that

93. Often seized upon by sneering British critics as an example of the silliness of All-Things-American, it is necessary to deflate an oft-quoted urban myth. Yes, *London Calling* was indeed released in December 1979. In the UK. In America, it was released during the second week of January 1980, making its branding as 'album of the 80s' completely valid in the context of an American magazine. It actually takes a degree of anal-retentiveness to care about such minutiae but, while we're on the subject, if anyone can come up with a decent alternative to *London Calling* as 'album of the 80s', this author is sure *Rolling Stone* would be delighted to hear from you.

actually doesn't seem to contain any filler, made on the cheap which keeps CBS happy and sold at a righteous price.'

'Comparison to *Exile On Main Street* is unavoidable,' wrote John Piccarella in *Village Voice*. 'Both albums are surprisingly loose in the wake of more carefully produced single albums. Both expand on previous keyboard and horn experiments, and both extend recently discovered styles. The outlaw-amid-big-business conceit of *Exile* is echoed, with a moral commitment the Stones wouldn't dream of, in The Clash's rudeboy maverick rebellion.' 'Symbolically, the first important rock album of the 1980s,' added the *New York Times*' John Rockwell.

Yet not everyone was happy and, indeed, some listeners shared Garry Bushell's anger. 'I remember a skinhead in Berlin saying, "Vot is that? My grandmother likes 'Wrong 'Em Boyo'!"' noted Strummer years later. 'For him the clean sound of that album was a travesty!'

SANDINISTA!

UK: CBS FSLN 1, December 1980, [19] (LP/Cassette).
Columbia 463364-2, April 1989 (CD).
Columbia 495348 2, October 1999 (CD).

US: Epic 37037, December 1980 [24].

'The Magnificent Seven', 'Hitsville UK', 'Junco Partner', 'Ivan Meets GI Joe', 'The Leader', 'Something About England', 'Rebel Waltz', 'Look Here', 'The Crooked Beat', 'Somebody Got Murdered', 'One More Time', 'One More Dub', 'Lightning Strikes (Not Once But Twice)', 'Up In Heaven (Not Only Here)', 'Corner Soul', 'Let's Go Crazy', 'If Music Could Talk', 'The Sound of the Sinners', 'Police On My Back', 'Midnight Log', 'The Equaliser', 'The Call Up', 'Washington Bullets', 'Broadway', 'Lose This Skin', 'Charlie Don't Surf', 'Mensforth Hill', 'Junkie Slip', 'Kingston Advice', 'The Street Parade', 'Version City', 'Living In Fame', 'Silicone On Sapphire', 'Version Pardner', 'Career Opportunities', 'Shepherds Delight'.

Paul Simonon (bass, vocals), Topper Headon (drums, marimba, vocals), Joe Strummer (vocals, guitar), Mick Jones (guitar, vocals), Mickey Gallagher (keyboards), Tymon Dogg (vocals, violin), Norman Watt-Roy (bass), J P Nicholson (keyboards), Ellen Foley (vocals), Davey Payne (saxophone), Lew Lewis (harmonica), Ivan Julien (guitar). Ray Gascoigne (percussion), David Yates (brass), Gary Barnacle (saxophone), Bill Barnacle (brass), Jody Winscott (steel drums), Noel Tempo Bailey (steel drums), Anthony Nelson Steele (steel drums), Gerald Baxter-Warman (steel drums), Terry McQuade (vocals), Rudolf Adolphus Jordan (vocals), Den Hegarty (vocals), Luke Gallagher (vocals), Ben Gallagher (vocals), Maria Gallagher (vocals), Battersea (barking).

RECORDED: Pluto Studios, Granby Row, Manchester; The Power Station, 53rd Street, New York; Electric Lady, 8th Street, New York; Channel One, Kingston, Jamaica; Wessex Studio. February-September 1980.
RECORDED & MIXED: Bill Price.

PRODUCED: The Clash.
VERSION MIX: Mikey Dread.
ENGINEERED: Jerry Green, JP Nicholson, Lancelot Maxie McKenzie.

If *London Calling* was The Clash's *Exile On Main Street*, then *Sandinista!* is undoubtedly their *White Album*. A wildly ambitious, self-indulgent, schizophrenic fusion of politically provocative soundbites against a soundscape containing dozens of radically different musical styles. 'We went into Electric Lady after the American tour,' Strummer told David Hepworth in 1980. 'We made some music and it just kept going on and on.' And on. 'Every day we showed up and wrote phantasmagorical stuff,' Strummer remembered in 1999. 'Everything was done in first takes and worked out 20 minutes beforehand. It was the most beautiful time ever. To be in New York, in Jimi Hendrix's studio, everything on a roll.'

The first *Sandinista!* recording was actually made in Manchester. The instrumental 'Shepherds Delight' was completed in February 1980 at Pluto during the sessions that produced the 'Bankrobber' single. After the completion of the US leg of the 16 Tons tour, Simonon was required to be in Vancouver for six weeks, starting on 11 March, to film his role in the Lou Adler movie *Ladies and Gentlemen, The Fabulous Stains.*[94] Strummer, Jones and Headon checked into New York's Iroquois Hotel – inspired by stories of James Dean having stayed there – and got Epic to book them into The Power Station for a few days. The idea, at this stage, was simply to record some cover versions and to sketch out a few new songs with Bill Price and Mikey Dread, to be used on the collection of singles that it was the band's intention to release during 1980 (see 'Bankrobber'). 'Police On My Back' was the first song recorded.

After a few days jamming, The Clash moved across town to Electric Lady. Mickey Gallagher and fellow Blockhead, bassist Norman Watt-Roy, flew in to assist for five days, after which Jones and Strummer shared bass duties between them 'in Paul's style', as Strummer told *New York Rocker*'s Richard Grabel. A chance encounter with Strummer's old busking partner, Tymon Dogg, led to an invitation for him to join the sessions. 'It was an experiment in recording where you go into a studio, with all the pressure on you, without any material!' remembered Mickey Gallagher. 'The mood was very creative.'

'Mick Jones bringing in the new sound of New York. Simmo with his reggae thing, me with my rhythm and blues thing and Topper with all his soul chops. We could do that,' said Strummer in *Westway to the World*. Marcus Gray suggests that the musical direction The Clash took during this period

---

94. Also known as *All Washed Up*, this Nancy Down story of a female rock 'n' roll band was Simonon's acting debut (if one discounts *Rude Boy* as 'acting', in any real sense of the word).

may have been, in part, a response to harsh music press criticisms of the 'retrogressive tendencies' of their 1979 output. Whatever the reason, The Clash barely left the studio for the next three weeks. Strummer, along with Headon and lighting man Warren Steadman, built a sanctuary in the studio with flight cases. A bubble world, cut off from reality, it became known as the Spliffbunker, in which many songs were written and much weed was smoked. 'It was a place to retreat for musicians and groovers only,' remembered Strummer. 'It's a good system, because it stops everyone hanging out in the control room. The engineer can't work with all that babble. I wrote nearly all the lyrics on *Sandinista!* in the bunker.'

While in New York, the band (and Jones in particular) picked up on the still radically new hip-hop sounds coming out of radio stations like WBLS. 'Jonesey was always on-the-button when it came to new things,' Strummer noted in 1999. 'That stuff we made the week after he came back from Brooklyn with those Sugarhill records – it *still* rocks.' 'I was so gone with the hip-hop that the others used to called me 'Whack Attack',' Jones remembered in 1991. 'I'd walk around with my beatbox all the time and my hat on backwards.'

After three weeks in Electric Lady, The Clash, including the returned Simonon, flew with Mikey Dread to Jamaica to use the Channel One Studios in Kingston. 'We recorded 'Junco Partner' and it sounded *great*,' remembered Strummer. 'I was sitting at the piano figuring out the chords for the next song when Mikey tapped me on the shoulder and said, "Quick, we've got to go. The drugmen are coming to kill everyone!"' It subsequently emerged that the last foreigners to use Channel One had been The Rolling Stones, who had recorded some of *Emotional Rescue* there several months previously. They made sure they weren't bothered by the local drug barons simply by handing out lots of cash. Assuming that every white rock band was similarly loaded, The Clash were thus perceived as greedy and ripe for being taught a lesson. As on Strummer and Jones' previous visit to Jamaica, they ended up having to scuttle back to their safe European home with their tail between their legs. Less *The Harder They Come*, more Jacques Tati, as Strummer subsequently noted.

The recording of *Sandinista!* also saw the band's fourth change of management in four years. 'We're not very organised,' Strummer told *Smash Hits*. 'We're not like The Jam who've got a tight ship, with Dad running things. I'm glad we're the way we are, it's more exciting.' 'By *Sandinista!* it was all getting a bit weird,' remembered Peter Jenner. 'There were white powders going around in certain quarters of the band.' Things reached a head once the LP was completed. 'I tried to get the band to do something about Topper,' Jenner told *NME*'s Len Brown in 1989. 'I was told to fuck off and mind my own business.'

Having toured Europe in May and June, the band reconvened the *Sandinista!* sessions in August at Wessex. Bill Price tended to oversee the recording of backing tracks, while Jeremy Green was entrusted with overdub sessions. 'Mick was the one with the overall plan,' Green noted. 'Every track was written down with every overdub that would be needed. If it was done and acceptable, it was noted in a certain colour.' One evening during this period The Blockheads, who had been performing their single 'I Want To Be Straight' on *Top of the Pops* dressed as policemen, decided to visit their old mates. They burst into Wessex and Jones, thinking a raid was in progress, flushed his stash down the studio loos. When *NME* reported the prank a few weeks later, they hinted heavily at Headon's blossoming heroin problems, noting that Topper 'was last seen wearing a false beard and reading a paper upside down in the Gatwick departure lounge.'

Hearing some initial mixes of the New York sessions, Richard Grabel asked, as many journalists had over the previous two years, whether the American influence evident in their new material represented a betrayal of The Clash's British fans. 'Who gives a shit whether a donkey fucked a rabbit and produced a kangaroo? At least it hops and you can dance to it,' was Strummer's suitably surreal reply. It's also worth noting that The Clash's attitude towards America in general was hardly fawning – the lyrics of 'Charlie Don't Surf' and 'Washington Bullets' make that very clear.

Having previously succeeded in releasing a double-LP, The Clash now went one stage further. With enough material for a triple, they presented *Sandinista!* to CBS. Furthermore, they insisted, it should retail at less than six pounds, thus maintaining Strummer's July 1979 boast to Garry Bushell that there would never be a Clash LP at that price. To their surprise, CBS agreed, with just two conditions. Firstly that the package would count as one LP, not three, towards The Clash's recently extended ten-record deal. And secondly, that the band would forego all claims to performance royalties on the first 200,000 copies sold. In the interests of getting the LP out in the format they wanted, The Clash agreed. 'To do that in Thatcher's Britain, during a recession, was a flamboyant gesture,' Strummer told Vic Garbarini. Asked by *Rip It Up*'s Duncan Campbell how CBS had responded, Jones noted: 'If it had happened in Japan, all the executives would have killed themselves.'

When all 36 tracks were assembled, the task of banding them up fell to Jones and Bill Price. In fact, there are actually 38 songs on *Sandinista!*, but The Clash's obsession with having six songs per side meant that Mikey Dread's version of 'The Crooked Beat' ('The Crooked Dub') was merely included as an extension of the main song. Similarly, Maria Gallagher's dreadful singalong to 'The Guns of Brixton' was tacked onto the end of 'Broadway'.

Some sides were much stronger than others; the sixth in particular, while conceptually dazzling and linked by several amusing Strummer soundbites, is among the most wilfully anti-commerical bits of vinyl a major rock group has ever released. 'Only bold men go there,' Strummer noted wryly in 1988. Several songs were also linked by radio samples and studio chatter. Once completed, Strummer's lyrics were given to the *Guardian* cartoonist Steve Bell to illustrate for the album's insert, titled *Arm-agideon Times No. 3*. Like *London Calling*, *Sandinista!* featured a moody Pennie Smith cover shot of the band lined-up against a wall behind Kings Cross station.

Sandinista! was generally crucified in the UK music press, albeit with some backhanded praise given to The Clash for at least trying to be different. David Hepworth, in *Smash Hits*, was typical of many reviewers when noting that 'we should be grateful that they're let down by ambition.' Nick Kent, in *NME*, considered *Sandinista!* 'ridiculously self-indulgent' and added: 'this record is strong testimony that The Clash have – temporarily at least – lost a grip on their bearings and find themselves parked in a cul-de-sac.' Offended by Greil Marcus' accusation that Kent himself had started a 'snivelling backlash' against The Clash in the UK via his review of *Give 'Em Enough Rope*, Kent responded by expressing distaste for the 'absurdly sycophantic reviews' The Clash had been receiving in America. 'The Clash will survive,' he concluded. 'Why they bother to is the really painful question that *Sandinista!* forces me to ask.'

'A floundering mutant of an album,' noted *Melody Maker*'s Patrick Humphries. 'The odd highlights are lost in a welter of reggae/dub overkill.' *Sounds*' Robbi Millar was more positive, finding 'an adventure of diversity and wit, excellence and dross. When it is good it is *very* good.' 'Loose, occasionally anarchic, sometimes fun, always different,' wrote *Record Mirror*. The standard line for most reviewers of *Sandinista!*, however, was voiced by *Trouser Press*'s Ira Robbins. 'This would have made a *great* album and a half.'

In the American mainstream press, it was a very different story. 'If The Clash, by insisting on their own heroism, continue their willingness to gamble it all away and *still* keep winning, they may yet inspire a viable rock-culture politics,' wrote *Rolling Stone*'s John Piccarella. '*Sandinista!* is an everywhere-you-turn guerrilla raid of vision and virtuosity. A sprawling, scattered smoke-screen of styles, with an expanded range that's at once encyclopaedic and supplemental.' The *New York Times*' Debra Rae Cohen considered that *Sandinista!*'s 'initially daunting two-hour sprawl turns out to be structured with both passion and purpose, skilfully paced to provide – like a live performance – breathing-spaces, humour, and moments for reflection. While much of the music is a far cry from The Clash's original two-minute skirmishes, the record fulfils the promise of those early songs, extending their struggle by universalising it.'

Sandinista! has, in fact, aged remarkably well – an obstinately eclectic collection of world music that was a decade or more ahead of its time. A major influence on the Madchester/baggy dance-rock fusion of the late 80s, *Sandinista!*'s best songs still sound fresh and contemporary today. The CD age has finally done the music justice, revealing a particular soundscape, a new world to go to for two and a half hours while only forcing listeners out of their seats once in order to change discs. As John Floyd wrote in 2002, 'Those looking to score the soundtrack for the next round of World Trade Organisation protests, whether they be hip-hoppers picking up the torch from fallen prophets Public Enemy or the Zapatista-feting Rage Against the Machine, could do a lot worse than look to *Sandinista!* for inspiration.' In *The Irish Times*, Michael McCaughren noted, 'The first time I heard mention of Nicaragua's Sandinista revolution was on the cover of the 1980 Clash album, bought with Christmas pocket money. Five years later I found myself lying in bed with dengue fever in a dusty village in rural Nicaragua, a punk-rock political journey inspired by The Clash's magnificent triple album.'

In 1998, Simon Goddard, in *Uncut*, offered the opinion that *Sandinista!* was 'the most innovative rock album ever made.' Examining the work almost two decades after its release, Goddard noted: 'evidence suggests that The Clash's only crime was to credit their audience with a fearless thirst for the shock of the new that, depressingly, turned out to be wildly optimistic.'

For one person at least, *Sandinista!* was always a source of immense pride. Although in 1989 Strummer considered the LP 'overindulgent', a decade later he had recovered his enthusiasm. 'We recorded all that music in one spot at one moment. For better or worse, *that's* the document,' he noted in 1999. 'I stand by all of it,' he told *Uncut*'s Gavin Martin. 'Ask the skinheads in Perth, a place that's 3500 kilometres from the nearest city. They take acid and listen to it all night.' While Jones amusingly commented that he saw the triple LP as 'a record for people on oil rigs or arctic stations,' Strummer remained, until the day he died, defiantly protective of *Sandinista!* 'I'm proud of it,' he said in *Westway to the World*. 'It's a magnificent thing. I wouldn't change it even if I could ... It's outrageous. And then, to release it like that, it's triply outrageous!'

COMBAT ROCK

UK: CBS FMLN 1, May 1982, [2] (LP/Cassette).
CBS 40 32787, November 1986 (LP/Cassette).
Columbia 32787, January 1991 (CD).
Columbia 495349 2, October 1999 (CD).

US: Epic 37689, May 1982, [7].

*'Know Your Rights', 'Car Jamming', 'Should I Stay Or Should I Go', 'Rock the Casbah',
'Red Angel Dragnet', 'Straight To Hell', 'Overpowered By Funk', 'Atom Tan', 'Sean Flynn',
'Ghetto Defendant', 'Inoculated City', 'Death is a Star'.*

Topper Headon (drums, percussion, bass, piano), Mick Jones (guitar, piano, harmonica, vocals), Paul Simonon (bass, vocals), Joe Strummer (vocals, guitar), Allan Ginsberg (vocals), Ellen Foley (vocals), Joe Ely (vocals), Futura 2000 (vocals), Tymon Dogg (piano), Poly Mandell (keyboards), Gary Barnacle (saxophone), Kosmo Vinyl (vocals).

RECORDED: Marcus Music, Kensington Gardens, London; Ear Studios, Preston Road, London; Electric Lady, New York. April 1981-January 1982.
MIXED: Glyn Jones.
PRODUCED: The Clash.
ENGINEERED: Joe Blaney, Jerry Green, Eddie Garcia.

The product of three different recording locations, *Combat Rock* was intended from the outset to be a distillation of the musical experimentation that had enriched *London Calling* and *Sandinista!* But at its heart lay a dichotomy that would ultimately pull The Clash apart. Strummer wanted a single LP, full of good old fashioned rock 'n' roll. Jones wanted another sprawling-experimental *Sandinista!*-style collection of ambient textures and radical new sounds. Believing that Epic had failed to push their last record directly because of economic considerations, Strummer told *RAM*'s Keri Phillips, as sessions got underway, 'if my tape operator wants a copy of *Sandinista!* – and remember we're not in Peru or Baghdad or Bombay, we're here in New York, supposedly the centre of the Western World – he can't even buy it. That's why [*Combat Rock*] is gonna be one record.'

The sessions in April and September 1981 had produced a series of demos, most (though not all) of which were re-recorded in the expensive splendour of Electric Lady either side of Christmas 1981. In such an environment, grandiose excess manifested itself in all sorts of ways – particularly musically. 'Does *everything* have to be a raga?' Bernard Rhodes is reported to have asked after sitting through seven and a half minutes of 'Sean Flynn'. It might have given Strummer his hilarious opening line to 'Rock the Casbah', but Rhodes *did* have a point. [95]

---

95. '*Rāga*' is an Indian term meaning an improvised harmonic structure. In the West, interest in Hindustani classic composition, particularly the sitar work of Ravi Shankar, was high among the more cerebral of the 60s groups. Introduced to Shankar's music by Roger McGuinn and Dave Crosby of The Byrds (who themselves experimented with the form on their 1966 song 'Why?', described in contemporary interviews as 'raga-rock'), George Harrison's zealous conversion to such sounds had a huge impact on The Beatles' studio work 1966-68. Through this, the influence of raga was implicit in rock music (Brian Jones' use of a sitar on The Rolling Stones' 'Paint It Black' and the incorporation of the pseudo-Indian drone into The Kinks' 'See My Friend', The Who's 'The Good's (cont. opposite)

Then, to top it all, Headon was arrested at Heathrow for possession of heroin. When he appeared at Uxbridge Magistrates Court on 17 December, his barrister pleaded that he was 'a valuable member of a band, recently voted one of the world's top five drummers.' Topper received a fine of £500.

With its working title of *Rat Patrol From Fort Bragg*, the LP was due to be completed in early January 1982, before The Clash embarked on their ground-breaking tour of Japan, Australia, New Zealand and South East Asia. But overdubbing and, indeed, recording was still taking place with the tour just days away. The LP was behind schedule for its intended April release – and way over-budget. Tempers reached breaking point when Strummer accused Jones of sabotaging the band by insisting that the LP had to be recorded in New York. 'He said "I was only joking,"' Strummer told Richard Cook in 1984. The situation reached such animosity, with Strummer describing his partner as often acting 'like Liz Taylor in a filthy mood,' that Strummer and Jones made sure they weren't in the studio together, recording their respective overdubs at different times to avoid further confrontation.

In late January, Jones presented the rest of the band with a 15-track 65-minute double-LP that included all the songs The Clash had worked on at Electric Lady except 'Overpowered By Funk' and 'Long Time Jerk'. Strummer later referred to it as a 'home movie mix' and rejected it. 'I don't believe anyone is so great that they don't write crap sometimes,' he told Bill Holdship in 1984. 'Mick wouldn't have that ... I'm supposed to be his buddy and partner. I said, "Mick, I don't think you can produce." And it was, "You bastard! I thought you were my friend!"'

The Far East tour was about to get underway so a compromise was reached whereby studio time was booked in Australia for the whole band to work on a new mix. 'It's all very well being heard by cult freaks, but I want to get through to the creep who's filling his head with "Stuff 'er on the bed and shove it to her!"' Strummer stated at a Sydney news conference. 'We were trying to re-mix *Combat Rock* after gigs,' Headon remembered in 1991. 'You can imagine what your hearing's like. They said, "You have a go at mixing it." I tried to be all professional, slide the bass up a bit, oh I can't hear the drums ... By the time I'd finished every fader on the desk was on full.' And still the fighting continued. 'I remember having a two-hour argument with Mick about the level of the bass on 'Know Your Rights',' Simonon noted in *Westway to the World*. 'I wanted it louder and deeper, a reggae sound. I think he'd got

95. (cont.) Gone' and The Yardbirds' 'Evil Hearted You'). By the turn of the decade, via another Shankar devotee, Led Zeppelin's Jimmy Page, such cross-genre fusion was a key element in the more pretentious and self-indulgent end of progressive rock. It was probably something along these latter lines that Rhodes was suggesting.

bored of playing guitar by then. He had equipment that would make it sound like a harpsichord, or an orchestra.'

With the LP's mixing in chaos, The Clash few to Thailand in March. 'We went mad,' Jones told James Brown in 1991. 'It was like *Apocalypse Now*. When you go that far away it takes time to get back.' Metaphorically as well as literally, it seems. During the trip, the band had their money stolen, marooning them in their hotel. Then Simonon became sick with what was initially diagnosed as a twisted colon (it turned out to be food poisoning). It was during this period that Pennie Smith took the anguished photo that would grace *Combat Rock*'s cover. She subsequently claimed that she, physically and conceptually, saw the group fall apart before her eyes during the session on a railway siding outside Bangkok.

'There was too much music to fit on a single album,' remembered Kosmo Vinyl. 'We decided to get some outside help. Bernard kept going on about Gus Dudgeon. I was thinking how is a bloke that's done all those weedy orchestral Elton John records going to be able to mix The Clash? The day we went to see him, Bernard said, "I've been getting his name wrong, it's Glyn Johns."' Johns was a veteran of the 1960s London music scene, having worked with The Rolling Stones, The Who, The Beatles and The Faces. Johns didn't particularly like mixing material that he hadn't recorded himself but he was sufficiently intrigued by what he heard to agree to work with The Clash.

He booked into Wessex at the end of March 1982, faced with the nearly impossible task of producing something that would satisfy everyone. 'The Beautiful People Are Ugly', 'Kill Time', 'Cool Confusion' and 'First Night Back In London' were dropped (the latter two would subsequently become B-Sides; the former remains unreleased). 'Overpowered By Funk' was put back and Strummer re-recorded his vocals for 'Know Your Rights'. Jones did likewise for 'Should I Stay Or Should I Go', cleaning up some of the lewd lyrics. 'Mick's attitude was that I ruined his music,' Strummer told *Creem* in 1984.

Combat Rock was released in early May, coinciding with the outbreak of hostilities in the South Atlantic. Reviewing the album for *NME*, X Moore declared it 'an inadvertent counterblast to The Falklands, too important to be snidely lumped with the other dross, by a band too important to tear themselves apart.' *Sounds*' Dave McCullough noted that The Clash 'aren't static anymore, but sailing into their own Heart of Darkness, trying to settle those wild contradictions they seemed doomed by.' He praised *Combat Rock*'s lyrics and 'strange musical landscapes' and gave it five stars. Adam Sweeting in *Melody Maker* disliked 'Know Your Rights' and was unhappy with the 'hard dry mix' but found 'the music increasingly effective.' Sweeting, too, picked up on *Combat Rock*'s cinematic imagery, noting that 'Red Angel

Dragnet' 'isn't *really* about the people's fight against street violence, it's about a Martin Scorsese movie.' In the US, *Combat Rock* was generally well received, although *Creem*'s Richard Meltzer declared it a 'relative piece of shit.'

The Clash's most successful LP in both the UK and the US, it's certainly true that *Combat Rock*'s success, taken in isolation, says more about their new audience than it does about the band's musical progression. *Combat Rock*'s cluttered lyrics and inelegant stubs at outré musical forms render the LP somewhat gauche beside *London Calling*'s groundbreaking and urbane recontextualisation of The Clash's basic sound, and positively anaemic compared to the breathtaking sophistication and depth of *Sandinista!* Nevertheless, there is much to admire here.

CUT THE CRAP

UK: CBS 26601, November 1985, [16] (LP/Cassette).
Columbia 465110-2, April 1989 (CD).
Columbia 495350 2, January 2000 (CD). Includes additional song 'Do It Now'.

US: Epic 40017, November 1985, [88].

'Dictator', 'Dirty Punk', 'We Are The Clash', 'Are You Red..Y', 'Cool Under Heat',
'Movers and Shakers', 'This Is England', 'Three Card Trick', 'Play To Win', 'Fingerpoppin'',
'North and South', 'Life Is Wild'.

Joe Strummer (vocals, guitar), Paul Simonon (bass, vocals), Nick Sheppard (guitar, vocals), Vince White (guitar, vocals), Pete Howard (drums), Michael Faye (drums), Herman Wagner (keyboards, synthesisers), Norman Watt-Roy (bass).

RECORDED: Munich.
MIXED: Mayfair, London.
PRODUCED: José Unidos
ENGINEERED: Ulli Rudolf, Simon Sullivan.

According to every authorised retrospective (until 2003), Mick Jones' departure from the band in September 1983 was effectively the end of The Clash. Actually, at the time it was seen as a new beginning – at least, within the band itself. 'Bernie's idea was to see if the original idea of The Clash would still stand up in the eighties,' Strummer told Sean O'Hagan in 1988. 'I thought the idea was impressive, but it didn't work in practice. I didn't realise his full motives until it was too late.'

During October and November 1983 a series of adverts were placed in *Melody Maker* seeking a 'young, hard guitarist' (under 25, over 5'9"!). Auditions were held at Camden's Electric Ballroom and one of the first to apply was Nick Sheppard, who had previously been in Bristol punk band The Cortinas. He was soon joined by another guitarist, Vince White, and the new five-piece Clash toured the US and Europe extensively throughout 1984. 'I don't want to record until we've got the group into a unit,' Strummer told *Jamming*'s Ross Fortune in May. The original intention had been that The Clash would record at Lucky Eight Studio, newly built on the site of Rehearsal Rehearsals.

'At one point, I was given a tape of songs numbered one to five,' remembered Sheppard. 'They had no lyrics, just Joe playing mad riffs over a drum machine. They made no sense whatsoever.' Recording finally got underway in December in Munich. Bernard Rhodes chose the studio, mainly, according to Sheppard, 'because it was cheap. It was also out of the way. A very early digital studio. It was owned by a millionaire who made his money in construction after the war.' The backing tracks were almost entirely recorded by Strummer and engineer Ulli Rudolf, with drums and keyboards added by session musicians Michael Faye and Herman Wagner. Sheppard flew to Munich in January 1985 and was subsequently joined by Howard and White. 'I'm on all the songs,' he told Marcus Gray. 'I would say Vince is as well. Paul wasn't really involved much but he did play on a couple of tracks.' Pete Howard's contributions were limited to two songs that the five-piece Clash recorded live in the studio in one afternoon, 'Do It Now' and 'Sex Mad Roar' (both of which appeared on the B-Side of the 'This is England' single).

Having wrested control of the project away from Strummer, Bernard Rhodes oversaw the mixing of *Cut the Crap* in Mayfair with engineer Simon Sullivan. 'I had a terrible time with Bernie in the end,' Strummer told Sean O'Hagan. 'In a nutshell, in order to control me, he destroyed my self-confidence.' Rhodes also received a co-songwriting credit on all of the LP's songs (even 'This is England', which had previously appeared on a single and been credited to The Clash). 'He served as a sounding board for me, but I thought it was a bit cheeky all the same,' Strummer told Bill Flanagan in 1988. 'That's not to say he didn't write *anything*, but I wouldn't have said it was half-and-half.'

With its title taken from dialogue in the movie *Mad Max 2: The Road Warrior* – a post-apocalyptic nightmare full of characters with mohican haircuts – most of *Cut the Crap*'s songs inhabit the same fantasy universe. Shot through with an occasional proto-realistic lyric here and there but, essentially, a Hollywood version of life in the urban jungle in the last days of the 20th century.

By the time that *Cut the Crap* was released in November 1985, the band were already, effectively, history. However, any lingering doubts in Strummer's mind about trying to flog a dead horse and keep The Clash going were assassinated by the reviews the LP received. Mat Snow's *NME* review was as harsh a critique as The Clash had ever received. Describing the cover as 'a marketing director's idea of Ye Style Punke', he considered that the band's sound had been reduced to 'snub nosed guitars bullying the trooper and railing at the bastions of privilege.' Adam Sweeting, at *Melody Maker*, was less sarcastic, if equally disappointed. 'Guess what? it's CRAP! And it doesn't cut it. Football chants, noises of heavy meals being regurgitated over pavements and a mix that Moulinex would be ashamed of ... It's painful.' *Cut the Crap* did receive one approving contemporary review, at *Sounds*, where Jack Barron gave the LP four and a half stars and declared that the band 'don't miss Mick Jones, and have finally managed to lucidly stitch together their love of ethnic musics with gut-level rock.'

Subsequently, *Cut the Crap* has become a virtual industry byword for 'a terrible mistake made by a major rock group', to such an extent that, apart from the inclusion of 'This Is England' on 2003's *The Essential Clash*, every other posthumous Clash release has ignored the LP's existence. It's odd, therefore, that Jon Savage in his seminal punk treatise, *England's Dreaming*, should consider *Cut the Crap* 'much maligned on release in an England grown cold' and that it was 'an ambitious and moving state-of-the-nation address with innovative use of rap rhythm and atmosphere.' It's actually none of those things or anything even remotely like them and it beggars belief that a writer as good as Savage could hold this LP in higher regard than *Give 'Em Enough Rope*, let alone *London Calling*.

Before *Cut the Crap* was even released, Strummer had decided he didn't want to carry on with The Clash. The 23 November 1985 *NME* carried a brief statement to the effect that Sheppard, White and Howard had left the band. 'I think about those guys sometimes,' Strummer told Sean O'Hagan in 1988. 'I hope it didn't fuck up their lives too much because they were good people in a no-win situation.'

FROM HERE TO ETERNITY

UK/US: Columbia 496183-2, October 1999.

'Complete Control', 'London's Burning', 'What's My Name', 'Clash City Rockers',
'Career Opportunities', '(White Man) In Hammersmith Palais', 'Capital Radio',
'City of the Dead', 'I Fought the Law', 'London Calling', 'Armagideon Time',
'Train In Vain', 'The Guns of Brixton', 'The Magnificent Seven', 'Know Your Rights',
'Should I Stay Or Should I Go', 'Straight To Hell'.

RECORDED: Victoria Park, Hackney, 30 April 1978; Music Machine, Camden 26 July
1978; the Lyceum, London, 3 January 1979[96]; the Odeon, Lewisham, 18 February 1980;
Bond's International Casino, New York, 13 June 1981;
the Orpheum Theater, Boston, 7-8 September 1982;
Shea Stadium, New York, 13 October 1982.

96. Both the Music Machine and Lyceum dates are incorrectly given on the sleeve as 27 July 1978 and 28 December 1978 respectively.

'London's Burning', 'What's My Name' and 'City of the Dead' feature some instrumental overdubs recorded during January and February 1979 at AIR and Wessex studios 'to repair technical deficiencies on the original live recordings.'

PRODUCED: The Clash.
MIXED: Bill Price.

A Clash live LP had been planned for many years (Strummer, for instance, had mentioned the idea to Paul Du Noyer in 1981). Indeed, it was with a view to such an eventuality that Glyn Johns recorded the October 1982 Shea Stadium gig. Once all of the band agreed to the project, Jones spent most of 1998 working with Bill Price on various live tapes. Just months before *From Here to Eternity* was released, the project was still going under the title *On the Road with The Clash* and was planned as a double CD with performances stretching back to 1976. In the event, the released CD featured 17 songs culled from nine concerts recorded between 1978 and 1982.

While Jones worked on the music, Simonon was put in charge of art direction and designed the cover. Strummer explained to the MTV Radio Network that he allowed his former bandmates to take the lead on the project so that he could focus his energies on his Mescaleros LP *Rock Art and the X-Ray Style*. When asked about The Clash live experience, Strummer recalled that the intense and volatile nature of the group's shows (and audiences) often caused him to focus more on what was going on in the crowd than what he was supposed to be playing. 'It's almost too intense for me [listening to *From Here to Eternity*],' he noted. 'When we were recorded live, which wasn't that often because the company had to send out a mobile truck, I felt it was unfair. I was the controller of the riot. It was my job to make sure that when two gangs in the audience kicked off, I could see who the biggest guy was and go out there and lamp him to chill everyone out. Or, I would see some girl getting jammed against a barrier and I'd stop everything. I [was] dealing with this kind of activity so I didn't care what chord I was playing.' Strummer told the UK music press that 'The past is like a room full of treacle. You think you can just walk in and out again but you can't. I just felt a terrible bad energy going back to the past, so I said to Mick and Paul, "Can you guys carry this because I can't hack it?"'

From Here to Eternity was favourably reviewed. In *Q*, Paul Du Noyer described it as 'a record of The Clash in their element.'

COMPILATIONS

BLACK MARKET CLASH

US: Nu-Disk 4E 36846, November 1980 [74].
UK: Columbia 468763 2, September 1991.

*'Time Is Tight', 'Capital Radio One', 'Bankrobber', 'Pressure Drop', 'The Prisoner',
'City of the Dead', 'Cheat', 'Armagideon Time', 'Justice Tonight'/'Kick It Over'.*

A beautifully packaged 10-inch mini-LP of mostly UK B-Sides released in the US in 1980. The main bonus was the inclusion of the band's otherwise unavailable cover of Booker T's 'Time Is Tight'. The LP sold heavily both in America and, on import, overseas and was eventually released in Britain in 1991.

THE STORY OF THE CLASH, VOL. 1

UK: Columbia 460244-1, March 1988 [7] (LP/Cassette/CD).
Columbia 495351 2, November 1999 (CD).

US: Epic E2K 44035

*'The Magnificent Seven', 'Rock the Casbah', 'This is Radio Clash',
'Should I Stay or Should I Go', 'Straight To Hell', 'Armagideon Time', 'Clampdown',
'Train In Vain', 'The Guns of Brixton', 'I Fought the Law', 'Somebody Got Murdered',
'Lost in the Supermarket', 'Bankrobber', '(White Man) In Hammersmith Palais',
'London's Burning', 'Janie Jones', 'Tommy Gun', 'Complete Control', 'Capital Radio One',
'White Riot', 'Career Opportunities', 'Clash City Rockers', 'Safe European Home',
'Stay Free', 'London Calling', 'Spanish Bombs', 'English Civil War', 'Police & Thieves'.*

CBS had been pushing for a Clash *Best Of* collection for some time and, finally, in 1987 the band agreed. Mick Jones compiled the collection, with assistance from Simonon's wife Tricia Ronane, while Strummer provided a very amusing set of sleevenotes under the pseudonym of Albert Transom. He was also responsible for the sarcastic 'Vol. 1' after the proposed title, *Revolution Rock*, had been vetoed by CBS. A fair retelling of the band's finest moments (in no particular order), the main bonus was the inclusion of the difficult-to-obtain *NME* version of 'Capital Radio', complete with part of Tony Parsons' interview with The Clash.

The CD was generally well received, albeit with a few pointed barbs at the 'turning rebellion into money' nature of a repackaged hits compilation.

For example, *NME*'s Steven Wells found it ironic that this 28-track blast of joyous freedom-expression was being put out by a subsidiary of a Japanese multinational corporation. 'One of rebel rock's silly little contradictions,' he concluded. Strummer, who had once proudly declared that there would never be a Clash LP retailing at £6 or above, was forced by ITV's *Night Network* to defend the CD's recommended retail price of £22.99. 'The LP is dead,' Strummer noted. 'Don't blame me that it's come out on CD. *I* don't even have a player yet! It's a retrospective, you can buy it if you want, or just ignore it.'

THE SINGLES COLLECTION

UK: Columbia 468946-2, November 1991 [68] (CD/Cassette).

'White Riot', 'Remote Control', 'Complete Control', 'Clash City Rockers', '(White Man) In Hammersmith Palais', 'Tommy Gun', 'English Civil War', 'I Fought the Law', 'London Calling', 'Train In Vain', 'Bankrobber', 'The Call Up', 'Hitsville UK', 'The Magnificent Seven', 'This Is Radio Clash', 'Know Your Rights', 'Rock the Casbah', 'Should I Stay Or Should I Go'.

A very disappointing example of product put together without the co-opera-tion of any members of the band and displaying all the lack of imagination that went into its visual counterpart, *This Is Video Clash*. *The Singles Collection* is a shoddily packaged attempt to milk the UK success of the 'Should I Stay Or Should I Go' reissue single. It's not even complete ('This Is England' is conspicuous by its absence). Most of the reviews the CD received were of the 'the music's great but don't bother with this collection' type.

CLASH ON BROADWAY

US: Columbia 469308-2, November 1991 (CD/Cassette).
UK: Columbia 469308-2, June 1994.

'Janie Jones' (Demo), 'Career Opportunities' (Demo), 'White Riot', '1977', 'I'm So Bored With The USA', 'Hate & War', 'What's My Name', 'Deny', 'London's Burning', 'Protex Blue', 'Police & Thieves', '48 Hours', 'Cheat', 'Garageland', 'Capital Radio One', 'Complete Control', 'Clash City Rockers', 'City of the Dead', 'Jail Guitar Doors', 'The Prisoner', '(White Man) In Hammersmith Palais', 'Pressure Drop', '1-2 Crush On You', 'English Civil War' (live), 'I Fought the Law' (live), 'Safe European Home', 'Tommy Gun', 'Julie's Been Working for the Drug Squad', 'Stay Free', 'One Emotion', 'Groovy Times', 'Gates of the West', 'Armagideon Time', 'London Calling', 'Brand New Cadillac', 'Rudie Can't Fail', 'The Guns of Brixton', 'Spanish Bombs', 'Lost in the Supermarket', 'The Right Profile', 'The Card Cheat', 'Death Or Glory', 'Clampdown', 'Train In Vain', 'Bankrobber', 'Police On My Back', 'The Magnificent Seven', 'The Leader', 'The Call Up', 'Somebody Got Murdered',

*'Washington Bullets', 'Broadway', 'Lightning Strikes (Not Once But Twice)' (Live),
'Every Little Bit Hurts', 'Stop the World', 'Midnight To Stevens', 'This Is Radio Clash',
'Cool Confusion', 'Red Angel Dragnet', 'Ghetto Defendant', 'Rock the Casbah',
'Should I Stay Or Should I Go', 'Straight To Hell', 'The Street Parade'.*

Put together by Kosmo Vinyl with the full co-operation of the band, the 3-CD *Clash On Broadway* is the definitive Clash compilation. It includes two of the 1976 Guy Stevens demos, three previously unreleased studio tracks and three live recordings together with the original, unedited version of 'Straight To Hell'. Once again the discography included with the package, and indeed the package itself, completely ignores the existence of *Cut the Crap*. 'I think that was a pathetic attempt not to offend Mick,' Strummer told Sean Egan in 2000. The set was assembled primarily with America in mind, but import sales eventually led to a British release three years later. 'The suits could never swallow The Clash,' wrote *Vox*'s Mike Pattenden in 1994. 'They were too jagged, too fucking unpalatable. For that reason, a Clash boxed-set can't but seem an incongruous monument.'

SUPER BLACK MARKET CLASH

UK/US: Columbia 474546-2, November 1993 (CD).
Columbia 495352-2, November, 1999 (CD).

*'1977', 'Listen', 'Jail Guitar Doors', 'City of the Dead', 'The Prisoner', 'Pressure Drop',
'1-2 Crush On You', 'Groovy Times', 'Gates of the West', 'Capital Radio Two',
'Time Is Tight', 'Justice Tonight'/'Kick It Over', 'Robber Dub', 'The Cool Out',
'Stop the World', 'The Magnificent Dance', 'This Is Radio Clash',
'First Night Back In Town', 'Long Time Jerk', 'Cool Confusion', 'Mustapha Dance'.*

This excellent 21-song compilation rounds up most of the obscure corners of The Clash's discography. Once again, it was compiled by Kosmo Vinyl, along with project director Gary Pacheco, and lovingly remastered by Bill Price. The cover, by Rocco Redondo, features a lone rasta facing an intimidating line of police. It's one of the most provocative and memorable images associated with The Clash.

THE ESSENTIAL CLASH

UK/US: Columbia 510998-2, March 2003. (CD)

*'White Riot', '1977', 'London's Burning', 'Complete Control', 'Clash City Rockers',
'I'm So Bored With The USA', 'Career Opportunities', 'Hate & War', 'Cheat',
'Police & Thieves', 'Janie Jones', 'Garageland', 'Capital Radio One',
'(White Man) In Hammersmith Palais', 'English Civil War', 'Tommy Gun',
'Safe European Home', 'Julie's Been Working for the Drug Squad', 'Stay Free',*

'Groovy Times', 'I Fought the Law', 'London Calling', 'The Guns of Brixton', 'Clampdown', 'Rudie Can't Fail', 'Lost in the Supermarket', 'Jimmy Jazz', 'Train In Vain', 'Bankrobber', 'The Magnificent Seven', 'Ivan Meets GI Joe', 'Stop the World', 'Somebody Got Murdered', 'The Street Parade', 'Broadway', 'Radio Clash', 'Ghetto Dependant', 'Rock the Casbah', 'Straight To Hell', 'Should I Stay Or Should I Go', 'This Is England'.

Assembled by Jones to coincide with The Clash's inauguration into the Rock & Roll Hall of Fame, the events of Christmas 2002 conspired to make *The Essential Clash*, and its DVD counterpart, a tribute to Strummer. The collection is a fine starting point for anyone looking to get into The Clash and, notably, it regards 'This Is England' as officially part of The Clash's legacy.

THE CLASH ON SCREEN

WHITE RIOT PROMO (17 April 1977)

Shot in a film studio in Dunstable, The Clash, including Headon just a week after he had joined the band, performed versions of 'White Riot', '1977' and 'London's Burning' live before an audience consisting of the camera crew and a hugely impressed Tony Parsons. Their backdrop was Sebastian Conran's blow-up of Rocco Macauley's celebrated *The Clash* back cover. Directed by Lindsay Clinell, the short film also included interview clips with Parsons and the band relaxing around a pool table. At the time, however, there were few places where the film could be shown. (It was played, in-store, at Marble Arch's Virgin Record shop although, as *Last Gang In Town* notes, 'the few dozen record purchases this possibly inspired hardly justified the expense of [the film's] making.') Subsequently, performance clips were used in a 1989 BBC2 Jones retrospective, *That Was Then This Is Now*, a 1991 MTV *Rockumentary* and in *Westway to the World*, while all three songs featured, in full, on *The Essential Clash* DVD.

THE PUNK ROCK MOVIE

An infamous, colour super-8 film documentary, shot during the first half of 1977, which captured punk at the very moment that it was rocketing into mainstream British culture. Mainly filmed at the Roxy Club by resident DJ Don Letts, this quasi home-movie, presented without narration, features shaky, sometimes virtually unwatchable footage, while the sound quality is frequently appalling. But, viewed purely as a historical document (and occasionally in musical terms), *The Punk Rock Movie* is invaluable.

In addition to several Sex Pistols performances, the film also captured Generation X, The Slits (hilariously playing at a girls' school), Johnny Thunders and The Heartbreakers, Wayne County, X Ray Spex and Siouxsie and The Banshees. Letts briefly attempted more traditional documentary-style clichés when he interviewed a young punkette who had recently lost her retail job because of her outrageous attire. For the most part, however, *The Punk Rock Movie* lived up to its name. Without any adornments, it was a grainy snapshot of a single *frantic* moment in time, conveying the raw, spontaneous energy of punk's zenith before jaded commercialisation turned it into just another fashion trend.

The Clash live footage features two extraordinary versions of 'White Riot', plus clips of 'Garageland' and '1977', all filmed during dates on the White Riot tour.

PUNK IN LONDON

Aware of the new musical sensation going on in London, German producer Wolfgang Büld came to England in the summer of 1977 to shoot live footage and interviews with numerous punk bands. He didn't get to film The Clash on that occasion – they were out on tour and he had to make do with interviewing Roadent instead. The roadie subsequently became something of a celebrity in Germany due to his appearance and his pithy comments. Büld did manage to shoot much exciting live footage of The Adverts, The Jam, Chelsea, The Killjoys (featuring a very young Kevin Rowland) and Subway Sect – the latter performing in Rehearsal Rehearsals.

Büld eventually caught up with The Clash in Munich in early October 1977. *Punk In London* – subsequently released theatrically in 1978 and on video in the early 1980s – featured performances of 'Hate & War', 'Police & Thieves' and 'Janie Jones', plus a short snippet of 'Complete Control' and brief interviews with a forthright, aggressive Jones and a considerably more relaxed Simonon. The 2001 Salvation DVD release added more live Clash footage, 'London's Burning', 'Complete Control', 'The Prisoner' and 'Garageland'. Fiery stuff it is too, capturing the power and passion of the 1977 Clash on stage. Particularly amusing is a moment during 'Garageland' when a cameraman wanders on stage for a close-up only to be prodded off with the microphone stand by Strummer.

SO IT GOES
(Granada, 27 November and 11 December 1977)

An arts and music programme made by Granada and, at least initially, broadcast purely in England's North West. The show was hosted by its producer Tony Wilson (during the first season, it was co-hosted by Clive James). Wilson was undoubtedly a musical visionary – his subsequent success as head of the Factory label proves that – but guests on the initial instalments of *So It Goes* will give readers an idea of what a cultural wasteland the show existed in. The Soft Machine and Kiss were considered to be at rock's cutting edge in mid-1976.

All that changed in August when *So It Goes* featured the television debut of the (at the time still unsigned) Sex Pistols, performing 'Anarchy in the UK'. 'We expected others to follow us and feature punk groups,' Wilson noted in 1988. 'They were either too dumb or too scared.' So for the next year, with the exception of the odd clip here or there, *So It Goes* was the only place on television where you could actually see a punk band. Naturally, they wanted The Clash badly.

The band's show at the Elizabethan Ballroom in Manchester on 15 November 1977 was filmed (as was the set by support group Siouxsie and The Banshees – their first TV appearance). Four Clash songs were eventually broadcast: 'Capital Radio' and 'Janie Jones' on 27 November and 'What's My Name?' and 'Garageland' on 11 December, the final show of the series. They remain some of the most memorable images of The Clash at this point in their career, drowning in a shower of spittle arcing majestically out of the audience. (Some of this ends up on one of the camera lenses, making footage from over Jones' shoulder appear as if it's been shot through a Vaseline filter.) It's a frantic, rough-as-sandpaper performance, with Strummer so excited that, at times, he can only move in tense spastic jerks and yell unintelligible babble into the microphone. Tunes are virtually non-existent, especially on 'Janie Jones' where the entire first verse seems never to deviate from a flat monotone. 'Anybody want it to sound like the record?' Strummer asks. 'No, me neither.'

The band look incredible. Strummer's battered black Telecaster, covered in numerous stickers, was discarded after the first song, leaving him leaping about in his bondage pants. His baseball boots become a prominent feature when he falls over at the end of 'What's My Name?' Simonon, with his electric blue shirt opened to reveal a well-muscled chest, prowls the stage like an angry tiger, his Rickenbacker bass splattered with Rauschenburg-inspired paint splashes. Jones, in a white-with-red-flashes military jacket, is the essence of sweaty cool. At the back, Headon looks like a cartoon Tasmanian Devil on the few occasions that we actually catch a glimpse of him. Strummer's ad-lib in 'What's My Name?' ('Here we are, on TV/What does it mean to me?/What does it mean to you?/FUCK ALL!') remains the most indelible image of The Clash in their full piss-and-vinegar fury.

All four songs were repeated on two Channel 4 retrospectives in the late 1980s (*The Way We Were* and *Punk*) and clips have subsequently appeared in several other documentaries, and also in *Westway to the World*. 'They played a dynamic set, fed from the audience's energy,' Johnny Green remembered, vividly describing a moment before 'Garageland' where Joe tripped over his own feet, fell to the floor, bashed out the rhythm on the wooden drum rise 'and [then] leapt up like a voodoo jack-in-the-box.'

TISWAS (ATV, 28 January 1978)

A typically anarchic edition of the children's television programme presented by Chris Tarrant and his foxy sidekick Sally James. The usual good-natured disrespect was shown to Strummer and Simonon when they appeared. Jones and Headon decided not to sacrifice their Saturday morning lie-in.

SOMETHING ELSE (BBC2, 11 March 1978)

This early evening BBC2 show had a DIY ethic, and was devised and presented by teenagers in the various BBC provincial regions. It featured a mixture of topics, usually current social events and music. A discussion about how much of a drag unemployment was normally featured at some point. It, and other similarly worthy 'yoof' programmes, had perfectly valid intentions but, with hindsight, seem a rather silly attempt at right-on-ness by the Beeb. The genre meant well but was doomed to fail and was ruthlessly parodied by contemporary comedy programmes like *Not The Nine O'Clock News* ('Hey! Wow!') and *The Young Ones* ('Nozzin' Around'). On this edition The Clash performed 'Tommy Gun', with Strummer wearing a pair of shades to hide his hepatitis-yellowed eyes. The clip has subsequently been repeated on the BBC's *Sounds of the 70s*.

RUDE BOY

In April 1978, The Clash met independent filmmakers Dave Mingay and Jack Hazan, who ran a production company called Buzzy Enterprises, with a view to making a social document about Britain in the late 70s. 'We were honourable,' Strummer told Gavin Martin in 1999. 'We said "Okay, do what you want, just don't get in the way".'

With its opening shots of cheering Jubilee crowds and fireworks juxtaposed with vile racist graffiti in a crumbling London tower-block, *Rude Boy* was a virtually plotless series of grim snapshots of Britain at the fag-end of a dangerous decade. The story, such as it is, concerns Ray (Ray Gange), a Clash fan who works in a seedy Soho porn shop and drinks from dawn till dusk. Uneducated, bored, harbouring offensive, ill-informed opinions and keen to become a capitalist, Gange blags his way into a job on The Clash's road crew and then drifts aimlessly away at the movie's climax. There's also some stuff about a team of black teenage pickpockets being observed, and then arrested, by the law, and lots of footage of National Front and Anti-Nazi League demonstrations. And, always, the awful spectre of oncoming Thatcherism hovering on the horizon. The acting from all concerned (even the professionals) is very stilted and the political discussions, when they occur, are monosyllabic and one-dimensional (although, one suspects, quite an accurate reflection of views held by a large proportion of the intended audience). The Clash, when they aren't on stage, appear rather self-conscious and ill at ease.

So, *A Hard Day's Night* it isn't... 'In a very rough-edged imitation of a British film of the 60s – kitchen-sink with the drain backed-up, you might say – *Rude Boy* chronicles every ratty detail of Ray's life,' noted Janet Maslin in the *New York Times*. 'He works sporadically. He meets girls whose nonchalance borders [on] the comatose. Then he gets a job as a roadie for The Clash. He may or may not have been previously acquainted with the band. The plot gets vague, and the dialogue unintelligible on points like this.'

The film also includes a very hostile portrayal of Mick Jones, often said to be because he had annoyed the directors with too many overt displays of pop-star behaviour during the early days of shooting. Interestingly, however, Mick is the only member of the band who directly questions Ray's racist views. Strummer is presented as a somewhat confused idealist, good on rhetoric but a bit short on any actual answers, Headon as a dumb thug (having got tired of kick-boxing his punch-bag, he starts using Ray instead) and Simonon as likeable but something of a puppet of his girlfriend, Caroline Coon. The only one of the group's entourage who was portrayed in the least bit sympathetically was Johnny Green, who also turned out to be the best actor in the entire film.

During pre-publicity for the movie, it was suggested that Gange was, in real life, a member of The Clash's road crew, a myth that continues to crop up in retrospectives about The Clash to this day (Jon Savage states this in *England's Dreaming*, for instance). Although, for the most part, the band got on quite well with Gange – who was certainly a fan – he was never a part of their entourage, except on those occasions when filming was taking place. 'He was a total phoney, brought in by Mingay,' Johnny Green subsequently noted. 'He'd never worked for us.'

The Clash music included in the film is as follows:-

★ 'Revolution Rock' – snatches of an instrumental studio version, recorded at Wessex in July 1979, are used at various points in the film.
★ 'Police & Thieves' – from Birmingham Barbarellas, 1 May 1978.
★ 'Career Opportunities' – *The Clash* version is played on Ray's cheap dansette.
★ 'Garageland' – The Clash perform a very effective slower-than-usual version in a rehearsal studio (actually the delightfully named Black Hole in South London).

★ 'London's Burning' – from the Victoria Park Rock Against Racism show, 30 April 1978.
★ 'White Riot' – from the same source, and featuring Jimmy Pursey (and his comedy trousers) on additional vocals.
★ '(White Man) In Hammersmith Palais' – the first of four songs from the riotous Glasgow Apollo gig, 4 July 1978.
★ 'I'm So Bored With The USA' – same source.
★ 'Janie Jones' – same source.
★ 'White Riot' – same source.
★ 'The Prisoner' – from Aberdeen, 5 July 1978.
★ 'Tommy Gun' – from Dunfermline, 6 July 1978.
★ 'All the Young Punks (New Boots and Contracts)' – Strummer is shown adding vocals to the pre-recorded backing track in Basing Street Studios.
★ 'Stay Free' – Jones' highlight of the movie, recording his emotional vocals to an alternative (much more acoustic) version of the song in Basing Street. When he's finished he is (sort of) praised, rather sycophantically, by Ray Gange.
★ 'Rudie Can't Fail' – an alternate take, recorded at Wessex in July 1979, is heard at various points in the movie, and over the end credits.
★ 'Complete Control' – the first of three songs from Camden's Music Machine, probably on 26 July 1978, although most sources (including *From Here to Eternity*) suggest 27 July.
★ 'Safe European Home' – same source.
★ 'What's My Name' – same source.
★ 'Safe European Home' – a stage performance heard while Gange is in The Clash's dressing room, nicking their beer. Recorded on one of the Sort It Out tour dates, though identifying which one is impossible.
★ 'Piano Song' – Strummer, alone with Gange, sings this self-penned blues.
★ 'Let the Good Times Roll' – same source.
★ 'I Fought the Law' – from the Lyceum, 3 January 1979.

Additionally, the 2001 Salvation DVD release of the film included 'English Civil War' from the 3 January Lyceum show, and a wild version of 'White Riot', climaxing with a stage invasion, filmed at Dunfermline.

Dissatisfied with the sound quality of many of the live performances, The Clash agreed to some post-production doctoring and recorded overdubs. In *A Riot Of Our Own* Johnny Green dates these sessions as taking place in January 1979, firstly at Wessex and then at George Martin's AIR Studios on Oxford Street. The latter had lip-synch facilities which allowed a rough cut of the movie to be projected while the band played along to it. Green notes that Kate Bush was recording in another studio and that the band often assembled in the canteen to admire her arse. Green also suggests that, except for the performance of 'I Fought the Law', everything else in the film was re-recorded. Dave Mingay has insisted, however, that at least half of the live performances in the film were not overdubbed at all.

According to *Smash Hits*, although The Clash were 'quite happy with their own performances and, in particular, with the musical footage,' they considered the plot 'a flop.' They also expressed objections to the movies' 'political overtones' (probably to the subplot involving the black pickpockets). Perhaps jokingly, the band said that they would withdraw their objections if their fans were let in to see the film for free.

Rude Boy was given its world premiere at the Zoo Palast on 27 February 1980 as Britain's entry in the Berlin Film festival. *The Times*' David Robinson described it as 'impressionistic' and praised the picture as 'rough, bawdy, often funny, finally devastating. The spiritual deprivation of this world – social security and tower blocks cannot fill every human need – seem insoluble.' He also noted that the most significant fact about *Rude Boy* was that it revealed there were two voices in Britain, speaking quite different languages. 'The content of the film, and its value as a social document, are so vital in themselves that it's easy to overlook the technical achievement of *Rude Boy*, a British film made at a fraction of the cost of commercial pictures it outclasses in style as well as seriousness.'

Other critics were less impressed. The *Daily Mail*'s Margaret Hinxman asked 'Must we show off this foul view of Britain?' The *Observer*'s Tom Davies was, apparently, so incensed by the film that he punched Dave Mingay in the face. In the music press, *NME*'s Neil Norman considered *Rude Boy* 'an innovative piece of cinematic art ... a genuine cri de coeur for a generation on the retreat.' *Melody Maker*'s Paolo Hewitt, however, found it ironic that The Clash, of all bands, should be distancing themselves from a film with such a strong political message. One of the most interesting reviews was by the *Guardian*'s Derek Malcolm. 'Musically, the film is extraordinary ... there could not be a better advertisement for them or their records,' he noted. The fact that the 'them' in question were constantly referred to as 'The Slash' was a shade unfortunate, however.

The film proved to be a big hit in Europe, particularly France. Although there were only a few UK screenings during 1980, *Rude Boy* has subsequently enjoyed a long life on video and DVD, and is still available in both formats. If you never got a chance to see The Clash live, then you need to see *Rude Boy* at least once in your life.

ROCK REVOLUTION

The commercial video *Rock Revolution* includes extraordinary footage of The Clash live at Manchester Apollo on 2 July 1978, performing 'I'm So Bored With The USA' and 'London's Burning'. The Clash are on manic form throughout. During the first song, Strummer jumps down into the pit between stage and audience before being pulled back up by Jones.

ALRIGHT NOW
(Tyne Tees TV, recorded 4 March, broadcast 18 April 1979)

The brainchild of Sunderland drama teacher turned television producer Malcolm Gerrie, *Alright Now* was a strange mixture of kids' TV and the more adult tone of Gerrie's next project, *The Tube*, which was also produced at Tyne Tees' studios on City Road, Newcastle. *Alright Now* went out in a prime-time 7.00 pm slot (previously occupied by *The Muppet Show*) in the northern region but, sadly, was not networked.

Conscientious boycotters of *Top of the Pops*, The Clash agreed to do *Alright Now* precisely because they were allowed to perform live ('You can just plug in and play' said Strummer eagerly). Introduced by compere Den Hegarty (previously with Darts and with whom The Clash got on well), they performed 'English Civil War' while a split-screen displayed short biographies (Jones' biggest influence: 'Third-rate rock bands 67-73', Headon's hobby: 'Milking goats', Strummer's instrument: 'Rhythmnnn [sic] guitar'). The sartorial highlights were, undoubtedly Simonon's fluorescent pink socks and Jones' leather waistcoat.

Afterwards the band were interrogated by Hegarty and some local youths. (Sample question: 'How do you feel about being called a punk band?' Answer: 'It's better than being called a *New Wave* band!'). Jones assured one Geordie punk that he always considered that The Clash were better than The Pistols and Simonon showed off his prowess at the hand-jive. To finish the show, Jones sang a furious version of 'Hate & War' and then Strummer led the band into an embryonic arrangement of Desmond Dekker's 'The Israelites' with Hegarty on backing vocals.

After transmission had ended, following the obvious appreciation of their short set, the band did a couple more songs for the audience – one rumoured to have been 'Tommy Gun'. The kids promptly invaded the stage, leaving Jones stranded on the drum riser. 'The Clash played as loud as ever, which gave the TV soundmen huge problems,' remembered Johnny Green. The performance of 'English Civil War' was repeated on a 2003 Channel 4 Joe Strummer retrospective.

PUNK, AND ITS AFTER SHOCKS

Wolfgang Büld, who had previously produced *Punk In London*, was back in London in December 1979 and January 1980 to film a follow- up. At the Aylesbury Friars on 5 January he filmed The Clash and an eight-minute section appears in his film, subsequently released on video in 1992 (and still available in this format, albeit only in the US). After rentagob interviewee Bob Geldof has given his opinion that The Clash almost backed themselves into a corner with their political stance but were good enough to escape this trap, there's a clip of 'London Calling'. This is followed by a short interview with Strummer and Simonon, both dressed in their black crombies and trilbys. They explain the band's musical changes since Büld last filmed them. 'Instead of using the hammer, we're trying to be more subtle with it,' noted Strummer. From the same gig, 'Police & Thieves' is included in its entirety along with a 35-second clip of 'Complete Control', with Jones playing a black Gibson. Sartorial highlight: Strummer's yellow shirt.

The film also includes thrilling live footage of The Jam, The Police, The Specials, Madness, Ian Dury And The Blockheads[116], The Pretenders and The Kinks, among others. It was released under a variety of titles in different countries (*Rock: Ready for the Eighties?*, *British Rock* etc). As a snapshot of a golden period of superb British pop music (1979-80), it's a fine document. Plus, where else are you going to see a performance of Spizz Energi's 'Where's Captain Kirk?'!

TISWAS (ATV, 5 January 1980)

A second appearance on *Tiswas*, this time featuring the whole band being interviewed by the almost-legendary Sally James and then being attacked by Spit the Dog. Ah, happy days.

NATIONWIDE (BBC1, 18 January 1980)

Duncan Gibbins, a reporter with the BBC's early evening current affairs programme *Nationwide*, was in Dundee with The Clash on 18 January 1980 to

---

116. The Blockheads footage was filmed when they supported The Clash at the Aylesbury gig. It features Mick Jones guesting on a white-hot version of 'Sweet Gene Vincent'.

film a 12-minute documentary. This included memorable live clips of 'Clampdown', 'Revolution Rock', 'London Calling' and 'London's Burning'. The Clash were shown preparing for the gig, with Joe drinking honey and lemon and listening to inspirational speeches by Martin Luther King. Jones talked at length about CBS and Strummer about their various run-ins with the police. Fans were shown waiting outside the venue praising the band ('they're noo a rip-off!') and, later, several were let in through the window by Strummer and *Rude Boy* actor Terry McQuade.

Gibbins' voice-over began: 'The Clash don't sing soppy songs about teenage love or pick-ups at the local disco. They tell of White Riots, they warn of Armagideon Time, they shout about the cost of living. They say they have no allegiance to either the right or the left, and despite an almost contemptuous disregard for exposure on TV or radio, they are one of the most successful groups in Britain today.' Short clips from this interesting piece of reportage feature in *Westway to the World*.

FRIDAYS (ABC TV, 25 April 1980)

A weekly late-night US comedy series often criticised as a pale clone of NBC's *Saturday Night Live*. The format was certainly similar, with a live band playing each week. For The Clash's debut US TV appearance, Mick Jones chose to wear the nastiest purple zoot suit you've ever seen. Of all the dreadful fashion crimes your favourite bands have ever been guilty of, this is by far the most heinous. Thankfully, it only slightly distracts from excellent live-in-the-studio performances of 'London Calling', 'Train In Vain', 'The Guns of Brixton' and 'Clampdown'.

CLASH ON BROADWAY

'A lot of film was shot,' remembered Kosmo Vinyl in 1991, 'and a trailer was shown on MTV but, to be honest, the film was never finished.' [117]

Don Letts accompanied The Clash on their 1981 residency at Bond's in New York. He shot many hours of footage, including at least two full gigs and lots of material of The Clash at work and at play in and around New York. In May 1982 Chris Salewicz reported in *The Face* that Letts and Bernard Rhodes were 'currently negotiating with major distributors for an autumn release.' Then, everyone quietly forgot about the project.

---

117. The trailer, which was included as an extra on *The Essential Clash* DVD, includes some additional footage that doesn't appear in the released version of *Clash On Broadway*.

'As far as I know the reels were stored in a rental place in New York,' Strummer told *Mojo* in 1994. 'Bernie forgot to pay the rent and the footage was destroyed.' A cutting copy of approximately 30 minutes' worth of footage was discovered by Letts in a cupboard during the early 90s and this was subsequently assembled and included on the *Westway to the World* DVD. What remains of the film is a fascinating time capsule of furious live footage and scenes of mayhem and rioting in Times Square in the aftermath of that infamous concert cancellation. Perform-ances of 'London Calling', 'The Guns of Brixton', 'Safe European Home' (albeit with the *Give 'Em Enough Rope* version on the soundtrack), 'Charlie Don't Surf' and 'This Is Radio Clash', filmed at Bond's, are obvious highlights. There's also a highly revealing interview fragment with Headon, who notes that if he hadn't been a drummer he still believed he would have been 'infamous. Or, in prison, possibly.'

THE TOMORROW SHOW (NBC TV, 5 June 1981)

During the Bond's Club residency, The Clash appeared on this late-night talk show hosted by Tom Snyder and gossip columnist Rona Barrett. The Clash performed 'The Magnificent Seven' and 'This Is Radio Clash'.

THE KING OF COMEDY

In 1979, when acclaimed movie director Martin Scorsese (*Mean Streets, Goodfellas*) conceived a movie version of Herbert Asbury's book about 19th century Irish immigrants in America, *Gangs of New York*, he initially planned find a place in the film for The Clash. Both Scorsese and his usual leading man, Robert DeNiro, had become fans of the band and were often seen at their New York concerts during 1979 and 1980. Various complications (not least the band's schedule) caused the abandonment of this plan and Scorsese and DeNiro went off and filmed *Raging Bull* instead. [118] As compensation, in 1981 Scorsese offered The Clash a brief cameo in his next movie, *The King of Comedy*. In this, Strummer, Jones and Simonon play a group of street scum who briefly hassle DeNiro and Sandra Bernhard's characters. Clash fellow-travellers Kosmo Vinyl, Don Letts, Pearl Harbour and Ellen Foley also appear in the scene. 'Nil points for us that day,' Strummer told Gavin Martin. 'We just stood there, bumbling around.' Despite this, Scorsese remained a fan

---

118. *Gangs of New York* would eventually be released in 2002, starring Leonardo DiCaprio, Daniel Day-Lewis and Cameron Diaz.

of The Clash and featured 'Janie Jones' and 'I'm So Bored With The USA' on the soundtrack of his 1999 movie *Bringing Out The Dead*.

SATURDAY NIGHT LIVE (NBC TV, 9 October 1982)

The band's final TV appearance included live studio performances of 'Straight To Hell' and 'Should I Stay Or Should I Go'.

HELL W10

In the summer of 1983, with The Clash off the road (and soon to implode), Strummer – for reasons that he never fully explained – decided to try and hold the band together by making a film. A 30-minute, black-and-white, 16mm silent movie at that. Heavily influenced by his friend Martin Scorsese's work, and by British gangster films like *Performance* and *Get Carter*, *Hell W10* was shot in just two weeks. 'It was a disaster,' Strummer told *Film Comment*'s Graham Fuller in 1987. 'Luckily, the laboratory that held the negative went bankrupt and destroyed all the stock, so the world can breathe again.'

A tale of lowlife gangsters in west London, the film featured Simonon playing a street robber in a rasta cap, Jones as a vicious drug baron, Mr Socrates, with slicked-down hair and a white tuxedo, and Strummer as a uniformed (yet armed) police inspector with a Brigadier Lethbridge-Stewart moustache. The rest of the cast comprised various friends, roadies and fans of the band (including Kosmo Vinyl, Ray Jordan and Pennie Smith, who played a policewoman). As Jules Balme noted in 2003, 'the streets of W10 bear a closer resemblance to those of *The Blue Lamp* than *Notting Hill*, particularly with the use of older vehicles like the hood's Zodiac and Joe's long-suffering Morris Minor.' Viewed today, it's very much of the amateur-dramatics school of film production, but it's an interesting artefact all the same – and hugely violent.

Almost two decades after it was made, a copy of *Hell W10* was found, allegedly at a car boot sale in north London. With the addition of a soundtrack made of up of over 20 pieces of Clash music, the film was released as a bonus feature on *The Essential Clash* DVD. Hardly essential. But it's worth a look, if only for the use of material like 'Silicone On Sapphire', 'Atom Tan' and 'Mensforth Hill' on the soundtrack – a reminder of some of The Clash's more obscure moments.

THIS IS VIDEO CLASH

A thoroughly lazy, shoddy piece of product, *This Is Video Clash* was rushed out with indecent haste in March 1991 to capitalise on the astonishing success of the 'Should I Stay Or Should I Go' reissue. With its frugal running time of just 30 minutes, the video includes only those promo clips directed by Don Letts, with seemingly no attempt having been made to acquire anything from other sources. It's still available, but if you buy it you're a mug.

WESTWAY TO THE WORLD

The Clash's version of The Beatles' *Anthology*, this was an authorised documentary put together by Don Letts. A 50-minute version was shown on BBC2 in October 1999. The 85-minute 'director's cut', together with some additional interview material conducted by Mal Peachey, was released on video and DVD soon afterwards. Obviously, the major selling point was the inclusion of a plethora of previously unseen (and, in some cases, previously undocumented) footage – including live material shot by Don Letts and Julien Temple's black-and-white 8mm film of The Clash in 1976.

As a whole, the film is a bit fragmented when it comes to the chronology of The Clash's story. All the pieces are there, though not necessarily in the correct order. Nevertheless, the emotion that Strummer, Jones, Simonon and Headon display during their interviews is something to see. The Clash's influences – musical, social and political – are expressed by the band members, and their story is told with humour and intelligence. Terry Chimes, Tony Parsons, Johnny Green, Bill Price and Pennie Smith also lend their perspectives to The Clash's story. 'A new standard for rock documentaries' according to *Uncut*, *Westway to the World* is essential viewing for anyone who claims to be a Clash fan.

THE ESSENTIAL CLASH

For the most part, *The Essential Clash* is merely a DVD reissue of *This Is Video Clash* although, thankfully, it does include a few impressive extras – the Dunstable 'White Riot' promo film, the band being interviewed by Janet Street Porter in 1976, *Hell W10* – to make it a worthwhile purchase. Said to have been assembled prior to Strummer's death, the package includes a final note dedicating the project to the memory of 'our friend and colleague Joe Strummer.'

SPLIT!

BEYOND THE CLASH

'I don't think any of us would do it just for the money.'
Mick Jones, *Vox* 1991

Following his departure from The Clash in late 1983, Mick Jones spent some time working as a guitar for hire. He played on the debut LP by General Public, the band formed from the ashes of The Beat by Dave Wakelin and Rankin' Roger, and also appeared live with both Sigue Sigue Sputnik, featuring his friend Tony James, and Theatre of Hate. In early 1984 he began putting his own band together. The first recruits were bassist Leo Williams – once the barman at the Roxy – and Don Letts, whom Mick taught rudimentary keyboards. The big news, however, was the initial involvement of Topper Headon.

The drummer's heroin intake was now gargantuan. (Pete Townshend had recently paid for Headon to undergo the expensive Black Box treatment in Los Angeles. Within weeks, Headon was shooting up again.) Jones' offer came with the strict proviso that Headon get himself cleaned up. Perhaps inevitably, it didn't happen and it was soon announced that Topper would not be part of Mick's band – although the official reason given was the project's musical direction, with an emphasis on sampling and technology. His replacement was Greg Roberts. Top Risk Action Company and Real Westway were considered as band names before someone suggested Big Audio Dynamite.

BAD made their live debut in October 1984, supporting The Alarm. A further European tour followed, in early 1985, with U2. Sessions for BAD's first LP then took place at Sarm West, the former Basing Street studios where *Give 'Em Enough Rope* had been recorded. *This Is Big Audio Dynamite* was a cracking debut, containing a mixture of social comment lyrics and brave new musical landscapes. Highlights included a trio of bona fide classic singles, 'The Bottom Line', 'E=MC^2'[119] and 'Medicine Show'. The LP's cover photograph was provided by Dan Donovan, who subsequently joined the group on keyboards.

---

119. In reaching number 11 in the UK charts, 'E=MC^2' equalled The Clash's highest chart placing to date. Perhaps in celebration, Jones chose to finally make his debut on *Top of the Pops* to promote the single.

In early 1986, while Jones was on holiday in the Bahamas, Strummer met up with him and the pair made their peace over the issues that had caused The Clash's break-up. However, although Strummer broached the idea of reforming The Clash, Jones now considered that he had his own road to travel. He, like Strummer, had recently become a father – his daughter Lauren was born in 1984 – and he liked the vast musical experimentation that BAD afforded him. When he played Strummer *This Is Big Audio Dynamite*, Strummer's reported opinion was 'It's the worst load of shit I've ever heard in my life!' In a public gesture of reconciliation, however, both Strummer and Simonon appeared as policemen in BAD's video for 'Medicine Show'.

Having worked with Strummer again, producing Joe's contributions to the *Sid and Nancy* soundtrack, Jones invited his former partner to renew their songwriting collaboration on BAD's second LP. Recorded at Trident studios, *No. 10, Upping Street* ended up being co-produced by Strummer and contained five songs co-written by the pair – including the excellent 'V Thirteen' and 'Sightsee MC!' The LP, which also included the single 'C'mon Every Beatbox', was a Top 20 hit in late 1986.

Further BAD LPs followed – *Tighten Up Vol. '88* (1988, featuring the single 'Just Play Music') and the De la Soul-influenced *Megatop Phoenix* (1989). But the band's momentum was halted when Jones suffered an almost-fatal bout of pneumonia and Big Audio Dynamite disintegrated.[120] A second line-up, BAD II, produced the autobiographical *Kool-Aid* (1990) and *The Globe* (1991). The latter was the best thing Jones had recorded in years and was a big hit in both America and Australia, featuring the splendid title song and 'Rush', which, controversially, Jones had placed on the B-Side of the reissued 'Should I Stay or Should I Go' single. Jones also found time to appear on Aztec Camera's 1990 hit 'Good Morning Britain'.

In 1994 BAD II appeared at the Hammersmith Apollo memorial concert for Mick Ronson. A week later MTV carried a news report that Jones himself had died. Thankfully this proved to be erroneous. Mick Jones was alive, well, living in London and jamming with the likes of Saint Etienne and Primal Scream. In 1994, *Higher Power* was released, credited to Big Audio, while the following year Jones switched to the independent Radioactive label and put out *F-Punk*. His next venture, *Entering a New Ride* (1996), wasn't to the label's liking, so Jones set up a BAD website and used it to release samples from the rejected LP online. During the late 90s, Jones also tried his hand at video direction (for Shack's 'Oscar') and played guitar on his old mate Glen

120. After the break-up of the original BAD line-up, Letts, Roberts, Williams and Donovan collaborated on Screaming Target and then, minus Letts, Dreadzone.

Matlock's LP *Open Mind*. Having joined Strummer on stage in late 2002, in the aftermath of his ex-partner's death there were reports in early 2003 that Jones was recording an anti-war song called 'Why Do Men Fight?' with Tony James.

Topper Headon had spent much of early 1984 recovering from a seriously broken leg, received in somewhat bizarre circumstances. Then, in the summer, he went into Wessex studios with several friends from Dover – including most of the Barnacle family – and Jeremy Green as producer [121] to record a cover of Gene Krupa's 'Drummin' Man'. He had such a good time that he put together a session band, including Mickey Gallagher, James Eller and Isaac Hayes' guitarist Robert Johnson. 'Drummin' Man' was released as a single in June 1985 (backed by two instrumentals, including the spooky 'Du Cane Road'). Although well-reviewed, the single failed to chart.

Headon's subsequent LP, *Waking Up*, was released in January 1986. With song titles like 'Just Another Hit' and 'Monkey On My Back', there was little doubt concerning the inspiration behind much of Topper's writing. Like the single, *Waking Up* was well-received but didn't sell and Headon's contract with Phonogram was cancelled. By the end of 1986 he had been reduced to selling off his Clash gold discs to pay for drugs. Topper's lowest point came in November 1987, when he was jailed for 15 months for supplying heroin to a friend who subsequently overdosed. Even after his release, Headon continued to be affected by drug problems and, on at least one occasion, Jones and Strummer paid for him to spend some time in rehab.

A succession of health problems, and a severe car crash in the late 90s, further hindered Topper's recovery, but the advance that he was paid by Sony for *From Here to Eternity* enabled him to buy a home in Dover and begin to get his life back on the rails. The news in 2003 that Topper had played his first live dates in over two decades was welcomed by every fan of The Clash.

The last of The Clash's classic line-up to strike out on his own, musically, was Paul Simonon. Having spent much of 1987 allegedly riding with an LA motor-cycle gang, and working with Bob Dylan on *Down in the Groove*, the bassist formed a new band, Havana 3AM, which signed with the Japanese label Portrait Records and recorded an eponymous debut LP in Tokyo in early 1990. It was an interesting, if derivative, set of songs heavily influenced by late 50s and early

---

121. Jones had hoped to use Green as engineer on BAD's first LP. According to Green, Mick saw his production of Headon's sessions as a betrayal and asked Green, 'Do you want to work with Tolstoy or with Harold Robbins?!'

60s American music (notably 'Blue Motorcycle Eyes', 'Hole in the Sky', 'Surf in the City' and 'Blue Gene Vincent'). The band subsequently toured Japan and the US, but split up in 1992. Meanwhile, Simonon married the LP's cover star, and his new manager, Tricia Ronane. He also returned to his first love, painting, producing the cover for BAD's *Tighten Up Vol. '88* as a favour to Jones.

In 1995, Simonon successfully exhibited at John Martin's gallery in west London and has become an artist whose work is able to command high prices. According to Strummer, in whose West Country garden many of Simonon's landscapes were painted, Paul has a 'very punk rock' attitude towards painting. Simonon remains a charming and amusing interviewee, as his contributions to *Mongrel Nation* in 2003 proved.

For Joe Strummer, the final year of The Clash's existence had been both rewarding – with the birth of his daughter, Jazz Domino, in early 1984 – and painful. In March, Strummer's father died with, as Strummer would later note, 'a lot still unsaid.' Shortly afterwards, his mother, Anna, was diagnosed with cancer. Strummer spent much of 1985 visiting her. She died early the following year. This was, as Strummer noted on *Wired* in 1988, a strange time for him, with new responsibilities and much loss in rapid succession. 'I had to disassemble myself and put the pieces back together. I'd lost my parents and my group. You become a different person.' It's perhaps no coincidence that, during this period, Strummer re-established his relationships with several old friends like Tymon Dogg and Richard Dudanski, friendships that were to remain solid for the rest of his life. Having already apologised to Jones in private, Strummer spent 1986 doing so publicly. 'I did him wrong,' he told Gavin Martin. 'I really stabbed him in the back.'

Just before Christmas 1985, Strummer gate-crashed the end-of-shoot party for Alex Cox's movie *Sid and Nancy*, about Strummer's friend Sid Vicious. Cox, a huge Clash fan, cornered Strummer and asked him to write a song for the movie. After seeing a rough cut, and being tremendously moved by Gary Oldman's sympathetic central performance, Strummer wrote two songs, 'Love Kills' and 'Dum Dum Club', which he recorded with Jones producing, along with a series of instrumental pieces credited on the movie to Dan Wul. 'Love Kills' was released as a single in May 1986 and was a minor UK hit despite a savage review by Steven Wells in *NME*. After working with Jones on the second BAD LP, Strummer spent August 1986 in Almería acting in Alex Cox's next movie, a spoof Spaghetti Western named after one of Strummer's finest songs, *Straight To Hell*.

Strummer would subsequently write and produce several movie sound-tracks both for Cox (like 1988's *Walker*) and for other directors, as well as occasionally acting in movies like *Mystery Train* and *I Hired a Contract Killer*. After a one-off single, 'Trash City', in 1988, the following year Strummer finally produced his debut solo LP. *Earthquake Weather* was an admirably eclectic collection of R&B, reggae, rockabilly and jazz with titles like 'Gangsterville', 'Island Hopping' and 'Leopardskin Limousines'. Just what you'd except from Joe Strummer, frankly. The LP, which included at least one song written during The Clash's final days ('Shouting Street'), was recorded with a new band, The Latino Rockabilly War, with whom Strummer toured over the next couple of years. This included drummer Jack Irons, formerly of Red Hot Chili Peppers, and guitarist Zandon Schloss. He subsequently recorded material for a second LP in 1990 and 1991 but Sony declined to issue it.

In 1991, Strummer joined The Pogues on tour, deputising for the ill Shane MacGowan. According to those who saw his performances, they were among the finest of Strummer's life, passionately bringing a few of his Clash songs ('London Calling' for instance) into The Pogues set. When asked by Q about his post-Clash career, Strummer joked that he had 'spent 11 years watching *Match of the Day*'. In fact, his musical collaborations were varied and interesting. In 1995 he worked with crusty rockers The Levellers on their single 'Just the One'. He continued to contribute to film soundtracks, worked with Rat Scabies on a song for an Amnesty International LP, wrote with former Stray Cat Brian Setzer and helped out Black Grape and Keith Allen with their unofficial Euro '96 anthem 'England's Irie'. The latter song, a Top 10 hit, finally saw Strummer appearing on *Top of the Pops* 19 years after The Clash had first refused to have anything to do with the show.

In 1996 Strummer recorded some dance tracks with The Grid's Richard Norris, though the project remained unreleased. Following the end of his first marriage, in the mid-1990s Strummer remarried and relocated to a farmhouse in Somerset. He recorded a series of shows for the BBC World Service in 1998 and, the following year, formed a new band, The Mescaleros, and signed to Mercury via his own Casbah Records. The core of the band was Antony Genn, Scott Shields, Pablo Cook, Martin Slattery and Richard Fleck, while Black Grape's Ged Lynch, Richard Norris and Dave Stewart also contributed to the sessions for *Rock Art and the X-Ray Style*. Released in 1999, the CD got Strummer his best series of reviews since *London Calling*, *Uncut* describing it as a 'triumphant return by the former Clash legend ... an album brimming with hope and optimism ... mesmerising.' Q added that it was 'a joy ... worth spending both time and money on.'

On songs like 'Tony Adams', 'The Road To Rock 'n' Roll', 'Diggin' the New', the single 'Yalla Yalla' and 'Willesden to Cricklewood', Strummer had finally rediscovered his love of wordplay. The Mescaleros toured extensively during

1999 and 2000, including a support stint to the recently reformed The Who, which inevitably brought to mind The Clash's stadium gigs in 1982. Their live repertoire was heavily weighted towards The Clash's back catalogue, although Strummer defended his right to play 'White Man', 'Rock the Casbah' and 'White Riot', telling *Metro* that since no one else was playing them it seemed a shame to ignore such good songs.

In October 2000 Strummer was presented with the 'Inspiration' award by *Q* magazine in recognition of his 25 years' service to the music industry. The following year, with his old friend Tymon Dogg added to the Mescaleros' ranks in place of the departed Genn, Strummer and friends recorded *Global A Go-Go*, another collection of mature and thoughtful songs incorporating decades of different influences and musical styles. On 'Bhindi Bhagee', Strummer noted the difficulty in pigeonholing his new direction when he is asked, in the song, what sort of music he plays. 'Well, it's kinda, like... *you know*,' he mumbles with a grin.

The Mescaleros played all around the world in 2002, although one of their final dates of the year was back on their home-boy turf, a benefit show for striking firemen in London. Famously, Mick Jones was persuaded to join the band on stage for the encore. Just over a month later, Joe Strummer was dead.

Strummer's bandmates are said to be sorting through possible tracks for a posthumous album which may include 'Long Shadow', a song Strummer recorded with Beck guitarist Smokey Hormel. Just before his death, Strummer had been working with Bono and Dave Stewart on a piece to be used at an AIDS benefit concert. The ten-minute '48864' was named after the prison number worn by the concert's organiser, Nelson Mandela. There were many such projects kicking around in Joe Strummer's mind. Tragically, on 22 December 2002, they died along with him.

On 20 April 2003, Strummer's first band, The 101ers, reformed for the first time in 25 years for a show at the Notting Hill Tabernacle. Billed as *A Benefit Gig in Memory of Joe*, guests included Wilko Johnson and Mick Jones. 'There was a great vibe in the hall,' noted Richard Dudanski. 'We managed to represent a pretty large chunk of Joe's musical life.' The show also launched the Summerville Charitable Trust, set up by Strummer's widow Lucinda. The aim is to help young kids from disadvantaged backgrounds who want to put a musical project together. Also, a Joe Strummer Memorial Forest was said to be planned for the Isle of Skye.

'If I owe anyone, I owe Joe,' wrote Billy Bragg in *Uncut*'s Strummer tribute. It was something felt by many fans and fellow musicians alike. On 23

February 2003, at the Grammy Awards in New York, Bruce Springsteen and Elvis Costello led a superstar tribute band into a blazing version of 'London Calling'. Two weeks later, across the city at the Waldorf-Astoria hotel, The Clash were among the inductees in the Rock & Roll Hall of Fame.

Before Strummer's death, it had been rumoured that The Clash would reform for the induction and play together for the first time in almost 20 years. In the event, there was no reunion. 'I sadly miss my big brother, Joe, with whom I shared my most life-changing experiences,' Simonon said. 'Joe had so much integrity and inspired us all.' Jones, meanwhile, dedicated the group's award to 'all the garage-bands who might have never dreamed of this kind of moment.'

When I heard about Joe Strummer's death, my mind went back 25 years to that night in November 1978 at Middlesbrough and to the encore when The Clash played 'Janie Jones', 'Garageland', '1-2 Crush On You', 'Complete Control' and 'White Riot' in one furious, seamlessly segued eight-minute burst of manic energy. To a band who, on the right night, with the right crowd, did things that few bands, before or since, could *dream* of matching. The Clash were about power, yes, but more importantly, they were about passion and a bond between the performer and the audience. A shared experience that, at times, came close to a shared identity. The band from the gutters who made those of us who listened to them look up to the stars.

We'll never see another one like them. Perhaps that's just as well. The Clash were more than enough for one lifetime.

SINGLES DISCOGRAPHY

'There were these hippies who lived across the road. They used
to scream abuse at me because I bought records by The Clash ...
I set fire to their house in the name of rock 'n' roll. They
were complacent, soulless, dope-smoking dead-heads, too stoned
to live.'
Bobby Gillespie, *NME* 1987

UK SINGLES
1977
Mar   White Riot/1977 (CBS 5058) [38]
May   Remote Control/London's Burning (Live) (CBS 5293)
Sep   Complete Control/City of the Dead (CBS 5664) [28]
1978
Feb   Clash City Rockers/Jail Guitar Doors (CBS 5834) [35]
Jun   (White Man) In Hammersmith Palais/The Prisoner (CBS 6383) [32]
Nov   Tommy Gun/1-2 Crush On You (CBS 6788) [19]
1979
Feb   English Civil War/Pressure Drop (CBS 7082) [25]
May   *The Cost of Living* EP (I Fought the Law/Groovy Times/Gates of the West/Capital Radio
         Two) (CBS 7324) [22]
Dec   London Calling/Armagideon Time (CBS 8087) [11]
1980
Jan   London Calling/Armagideon Time/Justice Tonight/Kick It Over (CBS 12 8087)
Aug   Bankrobber/Rockers Galore ..... UK Tour (CBS 8323) [12]
Nov   The Call Up/Stop the World (CBS 9339) [40]
1981
Jan   Hitsville UK/Radio One (CBS 9480) [56]
Apr   The Magnificent Seven/The Magnificent Dance (CBS A 1133/CBS A 12 1133) [34]
Nov   This Is Radio Clash/Radio Clash (CBS A 1797) [47]
Nov   This Is Radio Clash/Radio Clash/Outside Broadcast/Radio 5 (CBS A 13 1797)
1982
Apr   Know Your Rights/First Night Back In London (CBS A 2309) [43]
Jun   Rock the Casbah/Long Time Jerk (CBS A 2479) [30]
Jun   Rock the Casbah/Mustapha Dance (CBS A 13 2479)
Sep   Should I Stay or Should I Go/Straight To Hell (CBS A 2646) [17]
Nov   Complete Control/London Calling/Bank Robber/Clash City Rockers (CBS A40 2907)
1985
Sep   This Is England/Do It Now (CBS A 6122) [24]
Sep   This Is England/Do It Now/Sex Mad Roar (CBS TA 12 6122)
1988
Mar   I Fought the Law/City of the Dead/1977 (CBS CLASH1) [29]
Mar   I Fought the Law/Police On My Back/48 Hours (CBS CLASH T/C1)
Apr   London Calling/Brand New Cadillac (CBS CLASH2) [46]

| Apr | London Calling/Brand New Cadillac/Rudie Can't Fail (CBS CLASHT2) |
| Apr | London Calling/Brand New Cadillac/Rudie Can't Fail/The Street Parade (CBS CLASHC2) |

1990

| Jul | Return to Brixton/Return to Brixton (SW2 Mix) (CBS 656072-7) [57] |

1991

Feb	Should I Stay Or Should I Go/BAD II: Rush (Columbia 656667-7) [1]
Feb	Should I Stay Or Should I Go/Rush/ Rush Dance Mix/Protex Blue (Columbia 656667-6)
Feb	Should I Stay Or Should I Go/London Calling/Train In Vain/I Fought the Law (Columbia 656667-5)
Apr	Rock the Casbah/Mustapha Dance (Columbia 656814-7) [15]
Apr	Rock the Casbah/Mustapha Dance/The Magnificent Dance (Columbia 656814-6)
Apr	Rock the Casbah/Tommy Gun/(White Man) In Hammersmith Palais/Straight To Hell (Columbia 656814-5)
Jun	London Calling/Brand New Cadillac (Columbia 656946-7) [64]
Jun	London Calling/Brand New Cadillac/Return to Brixton (Columbia 656946-6)
Jun	London Calling/Brand New Cadillac/The Call Up/London's Burning (Columbia 656946-5)
Oct	Train In Vain/The Right Profile (Columbia 656-7)
Oct	Train In Vain/The Right Profile/Train In Vain/Death Or Glory (Columbia 656-5)
Oct	Train In Vain/The Right Profile/Groovy Times/Gates of the West (Columbia 656-2)

US SINGLES

1979

| Jul | I Fought the Law/(White Man) In Hammersmith Palais (Epic 50738) |

1980

| Mar | Train In Vain (Stand By Me)/London Calling (Epic 50851) [27] |

1981

| Feb | Hitsville UK/Police On My Back (Epic 51013) |
| Apr | The Magnificent Seven/The Call Up/The Magnificent Dance/The Cool Out (Epic 02036) |

1982

May	Should I Stay or Should I Go/Innoculated City (Epic 03006)
Jun	Rock the Casbah/Long Time Jerk (Epic 03245) [8]
Jul	Should I Stay Or Should I Go/First Night Back In London (Epic 03061) [45]

1983

| Feb | Should I Stay Or Should I Go/Cool Confusion (Epic 03547) [50] |

1988

| Aug | London Calling/The Magnificent Seven/Rock the Casbah/I Fought the Law (Epic 49-06899) |

IMPORTANT OVERSEAS SINGLES

1979

| May | I Fought the Law/Groovy Times (CBS 7324) – Europe |

1980

| Jun | Rudie Can't Fail/Bankrobber/Rockers Galore ..... UK Tour (CBS 8363) – Holland |
| Jun | Train In Vain/Bankrobber/Rockers Galore ..... UK Tour (CBS 8370) – Europe |

1981

| Feb | 1981 Somebody Got Murdered/Hitsville UK (CBS A 1310) – Spain |

1988

| Jun | This Is Radio Clash/Radio Clash/The Magnificent Dance/The Magnificent Seven [edit] (CBS 651653 3) – Europe |

BIBLIOGRAPHY

The following books, articles, interviews and reviews were consulted in the preparation of this text:

Abowitz, Richard, 'Notes on the Passing of Joe Strummer', *Las Vegas Weekly*, 1 January 2003.

'A Phlash of The Clash', *Killer Children*, November 1979.

'Are You Ready for British Punk?', *Trouser Press*, December 1976.

Bangs, Lester, *Psychotic Reactions and Carburetor Dung*, Random House, 1987.

Bangs, Lester, 'Lester Bangs Meets The Clash', *NME*, 10-24 December 1977.

Bangs, Lester, 'The Fire Next Time', *Soho Weekly News*, 5 March 1980.

Bennett, Clive, 'Clash: Rainbow', *The Times*, 11 May 1977.

Binelli, Mark, 'Titans of The Clash', *Rolling Stone*, 17 April 2003.

Birch, Ian, 'Clash – Music Machine', *Melody Maker*, 25 July 1978.

Black, Johnny, 'Destination Nowhere', *Mojo*, December 1996.

Bockris, Victor, *Keith Richards: The Biography*, Hutchinson, 1992.

Brown, Cecil, 'Godfather of Gangsta', *The Guardian*, 9 May 2003.

Buckley, Jonathan and Ellingham, Mark [eds], *Rock The Rough Guide*, Rough Guides Ltd, 1996.

Burchill, Julie and Parsons, Tony, *The Boy Looked at Johnny: The Obituary Of Rock 'n' roll*, Pluto Press, 1978.

Burchill, Julie, 'Mindless Aggreshunn On Hippy Farm', *NME*, 12 November 1977.

Bushell, Garry, 'Clash/The Specials – Aylesbury', *Sounds*, 8 July 1978.

Bushell, Garry, 'Tour Notes', *Sounds*, 25 February 1979.

Cain, Barry, 'The Clash: *The Clash*', *Record Mirror*, 9 April 1977.

Carson, Tom, 'The Clash Conquer America', *Rolling Stone*, 25 April 1979.

Carson, Tom, 'The Clash: Street-Fighting Men', *Rolling Stone*, 18 October 1979.

Caws, Matthew, 'Interview with Mick Jones', *Guitar World*, December 1995.

Chaillet, Ned, 'The Clash: Lyceum', *The Times*, 20 October 1981.

Childs, David, *Britain Since 1945: A Political History*, Routledge, 1997.

Clarke, Peter F., *Hope and Glory: Britain, 1900-1990*, Penguin Books, 1997.

Christgau, Robert, 'The Clash See America – Second Most Intense Rock Band Ever,' *Village Voice*, 5 March 1979.

'The Clash's First American Tour', *Q*, May 2001.

Cocks, Jay, 'The Best Gang In Town', *Time*, 5 March 1979.

Cohen, Debra Rae, 'For The Clash, Music is Part of The Message', *New York Times*, 24 May 1981.

Collins, Andrew, 'Joe Strummer: Cash For Questions', *Q*, November 1999.

Coon, Caroline, *1988: The New Wave Punk Rock Explosion*, Omnibus, 1982.

Coon, Caroline, 'New Faces', *Melody Maker*, 13 November 1976.

Coon, Caroline, 'Harlesden Colliseum', *Meldoy Maker*, 9 April 1977.

Cooper, Mark, 'Doubt and Desperation on the Edge of Town: From Garageland to Hell with Joe Strummer of the Clash', *Record Mirror*, 24 July 1982.

Cook, Richard, 'Three Convictions on the Road from Hell', *Sounds*, 5 August 1982.

Cope, Julian, *Head On*, Magog Books Limited, 1994.

Cornell, Paul, Day, Martin and Topping, Keith, *The Guinness Book of Classic British TV* [2nd ed], Guinness Publishing, 1996.

Cousins, Christine, 'The Clash: Fair Deal', *NME*, 6 August 1982.

Crawley, Philip, 'Hell and High Water', *The Journal*, 28 October 1977.

Cromelin, Richard, 'Strummer On Man, God Law – And The Clash', *Los Angeles Times*, 31 January 1988.

Crowley, Gary, 'Jam today, tomorrow & yesterday', *The Face*, June 1980.

Dadomo, Giovanni, 'The Screen On The Green', *Sounds*, 5 September 1976.

Dalrymple, Henderson, *Bob Marley: Music, Myth and the Rastas*, Carib-Arawak, 1976.

Davis, Julie, *Punk*, Davison Press, 1977.

Day, Martin and Topping, Keith, *SHUT IT! A Fan's Guide to 70s Cops on the Box*, Virgin Publishing, 1999.

Dennis, Jon, 'Punk Legend Joe Strummer Dies', *The Guardian*, 23 December 2003.

Denselow, Robin, 'The Clash at the Brixton Academy', *The Guardian*, 17 March 1984.

Dibblin, Jane, 'The Clash in Top Gear', *The Journal*, 13 June 1980.

Doggart, Peter, 'Career Opportunities: The Legacy of The Clash', *Record Collector*, November 1999.

Driver, Jim [ed], *The Mammoth Book of Sex, Drugs & Rock 'n' Roll*, Robinson, 2001.

Dudanski, Richard, 'Clang! Clang! Go The Jail Guitar Doors', *Uncut*, March 2003.

Dutton, David, *British Politics Since 1945: The Rise, Fall and Rebirth of Consensus*, Blackwell, 1997.

Egan, Sean, *Animal Tracks*, Helter Skelter Publishing, 2001.

Egan, Sean, 'Joe Strummer: Before and After', *Record Collector*, August 2000.

Egan, Sean, 'London's Burning', *Uncut*, February 2003.

Elwood, Phil, 'New Clash Lacks Some of the Old Fire', *San Francisco Examiner*, 23 January 1984.

Farren, Mick, 'The Titanic Sails at Dawn', *NME*, 19 June 1976.

''Fear and Loathing in W11', *International Times*, 1 September 1977.

Flanagan, Bill, 'The Exile Of Joe Strummer', *Musician*, March 1988.

Flanagan, Bill, 'Joe Strummer is alive and living near London – but even he isn't quite certain what he's doing there', *GQ*, June 1997.

Floyd, John, 'Viva *Sandinista!* Is The Clash still the only band that matters?' *Dallas Observer*, 2 March 2002.

'4-Letter Reply to Rock Band', *The Journal*, 4 December 1976.

Fricke, David, 'Clashing In: The World's Greatest Band's Great Gamble', *Rolling Stone*, 16 April 1981.

Fricke, David, 'The Clash: Convention Hall, Asbury Park', *Melody Maker*, 4 June 1982.

Frith, Simon, *Sound Effects: Youth, Leisure And The Politics Of Rock 'n' roll*, Pantheon, 1981.

Frith, Simon, 'Out on the Streets', *Melody Maker*, 26 January 1980.

Fuller, Graham, 'Combat Rocker', *Film Comment*, July 1987.

Fuller, Eric, 'Harlesden Roxy', *Sounds*, 4 November 1978.

Gael, Steve, 'Long Hot Strummer', *Melody Maker*, 15 February 1984.

Game, Peter, 'The Starsky and Hutch of the Valley', *Sun*, 8 March 1978.

Garbarini, Vic, 'Rude Boys: An Interview with Joe Strummer and Robert Fripp', *Musician*, June 1981.

Garrett, Susanne, 'What's that you've got in your pocket then, sonny?' *Sounds*, 28 March 1981.

Gilbert, Pat, 'The Clash On Broadway', *Record Collector*, June 1994.

Gilbert, Pat, 'Meltdown!', *Mojo*, October 1999.

Gilbert, Pat, 'Breakdown', *Mojo*, March 2003.

Gilmore, Mikal, 'The Clash: Anger on the Left', *Rolling Stone*, 8 March 1979.

Glassman, Judith, *The Year in Music: 1979*, Columbia House, 1979.

Goddard, Simon, 'The Trebleshooters', *Uncut*, November 1998.

Goddard, Simon, *The Smiths: Songs That Saved Your Life*, Reynolds & Hearn, 2002.

Goldberg, Michael, 'The Clash: Revolution Rock', *Down Beat*, December 1982.

Goldberg, Michael, 'A Fired-Up Joe Strummer Brings His New Clash to America', *Rolling Stone*, 1 March 1984.

Goldman, Vivien, 'Clash Make It Good', *Melody Maker*, 2 January 1980.

Grant, Neil, *Illustrated History of 20th Century Conflict*, Hamlyn, 1993.

Gray, Marcus, *Last Gang in Town: The Story and Myth of The Clash*, Fourth Estate, 1995.

Gray, Marcus, *Return of the Last Gang in Town*, Helter Skelter Publishing, 2002.

Green, Johnny and Barker, Garry, *A Riot Of Our Own: Night and Day with The Clash*, Indigo, 1997.

Gruen, Bob, *The Clash*, Omnibus Press, 2002.

Gunn, Keith, 'Whatever Happened To Revolution Rock?', *Melody Maker*, 4 April 1981.

Harron, Mary, 'Clash in NYC – Waiting For Ivan', *Melody Maker*, 28 September 1979.

Henke, James, 'Rebels With a Cause and a Hit Album', *Rolling Stone*, 17 April 1980.

Hepworth, David, 'John Peel: Forty Is More Fun', *Smash Hits*, 13 December 1979.

Hepworth, David, 'Who wants to be a millionaire?', *Smash Hits*, 1 December 1980.

Hibbert, Christopher, *King Mob*, Reader's Union, 1959.

Hilburn, Robert, 'Clash: Manifesto of Punk', *Los Angeles Times*, 17 September 1978.

Hilburn, Robert, 'Clash Crests on New Wave Punk Wave', *Los Angeles Times*, 20 January 1979.

Hilburn, Robert, 'Active or Passive: Two Rock Voices', *Los Angeles Times*, 4 February 1979.

Hilburn, Robert, 'Clash Specializes in High Energy', *Los Angeles Times*, 12 February 1979.

Hilburn, Robert, 'A Re-Formed Clash is Back on the Attack', *Los Angeles Times*, 22 January 1984.

Hilburn, Robert, 'Strummer Says he was Behind Clash Collision', *Los Angeles Times*, 9 August 1986.

Hills, Geoff, 'Go Johnny Go', *NME*, 2 October 1976.

Holan, Marc, 'Live Wire', *Cleveland Scene*, 26 August 1982.

Holden, Stephen, 'Rock-Rap: The Clash', *New York Times*, 5 September 1982.

Houpt, Simon, 'Keeping Up With Joe Strummer', *The Globe and Mail*, 2 November 1999.

Ingham, Jonh, 'Welcome to the (?) Rock Special', *Sounds*, 9 October 1976.

Jones, Allan, 'Doctors Orders', *Melody Maker*, 18 September 1976.

Jones, Allan, 'Banging on the White House Door', *Melody Maker*, 25 February 1979.

Jones, Allan, 'Death Or Glory: Joe Strummer 1952-2002', *Uncut*, March 2003.

Kaye, Lenny, 'Americlash', 1991.

Kelly, Danny, 'White Riot', in *Love is the Drug*, Aizelwood, John [ed], Penguin, 1994.

Kent, Nick, *The Dark Stuff*, Da Capo, 2002.

Kent, Nick, 'Just Watch This Screen', *NME*, 5 February 1977.

Kent, Nick, 'Mind Your Bollocks, Here Comes the Wrath of Sid', *NME*, 17 December 1977.

Kent, Nick, 'Pills and Thrills', *Guardian*, 12 April 2002.

Kinsella, Warren, 'The Clash', *Toronto Star*, 24 December 2002.

Klein, Howie, 'Clash Mania!', *New York Rocker*, March 1979.

Knabb, Ken [ed], *Situationalist International Anthology*, Public Bureau of Secrets, 1981.

Leech, Kenneth, *Brick Lane 1978: The Events And Their Aftermath*, St Botolph's Church Press, 1978.

Legum, Margaret, 'Punk Isn't Funny, It's Frightening', *The Times*, 11 June 1978.

'Let No Blame Fall On The Clash', *NME*, 22 July 1978.

Lott, Terry, 'Join the Fight Against the Front', *Record Mirror*, 8 April 1978.

Lupino, Gary, 'In Concert', *Cleveland Scene*, 22 February 1979.

Lydon, John, with Keith and Kent Zimmerman, *Rotten: No Irish, No Blacks, No Dogs*,
    Hodder & Stoughton, 1995.
McClelland, Colin, 'Belfast Christmas Dates', *NME*, 1 January 1978.
McCullough, David, 'Notre Dame Hall', *Sounds*, 14 July 1979.
McDonald, Ian, *Revolution in the Head*, Fourth Estate, 1994.
McKay, Simon, 'The Clash', *Eccentric Sleeve Notes*, January 1983.
McSmith, Andy, *Faces of Labour: The Inside Story*, Verso, 1996.
Marcus, Greil, *Lipstick Traces*, Secker and Warburg, 1989.
Marcus, Greil, 'Clash Warfare', *New West*, 25 September 1978.
Marcus, Greil, 'The Clash: Stay Free', *Rolling Stone*, 25 January 1979.
Marcus, Greil, Cave, Nick and Brown, Cecil, 'The Murder Mystery', *Mojo*, January 1996.
Marsh, Dave, *Before I Get Old: The Story of The Who*, Plexus Publishing, 1983.
Marten, Neville and Hudson, Jeffrey, *The Kinks: Well Respected Men*, Castle Communications, 1996.
Martens, Todd, 'Ex-Clash Singer Breaks Ground', *Daily Trojan*, 19 March 1997.
Martin, Gavin, 'Belfast', *NME*, 21 October 1978.
Martin, Gavin, 'Combat Rock', *Uncut*, September 1999.
Martin, Gavin, 'The Prefect Who Rocked the World', *Joe Strummer Resource*, 2002.
Marwick, Arthur, *British Society Since 1945*, Penguin Books, 1990.
Matlock, Glen, *I Was A Teenage Sex Pistol*, Omnibus, 1989.
'Mayhem: Guard Dogs For Poly Night Out', *Sunday Sun*, 3 December 1977.
Meslin, Janet, 'The Screen: *Rude Boy*', *New York Times*, 25 July 1980.
Middles, Mick, 'From the Vaults: White Riot Tour', *Classic Rock*, July 2003.
Millar, Robbi, 'The Rainbow', *Sounds*, 20 July 1979.
Miller, Russell, 'Who Are These Punks?', *Daily Mirror*, 2 December 1976.
Miles, Barry, *Ginsberg: A Biography*, Viking Press, 1990.
Miles, Barry, 'Cannibalism at Clash Gig', *NME*, 6 November 1976
Miles, Barry, 'Eighteen-Flight Rock and the Sound of the Westway', *NME*, 11 December 1976.
Miles, Barry, 'A Clash of Interests', *Time Out*, 15 December 1978.
Morely, Paul, 'The Rainbow', NME, 21 July 1979.
Morley, Paul, 'The Clash Take the Fifth', *NME*, 29 September 1979.
Morley, Paul, 'The Last Gang in the West Leaves Town', *NME*, 13 October 1979.
Morley, Paul, 'The Fastest Gang In Town', *NME*, 20th October 1979.
Morley, Paul, 'Cutting Edge', *Uncut*, February 2001.
Morse, Steve, 'The Clash at the Worcester Centrum', *Boston Globe*, 16 April 1984.
Moser, Margaret, 'Lubbock Calling: Joe Ely Remembers The Clash', *Austin Chronicle*, 19 May 2000.
Myers, Barry 'Music Machine', *Sounds*, 25 July 1978.
Nelson, Chris, 'Joe Strummer, A Razor-Edged Poet', *Calgary Sun*, 24 December 2002.
Nicholls, Mike, 'The Clash: Brixton Fair Deal', 6 August 1982.
'Obituary: Joe Strummer', *The Times*, 24 December 2002.
Palmer, Robert, 'Clash Melee Points Up Danger Of Overselling', *New York Times*, 3 June 1981.
Parson, Tony, 'Blank Generation Out On the Road', *NME*, 11 December 1976.
Parsons, Tony and Burchill, Julie, 'Fear and Loathing at the Roxy', *NME*, 19 March 1977.
Parsons, Tony, 'The Thinking Man's Yobs: Sten Guns In Knightsbridge? The Clash Napalm
    Cheltenham', *NME*, 2 April 1977.
Parsons, Tony, 'The Clash: *The Clash*', *NME*, 16 April 1977.
Parsons, Tony, 'Daddy, What Did *You* Do In The Sex Pistols?' *Smash Hits*, 27 December 1979.
Parsons, Tony, 'Touch That Dial!', *Smash Hits*, 15 May 1980.
Pearlman, Sandy, 'Give 'Em Enough Hope', *Joe Strummer Resource*, 2002.

Pegg, Nicholas, *The Complete David Bowie*, Reynolds & Hearn, 2002.

Penman, Ian, 'Harlesden Roxy', *NME*, 4 November 1978.

Perry, Mark, *Sniffin' Glue: The Catalogue Of Chaos 1976-77*, Faber & Faber, 2000.

Petridis, Alexis, 'Turn That Racket Down', *Guardian*, 16 April 2002.

'Police Quiz Punk Rockers', *The Journal*, 24 May 1977.

Piccarella, John, 'The Clash On Main Street', *Village Voice*, 4 February 1980.

Prophet, Sheila, 'The Clash at the Music Machine', *Record Mirror*, 30 July 1978.

Prophet, Sheila, 'The Lyceum', *Record Mirror*, 2 January 1979.

'Punk Rock Hits You, OK?', *The Sunday Sun*, 22 May 1977.

'*Q* Punk Special', June 2002.

Quantick, David, *Revolution: The Making of The Beatles' White Album*, Unanimous, 2002.

Rambali, Paul, 'A Concert For The People of Kampuchea', *NME*, 5 January 1980.

Rathhun, Keith, 'Pontiac, Michigan', *Scene*, 13 October 1982.

Reed, John, *Paul Weller: My Ever Changing Moods*, Omnibus Press, 1996.

Reid, Jim, 'The Return of the Last Punk in Town', *Record Mirror*, 19 July 1986.

Robbins, Ira, 'The Clash', *Trouser Press*, September 1977.

Robbins, Ira, 'Clash City Talkers: New York Meets Jones And Co.', *Trouser Press*, March 1979.

Robbins, Ira, 'Clash at the Controls?', *Trouser Press*, April 1981.

Robinson, David, 'Devastating and disarming rebels against society', *The Times*, 14 march 1980.

Rockwell, John, '*London Calling* Helps The Clash Live Up To Billing', *New York Times*,
    4 January 1980.

Rowley, Scott, 'Interview with Paul Simonon', *Bassist Magazine*, October 1999.

'Rude Boys Argue', *Smash Hits*, 3 March 1980.

Ruth, Emma, 'Leeds', *NME*, 8 July 1978.

Salewicz, Chris, 'Sort It Out Preview', *NME*, 7 October 1978.

Salewicz, Chris, 'Manchester Apollo', *NME*, 2 December 1978.

Salewicz, Chris, '1977 – Two Sevens Clash', *The History of Rock*, 1983.

Salewicz, Chris, 'The Triumphant Return of Mick Jones', *The Face*, March 1985.

Sangster, Jim, *Scorsese*, Virgin Books, 2002.

Sato, Masaru, 'Punk Hero Joe Strummer Rocks Again With Young Band', *Reuters*,
    25 November 1999.

Saunders, Red, 'Appreciation: The Sound of an Urban Revolution', *Socialist Worker*, February 2003.

Savage, Jon, *England's Dreaming: Sex Pistols and Punk Rock*, Faber & Faber, 1991.

Savage, Jon, *Time Travel – From The Sex Pistols to Nirvana: Po, Media and Sexuality, 1977-96*,
    Chatto & Windus, 1996.

Savage, Jon, 'The Clash: Live at the Rainbow', *Sounds*, 21 May 1977

Savage, Jon, 'The Clash: *Give 'Em Enough Rope*', *Melody Maker*, 11 November 1978.

Savage, Jon, 'Punk, Five Years On', *The Face*, November 1981.

Savage, Jon, 'Spit and Polish', *The Guardian*, 24 September 1999.

Scott, Jane, 'Clash Comes On Strong, Lacks Heart', *Cleveland Plain Dealer*, 12 May 1984.

Selvin, Joel, 'San Francisco', *San Francisco Chronicle*, 15 February 1979.

Selvin, Joel, '"New" Clash Plays Some Old favourites For SF Faithful', *San Francisco Chronicle*,
    23 January 1984.

Sexton, Paul, 'Strummer Honored With London Landmark', *Billboard*, 1999.

Shaar Murray, Charles, *Shots from the Hip*, Penguin, 1991.

Shaar Murray, Charles, 'Are you Alive to the Jive of the Sound of 75?', *NME*, 8 November 1975.

Shaar Murray, Charles, 'The Screen on the Green', *NME*, 5 September 1976.

Shaar Murray, Charles, 'Music Machine', *NME*, 30 July 1978.

Shaar Murray, Charles, 'Comrade, Goodbye', *Mojo*, March 2003.

Silverton, Peter, 'Greatness from Garageland', *Trouser Press*, February 1978.

Silverton, Peter, 'The Clash On TV', *Sounds*, 17 March 1979.

Silverton, Peter, 'The Clash Turn Pro (Sort Of)', *Sounds*, 29 September 1979.

Simmonds, Sylvie, 'The Clash Pearl Harbour Tour', *Sounds*, 17 February 1979.

Smith, Pennie, *The Clash, Before and After*, Plexus Publishing, 1994.

Smith, Pennie, 'Hippies – Will This Sinister Cult Catch On?', *NME*, 29 June 1978.

Smucker, Tom, 'Pop Music', *The Nation*, 31 May 1980.

Snowden, Don, 'The Clash in LA: Just the Best', *Los Angeles Weekly*, 23 February 1979.

Spenser, Neil, 'Is This What We Ordered?', *NME*, 21 May 1977.

Stevenson, Jane, "No Ordinary Joe', *Toronto Star*, 24 December 2002.

Stewart, Tony, 'The Return of the Avenger', *NME*, 25 December 1982.

Stokes, Geoffrey, 'The Clash's Romantic Rebellion', *Village Voice*, 1 October 1979.

Strummer, Joe, 'Diaries of the Pearl Harbour Tour', *NME*, 18 March 1979.

Sullivan, Caroline, 'Definitely not admitting defeat', *The Guardian*, 24 September 1999.

Sutcliffe, Phil, 'Middlesbrough Town Hall', *Sounds*, 20 November 1978.

Taylor, Steve, 'The Selling of a Myth', in *The Rock Yearbook 1982* (Clark, Al [ed]),
    Virgin Publishing, 1982.

Thompson, David and Christie, Ian [ed], *Scorsese on Scorsese*, Faber and Faber, 1989.

Thrills, Adrian, 'White Riot in Dunstable Queensway', *NME*, 1 February 1978.

Thrills, Adrian, 'Strummertime Blues', *Smash Hits*, 30 November 1979.

Topping, Keith, 'I'm With The Band', *Intergalactic Enquirer*, June 2003.

Tyler, Kieron, 'The Leper Messiah', *Mojo*, November 2000.

Tyner, Rob, 'Back in the UK', *NME*, 1 October 1977.

Valentine, Penny, 'Combat Rockers', *The History of Rock*, 1983.

Vare, Ethlie Ann, 'Struggle and Controversy Just Par for the Course', *Pulse*, March 1984.

Walsh, Steve, 'A Very Angry Clash', *Sniffin' Glue*, November 1976.

Ward, Ed, 'No Second Act in Punk?', *New York Times*, 30 December 2002.

Watson, Albert, 'Punk is A Four-Letter Word', *The Journal*, 6 December 1976.

Weatherman, Annette and Sands, Vermilion, 'Clash Landing', *Search and Destroy*, 1977.

Wenner, Jan [ed], *Twenty Years of Rolling Stone*, Ebury Press, 1987.

Westwood, Chris, 'Top Rank, Sheffield', *Record Mirror*, 7 July 1978.

Whitehead, Philip, *The Writing on the Wall – Britain in the Seventies*, Michael Joseph, 1985.

Widgery, David, *Beating Time – Riot 'n' Race 'n' Rock 'n' Roll*, Chatto, 1986.

Wigney, Allan, 'Strummer's Passing Musical Low of 2002', *Ottowa Sun*, 27 December 2002.